The Borzoi Reader
in Latin American History

VOLUME 2

Consulting Editor
LEWIS HANKE
University of Massachusetts, Amherst

The Borzoi Reader in Latin American History

VOLUME 2

The Nineteenth and Twentieth Centuries

———❖———

EDITED, WITH INTRODUCTIONS, BY

Helen Delpar
Florida State University

Alfred A. Knopf　　　　　*New York*

THIS IS A BORZOI BOOK
PUBLISHED BY ALFRED A. KNOPF, INC.

Foreword

The *Borzoi Reader in Latin American History, Volume 1 and 2* is designed to provide an introduction to Latin American civilization while conveying an appreciation of the diversity and complexity of the area. Volume 1 presents the colonial period and the growth of independence movements. Volume 2 describes nineteenth and twentieth century developments, with special sections on the Cuban and Mexican revolutions and on Peronism. Although this anthology cannot cover every aspect of Latin American history, it is the editor's hope that all the selections are both important and relevant. An attempt has been made to balance expository writings with more analytical material and to include selections by Latin American authors. A few of the articles, such as Bolívar's letter from Jamaica, will be familiar to specialists, but their intrinsic importance warrants their inclusion in a book aimed primarily at the beginning student.

Many of the readings in this collection have already appeared in the Borzoi series, and the editor gratefully acknowledges the cooperation of the editors of the earlier volumes who generously permitted use of material which they had excerpted or translated. The editor also thanks Lewis Hanke, general editor of the Borzoi series, for his assistance.

The editor of the present volume assumes all responsibility for choosing material from these books to be reprinted and for its presentation here.

Contents

✣ ONE ✣

THE NINETEENTH CENTURY
(1830–1914)

T he decades following the emancipation of the Spanish American colonies were characterized by political turbulence in most of the newly independent nations. Indeed, the turbulence was in many ways an outgrowth of the revolutionary struggle itself, for this struggle had eliminated the unifying and stabilizing authority of the crown, created a host of ambitious and unruly military leaders, and produced severe economic dislocation in many areas. Of the major nations, only Brazil escaped the effects of endemic revolution, but even there the years following the declaration of independence in 1822 saw the forced abdication of Emperor Pedro I in 1831 and several local uprisings during the minority of his son, Pedro II.

In the opinion of contemporary conservatives, the disorders of the postindependence period were but the natural consequence of the repudiation of the Spanish legacy of Catholicism, centralism, and authority and order in government. Liberals, on the other hand, tended to attribute most of Spanish America's failings to 300 years of tyrannical and obscurantist rule by Spain. The liberals' political program usually called for a reduction in the spiritual and temporal influence of the Church and for the adoption of political institutions such as federalism, which would eradicate all vestiges of Spanish influence. While liberals and conservatives debated, power was often seized by *caudillos,* or strong men, with scant appreciation for doctrinal niceties.

In addition to the political emancipation of the former colonies, perhaps the most important result of the independence movement was the more complete integration of the economies of Latin America with those of the Western world. In the years immediately after independence, Europeans hastened to take advantage of the seemingly dazzling economic opportunities available in Latin America, but all too often their dreams were shattered by the harsh realities of enterprise in an environment that was frequently hostile both culturally and geographically. After 1850 many foreign investments and enterprises did prove profitable, especially in Argentina, Brazil, Mexico, and Chile. By 1914 British investments alone totalled £750 million, largely in government bonds, railways, public utilities, mines, and meat packing.[1]

These infusions of foreign capital contributed to the expansion of trade and to improved transportation, particularly as a result of rail-

---

[1] Marvin D. Bernstein (ed.), *Foreign Investment in Latin America: Cases and Attitudes* (New York: Knopf, 1966), pp. 6–7.

road construction and the introduction of steam navigation to the major rivers. At the same time, however, the economic bonds forged in the nineteenth century between Latin America and Europe and, to a lesser extent, the United States, helped to perpetuate the colonial status of Latin America, for its national economies remained tied to the production of a single crop or mineral and subject to the vagaries of the world market. In addition, the foreign demand for agricul tural products served to reinforce the colonial heritage of the large estate ordinarily manned by a servile and inexpensive labor force. Finally, the nature of Latin America's economic relationship with Europe made it at times the victim of diplomatic or military pressure by foreign governments acting to protect the interests of their nationals.

The Spanish American Political Tradition

Glen Dealy

The failure of the Spanish American republics to establish stable and democratic governments in the decades after independence usually is attributed to the political inexperience of the ruling classes and to their misguided attempts to introduce alien and unsuitable political institutions. Both of these assumptions are challenged in this selection by Professor Glen Dealy of the Political Science Department of Oregon State University.

It is the purpose of this essay to raise some questions about a central dogma held by many writers on Latin American politics. A typical interpretation asserts that "there is little doubt that the Latin American ideal of government for more than a century and a half has been that of political democracy." This is largely taken for granted. While few members of the intellectual community now engaged in Latin American research are specifically studying political ideology, it appears to me that many of us, whether beginning with a consensus or a conflict model, implicitly assume Latin American approval of democracy. In this we are following a long academic tradition, albeit with new methods.

Most North Americans tend to believe that a stable, viable Latin America would be a democratic Latin America. They derive that conviction from scholarly perceptions of early nineteenth-century political thought in Latin America. And this democratic argument is based upon two propositions: that Latin Americans borrowed the form and substance of their government; and that they failed to implant the alien system because they lacked political preparation. Writers who make these assumptions see the United States and French polities evolving out of their past despite certain foreign borrowings of an ideological and institutional nature. By contrast they often portray

---

From Glen Dealy, "Prolegomena on the Spanish American Political Tradition," *Hispanic American Historical Review,* 48 (1968), 37–52. Reprinted by permission of the author and Duke University Press. Most footnotes deleted. Italicized bracketed note in the text is by Helen Delpar.

Latin American political leaders as having not merely repeated the words of their late-eighteenth-century teachers, but as having actually plagiarized from their fellow students on both continents. Overwhelming scholarly opinion credits France and the United States as the ideological source of both the structure and the substance of Latin American government since 1810, while the influence of Spain, the mother country, is minimized or ignored.

This belief is so extensively accepted that it would be difficult to find a textbook on Latin America in which the thesis is not somewhere stated. For example, one writer speaks of the independence movement as sweeping through Latin America "under ideological banners borrowed from the United States and France." Another notes that the Wars for Independence were "fought in the name of the same ideals and aspirations that accompanied the American and French revolutions." A historian summarizes this theme: "The political ideals of liberty, natural rights, equality before the law, and popular sovereignty, which were developed in England, given irresistible literary expression in France, and first put into practice in the United States . . . constituted the great spiritual force back of the heroic struggle of Spanish America for emancipation."

Latin American nations are charged with having similarly borrowed the structure and organization of their new governments. A modern author asks: "What, then, are the sources of the material embodied in most of the written constitutions of the area?" "The answer," he says, "is that much of this material is derived, not from Spanish or Latin American experience as one would expect, but rather from the constitutional norms and practices of France and the United States." One textbook holds that "most of the states drew up liberal republican constitutions based upon that of the United States or that of the defunct French Republic," while another declares that "many of the earlier constitutions were copied after that of the United States . . . and frequently the French pattern was followed." A leading sociologist writes: "The new South American nations, looking around for models to follow, found ready at hand the philosophies of the French and American revolutions," and an economist holds that "the constitutions which were adopted by the new Latin American states were largely inspired, if not copied, from that of the United States, while the 'generous ideas of the French Revolution' served as the ideological foundation for the new republics." The implication is that Latin America is running upon a borrowed ideology and borrowed institutions. In addition, it is usually observed that the ideology and institutions so appropriated were democratic, in contrast to Spanish authoritarian colonial tradition.

The second assumption usually made by scholars is that the initial failure of borrowed democracy in Latin America can be traced to the men who tried to implement this alien type of government. Such scholars hold that the leaders of the revolutionary era were politically naïve, inexperienced, and untutored in government. This idea is at least as old as Lord Bryce.[1] Regarding the revolutionary upper class he observed that none of them had "any experience in civil administration."

The belief was carried forward by leading historians during the first half of this century. "Except for his membership in the comparatively unimportant *cabildos,* or local councils, the Spanish American creole, or native-born white, had almost no participation in the government of the colonies," says one of these works. In another essay one reads of the post-independence period that "the turbulence was due to political inexperience." "From the political viewpoint, what was the heritage left to these new states by Spain?" asks still another writer. He answers that "in the first place, there was the negative condition of political inexperience." And a textbook published in 1950 states: "The political inexperience of the ruling classes was another great obstacle to republican government." A contemporary political scientist agrees: "Latin American politics lacks an adequate theory or rationale drawn from experience." Finally, one may cite one of the more influential books on Latin America to appear in recent years: "The intellectuals had little more than a theoretical understanding of what they proposed to achieve. They had been so effectively excluded from participation in government by Spain and Portugal, in collaboration with the Catholic Church, that nearly all their knowledge of the art of government and politics was academic."

Assuming that the revolutionaries lacked political experience, historians have often exculpated them for not having established a functioning democracy: "It was unreasonable to expect that the Spanish Americans, with no schooling in self-government, exhausted and brutalized by twelve years of warfare . . . should at once have understood the successful operation of free institutions."

Thus there is widespread agreement over the Latin American preference for democratic government as well as the cause for its initial failure in that area. These two beliefs are at the center of present interpretations of Latin American politics. The conclusion which follows from these assumptions is that for the last century and a half there has existed a constant ambivalence between the "real" Latin American government somehow rooted in the colonial tradition, and

---

[1] James Bryce, Viscount Bryce (1838–1922), English historian and statesman, wrote *South America: Observations and Impressions,* rev. ed. (New York: Macmillan, 1917). [H.D.]

the "unreal" governmental superstructure based upon borrowed constitutions and ideologies. Thus constitutional government grounded
in democratic principles is the persistent aspiration, the "unreal." But
the "real" Latin America continually comes to the fore in the form
of rigged elections, caudillos, and the general repression of individual
rights.

In contemplating the dualisms of "real" and "unreal," fact and
theory, achievement and aspiration, scholars as well as political figures
directly concerned with Latin America tend to agree that the hiatus
between adopted democratic theory and contrary practices must be
filled in. They have assumed that it is possible to join the "real" (the
sordid reality of Latin American politics) with the "unreal" (the
adopted democratic ideology) and that this juncture will inevitably
lead toward democracy.

This essay will examine some of these assumptions as they pertain
to Spanish America. It will develop the thesis that there exists but
a single Spanish American tradition, and that this tradition exhibits
a rather close unity between theory and practice. While scholars may
certainly have differing interpretations of just what comprises the
tradition, they cannot seriously maintain that Spanish American governments are any more schizophrenic than are those of the United
States, France, or any other nation of the Western world. Spanish
Americans in 1810 did not sever themselves from the ideals and practices of their colonial past or reject three hundred years of Spanish
colonial institutions. The assumption that the patriot leaders borrowed the bulk of their ideological concepts is subject to question.
Many scholars hold that they primarily reflected French or North
American liberal thought, despite what Spanish Americans themselves
asserted in the early 1800s. Political tracts of the independence era
show that their authors possessed a remarkable genius for adopting
the language, style, and enthusiasm of the age while retaining their
own non-democratic heritage almost intact. Although some of the
ideas utilized by the republicans had their genesis in French and
North American eighteenth-century political thought, these foreign
sources provided the patriots with a great catalog of ideas from which
to choose. One may readily admit that the Spanish Americans referred
extensively to these sources. Through selection, deletion, and rewrit-
ing it was quite possible, however, to appropriate a considerable
amount of non-democratic ideology from this ideological pool. An
analysis of twenty-seven of the first constitutions written throughout
Spanish America from 1810 through 1815 will demonstrate the dis-
crepancy between Spanish American political thought and allegedly
borrowed ideas.

Eighteenth-century political liberalism was almost uniformly and overwhelmingly rejected by Spanish America's first statesmen. Though there is wide variety in the form and content of the early charters, not one could be construed as embodying constitutional liberalism, however loosely that term may be defined. Spanish American constitutions of this early period all began with a view of human nature which paralleled that of our founding fathers. Man was seen as essentially Hobbesian. Experience had taught that one must "protect the public and individual liberty against the oppression of those that govern." Upon this premise they built their constitutional order. Essentially pessimistic, they sought to regularize men's activities and to eliminate the vicissitudes and uncertainties of politics.

The answer which they gave to the problem of order, however, was vastly different from that of Anglo-Saxon constitutionalists. Unlike them the Spanish Americans had no faith whatever in the possibility of neutralizing evil through institutional arrangements. At the heart of our own constitutionalism is the conviction, stated by Kant, "that it is only necessary to organize the state well (which is indeed within the ability of man) and to direct these forces against each other in such wise that one balances the other in its devastating effect, or even suspends it. Consequently the result for reason is as if both selfish forces were nonexistent. Thus man, although not a morally good man, is compelled to be a good citizen." This assertion presupposes a confidence in the instrument which one has created, a belief that a particular type of organization or deployment of men will actually neutralize evil.

The Spanish Americans displayed none of this confidence. Their constitutionalism is identified with both Greek and Christian thought and separated from Machiavelli and from those who followed in one crucial respect—it was based upon a fundamental relationship between state-craft and soul-craft. The drafters of Spanish American constitutions were unable or unwilling to make a distinction between external conduct and the goods of the soul. Thus, at the center of these documents is the conviction that only the morally good man could be a good citizen. "Consequently, he who is not a good son, good father, good friend, good husband, good master, good servant, cannot be a good citizen." They could not perceive politics as the satisfaction of interests in the style of Locke. Politics to them was the achievement of the common good. And this, in the tradition of Aquinas, had no automatic connection with private interest.

Subscribing to such a view, as one might suspect, they were also necessarily committed to other conclusions. If the rules and procedures of constitutional government could not be trusted to defeat self-interest, it seemed to follow that good government depended upon the recruitment of good men. The province of Barinas, Venezuela, provided in its *Plan de Gobierno* [*Plan of Government*] that officials must be of "known virtue, talent, and patriotism, proven in the community." In Argentina, for another example, we find that the election of the executive "will fall of necessity on a person of known patriotism, integrity, public repute, good habits, and aptitude for the office."

But of course, there could be no surer means of obtaining good men than by sanctifying the electoral process itself. Thus in order to thrust self-interest out of men's minds and thereby ensure the moral purity of the newly elected, some constitutions went so far as to provide that midway in the elections all of the voters should go as a group to attend Mass and hear a sermon: "For the success of the elections, divine help must be sought, and to this effect, the electors united in cabildo before voting will proceed to the church. They will hear a Mass of the Holy Spirit conducted by the priest, who will then intone the hymn *Veni Creator,* and will briefly exhort the electors to justice and impartiality in the election." By such electoral procedures, it was hoped that "those that are to vote will put aside all passion and interest, friendship, etc., and will choose persons of honesty, of the best possible education, and of good public repute."

Since most of the charters begin with a declaration of rights, commentators have assumed the existence of premises similar to those held in the United States and France. However, there is reason to suspect this conclusion. Spanish Americans, through a confusion in terminology, seem to have equated modern natural right doctrine with their own natural law tradition. The apparent similarities, perhaps coupled with a proclivity to perceive only those principles which the commentators wished to underscore, tended to hide from view the quite different assumptions underlying each constitutional system.

The most striking example of this confusion is the fact that a number of the constitutions provided that in their schools children should be taught the fundamentals of Roman Catholicism and some version of The Rights of Man and of the Citizen. The writers do not seem to have recognized that the first presupposed a hierarchical view of society, the second an egalitarian view. They wished, at the same time, to preserve the past and to embrace the new. In this they saw no conflict. Thus, in framing their bills of rights, they found no contradiction in almost uniformly establishing Catholicism as the state religion and prohibiting the free exercise of all other "cults"; abridging, if not abolishing freedom of speech and of the press; and in some cases even denying the right of peaceable assembly or of presenting collective petitions to the government.

But the contrast with modern Western constitutionalism is perhaps sharpest when we consider the matter of limitations upon power. Carl Friedrich defines a constitutional government as one based upon "the establishment and maintenance of effective restraints upon political and more especially upon governmental action." [2] And he considers these restraints to be rooted primarily in a division of power—between legislative, executive, and judicial and/or between central and local government. The notion of a limitation upon power was not new to the eighteenth century, but was firmly rooted in the medieval tradition. Yet, as Charles H. McIlwain has affirmed, there is no medieval doctrine of a separation of powers as the basis for limitation.[3]

Spanish Americans in 1810 were clearly thinking more in medieval terms. Limitation for them was not equivalent to separation of powers, although the constitutions formally provided for separation. A close reading shows that almost without exception overwhelming power was finally vested in one body. While others were more subtle, a Colombian constitution states with amazing frankness: "Only the Legislative Power has the authority to interpret, amplify, limit, or comment on the laws, always adhering, however, in these matters to the formalities that are required and which are prescribed for their establishment. The Executive and Judicial Powers must follow them to the letter and consult the Legislative Body in case of doubt."

Restraints were not procedural but moral. Following the Romans, the makers of Spanish American constitutions were charmed by the possibility of establishing a government based upon virtue. In some cases they provided for a body of moral censors to interpret this principle: "there will be a Senate of censure and protection . . . in order to sustain this Constitution and the rights of the people, to the end that either officially or through requirement by any citizen, any infraction or usurpation of all or each one of the three Powers—Executive, Legislative and Judicial—that is against the tenor of the Constitution may be claimed." In other constitutions it was left to moral education, sermons before elections, and elaborate tattle-tale procedures to hold men to a virtuous course of action.

Political responsibility in a constitutional democracy is primarily exacted through the electoral process. These early constitutions by contrast demonstrated their distrust of elections by turning to a colonial practice, the *residencia*. Under this system government officials were subjected to a judicial inquiry at the end of their term of office. Anyone could make a charge, and it would be duly investigated. The sweeping breadth of possible accusation is suggested by the Mexican

[2] Carl J. Friedrich, *Constitutional Government and Democracy* (New York: Ginn, 1950), p. 123.

[3] Charles H. McIlwain, *Constitutionalism: Ancient and Modern* (Ithaca: Cornell University Press, 1958), p. 142.

constitution of 1814 which provided prosecution "for the crimes of heresy and apostasy, and for crimes of state, especially for those of misfeasance, extortion, and the squandering of public funds." Thus not the hope of reelection but the fear of legal action was believed to keep men moral while they exercised political responsibility.

Constitutional government in early Spanish America can be set in relief by a consideration of *Federalist* paper No. 10. Madison had declared that "there are two methods of curing the mischiefs of faction. The one, by removing its causes; the other, by controlling its effects." But only a brief examination of the proposition led him to conclude that the "*causes* of faction cannot be removed; and that relief is only to be sought in the means of controlling its *effects*." The Spanish Americans soon came to the opposite conclusion—they believed that political diversity could be checked only by dealing with its causes. In pursuing this assumption to its logical conclusion, they fulfilled Madison's requisites amazingly well. He had suggested two methods by which the causes of faction might be removed, "the one, by destroying the liberty which is essential to its existence; the other, by giving to every citizen the same opinions, the same passions, and the same interests."

Certain provisions which tended to destroy liberty have already been described. For example, the establishment of a state church and the eradication or curbing of some basic political freedoms have been noted. But at the very core of the early constitutions was the attempt to achieve a uniformity of opinion, an attempt grounded in the belief that similar passions and interests were not only desirable but possible. The basis of this assumption was derived from a near unanimity in religious matters: "Since there can be no happiness without civil liberty, nor liberty without morality, nor morality without religion, the government is to look upon it (religion) as the strongest bond of society, its most precious interest, and the first law of the Republic." This unanimity in religion was held to be a natural course of affairs and one which could be readily extended to other parts of the socio-political order. In the negative sense, no freedoms were allowed which might be contrary to good customs, either public or private. On the positive side, a concerted effort was made to achieve unity through an active policy of political education. In Argentina, by way of illustration, a weekly news-sheet, the *Censor*, was to be established. Its principal object was "to reflect on all the procedures and unjust acts of the public functionaries and abuses in the country, showing the people their rights and true interests." No private educational institutions were allowed, and state schools were usually to be minutely supervised by the national congresses. Finally, the concluding statements of a constitution itself were often an injunction toward political unanimity: "Read it, study it, and make your children learn it. May the Constitution be your second catechism. Sustain it with your zeal and vigilance. . . ."

Although one might continue to enumerate these rather startling constitutional provisions, perhaps enough has been said to bring into question the conventional view that Spanish America engaged in wholesale borrowing of a liberal foreign ideology in its early governance. No attempt has been made to give a consistent outline of the political philosophy of Spanish America during the independence period. Rather, the goal has been to demonstrate that the preponderant weight of its political thought was derived from sources other than modern Western constitutional philosophy, broadly construed. The purpose has been to cast doubt upon the current notion that Spanish America lives as a split personality, ever striving to unify itself in the direction of its democratic superstructure adopted in 1810. This is a prescriptive myth. Democratic theory was not embraced at that time. The forms of government bore certain similarities to other constitutional democracies, and at times the language even sounded familiar, but the content was in many basic ways at the opposite pole.

The second argument—that the men who attempted to implant this allegedly alien type of government failed because they lacked political preparation—is also open to question. The founding fathers did have wide political experience prior to their wars for independence. During the first five years of the movement for independence in northern South America approximately twenty constitutional charters were drawn up in the provinces and capitals of the old viceroyalty of New Granada—present-day Ecuador, Colombia, Venezuela, and Panama. A list of the men who signed these fundamental documents may be representative of all Spanish America. Extensive research in the colonial archives of New Granada indicates the degree to which these men were politically active prior to the independence movements. Of the 468 men who signed these early charters, no fewer than 303 had served in the Spanish colonial government before the wars of independence began. Among these were 92 lawyers, 100 members of cabildos, 107 in lesser bureaucratic positions, 28 militiamen, and 104 clergymen.

Not only lawyers, but clergymen and militiamen as well were politically influential in colonial politics. To appreciate the import of the clerical figures one should recall that colonial Spanish America had operated under an integrated church-state governmental bureaucracy. Because of certain papal bulls, Spanish kings near the beginning of the sixteenth century were granted the *patronato real* in perpetuity. Thus the clergy came to serve at the pleasure of the kings of Spain rather than directly under the papacy. They soon became perhaps the most politically minded body of men in the Spanish bureaucracy.[4]

Almost by definition lawyers were part of the political structure of Spanish colonial government. In order to practice law before the royal *audiencia,* they must have first received a degree in law from one of the state administered colleges. Here they were educated in Roman civil law and canon law as well as the *Leyes de Indias.* In addition, they were obliged to serve a four-year apprenticeship to another lawyer. This training gave them a thorough grounding in the intricacies of colonial public administration. At the end of the designated period of preparation they were required to pass an oral examination and then more often than not they became an integral part of the Spanish bureaucracy. Frequently those following a military career were also deeply involved in political matters. It was by no means uncommon for them to be named to civil as well as military posts. Although as a group they tended to be less educated than the lawyers and clergy, normally they too had some formal education. Training in the *colegios* was geared toward the creation of future political elites, and those who chose a military career felt themselves to be a part of that elite group much as the lawyers and the clerics. Obviously the founders were experienced in the philosophy and intricacies of colonial government. The question is not only *how much* experience but *what kind* of experience they had. It is possible that the "failure" of Spanish American governments in 1810 as in 1966 is really not a failure to achieve democracy, but a triumph for the ideals and aspirations which were theirs since colonial days.

One must conclude, then, that neither lack of prior experience nor a borrowed political ideology can explain the failure of Spanish Americans to establish viable democracy as we know it. Rather, it would seem that they consciously chose to implement a system of government which in both theory and practice had much in common with their tradition. If this is the case, one may well hesitate before discarding contemporary Spanish American constitutionalism and philosophy as irrelevant to the "real" political process. We cannot operate upon the facile assertion that Spanish Americans have long suffered from the effects of their vain aspirations toward liberal constitutionalism. The revised

---

[4] However, I do not wish to convey the impression that clerical and secular officials always worked together harmoniously during the colonial days. A bibliography of the colonial church-state relationship may be found in Fredrick B. Pike, *The Conflict Between Church and State in Latin America* (New York, 1964), 233-235.

premises raise many questions. Central to our consideration, however, is whether those peoples still aspire to the type of "democracy" envisaged in 1810.

A brief glance at contemporary Spanish American constitutions elicits some striking parallels to those first charters of 1810—and some amazingly non-liberal, non-democratic propositions. As constitutions have come and gone during the past century and a half, the philosophic beliefs of the documents have become at times clouded and less explicit. Nevertheless, the direction of thought has maintained a most significant continuity since 1810. Throughout these years the vision has been essentially non-democratic; it still is.

⋙ 2 ⋘

The Defects from Which Mexico Suffers

Lucas Alamán

Few of the Latin American nations experienced greater political turmoil in the nineteenth century than did Mexico. In its first fifty years of independence the presidency was held by over thirty different individuals, only three of whom served out their full terms. Lucas Alamán (1792–1853), the statesman and historian who was Mexico's ablest nineteenth-century conservative, blamed many of his country's ills on the excessive powers of the states. In this reading, Alamán proposes the division of the states and the reestablishment of the system of territorial organization that had existed during most of the colonial period. He also urges his countrymen to confer political power upon men spiritually akin to the eighteenth-century viceroys of New Spain.

. . . Some of the defects from which the Mexican nation suffers are the result of the general course of things and of the spirit of the country, and are not easy to remedy with immediate measures. Just as the damage has developed gradually, so it must be remedied little by little as society profits from the mistakes of the past. Fortunately, these defects are no longer of such great importance. By imitating Europe we have created the problems ourselves, and they therefore can be resolved with the appropriate measures. If we are patient, it is still possible to avoid all of the mistakes and to gain all of the advantages of the experiences of the rest of the world.

Other defects from which we suffer are the result of our institutions. For the executive power, the problem lies in the feebleness of its actions and in the lack of effective protection for the citizens against the abuses of this same power. On the one hand, the executive power is weak in order to conform with the law. On the other hand, it is absolute in order to break it. As for the legislative power, the problem lies in its excessive functions and in the defective composition of the co-legislative bodies. The congress as it is now constituted is not only

From Samuel L. Baily (ed. and tr.), *Nationalism in Latin America.* (New York: Knopf, 1971), pp. 54–57. Copyright © 1970 by Samuel L. Baily. Reprinted by permission of Alfred A. Knopf, Inc.

useless, but an impediment to the regular order of any government which might be able to fill the needs of the nation. Regarding the states, the problem lies in their excessive power and in their inequality. These defects must be remedied in conformity with the country's traditions; otherwise the reform will not be popular or permanent. We must not attempt to alter drastically all that exists, but instead we must conserve the best features of the present system and suppress only that which is prejudicial and harmful.

One of our strongest traditions, and one which has contributed much to the origin, reestablishment, and conservation of the federal system, is that of loyalty to the locality or what is called provincialism. Reduced to just and prudent limits, provincialism should produce good results; it encourages greater care in the administration of the particular interests of each area and each state, and it stimulates education and useful works of leisure and decoration. This fondness for the place where one is born or is settled or owns property is observable in those attempts at revolution in which respect for and loyalty to the ancient capital of the nation is asserted. Thus, in 1823, we saw Colima separating itself from Guadalajara in order to deal directly, as a territory of the federation, with the government of Mexico. The same situation occurred in Orizaba, Mazatlán, Aguascalientes and other areas, and still others are inclined toward the same action. If existing states broke up into their constituent departments or districts, it would be to the advantage of all the departments. This alone, with the extensive consequences that it would have, would be enough to bring the nation out of all the difficulties in which it finds itself, by establishing a simple, symmetric, uniform and not-difficult-to-obtain order in all areas.

Before explaining these points, I must say that this [organization] would not be new; it would be the reestablishment of the ancient system of the government of New Spain before the creation of the intendancies that later became states. The principle is such that we can make exceptions with respect to those states of small size and population—Chiapas, Nuevo León, Querétaro and Tabasco—which should not be further divided. In executing this reform, it would be possible to add a part of those states of greater size and number of inhabitants to others, and to make all states roughly equal. France did this when it divided the ancient states and provinces into departments, and this division has greatly benefited that country because it has kept in power all of the governments that have come to power since the national assembly. . . .

In this manner, we would establish a system—symmetrical and uniform in all areas, economical to run, conforming with the opinions and traditions that have created it—adequate for the nation's government. The principles of the federation would be preserved and strengthened. The government's actions would hardly be felt and would not be contradictory, and therefore they would be more effective. The action of the congresses and governments of the states would be reduced to distributing local benefits and improvements. The state would be a paternal authority, but it would not become oppressive, as has happened in some cases, creating hate, exciting discontent and provoking revolution. The proprietor class would take a larger part in public affairs because it would be in its self-interest to do so. When it understood that this system depends upon it, the proprietor class would pledge itself to guarantee the system's continued existence. This would give birth to public spirit, now completely absent, and would reestablish the lost national character. Mexicans would have a name to honor, a country to defend, and a government to respect, not because of the fear of punishment, but because of the benefits it dispenses, the honor it acquires and the consideration it merits.

In order to obtain these goals, it is not essential that power fall on men of great capacity. Honor and integrity are all that is necessary. The skill with which the viceroys governed is due to these qualities. During the past century, they brought New Spain out of the condition of disorder and decadence to which it had been reduced during the last reigns of the Hapsburgs. Not only did they solve all of the existing administrative problems, but they also anticipated future problems. The Duke of Linares (1711–1716), the Marquis of Casafuerte (1722–1734), Bucareli (1771–1779), Revilla Gigedo (1789–1794)—they had no other secret. Apodaca (1816–1821), without other means than these, reestablished the public finances in circumstances much more difficult than the present ones. Their principles were those of Christian morality, and when they served the king faithfully, their loyalty was based on the firm belief that in this manner they were also serving God. On the same basis was formed the respectable class of employees that aspired to be promoted only by fulfilling its obligations, and to whose zealousness and intelligence is owed the efficiency of the offices of government. Because they were men, they at times transgressed and abused their positions. But when these men were clearsighted, like the Duke of Linares to whom "the most rigorous review is that of the viceroy's judgement by the Divine Majesty," it was impossible for them to fall into the excesses to which those who did not have this conviction succumbed.

In light of the above, it would be a good thing to name a commission, not to exceed three to five individuals, charged with the task of establishing the nation. This commission would not be opposed because of the small number of its members, because, in the fiction of the representative system, one can be represented by five as well as by one hundred. In accordance with the general plan that it might propose, this commission would have the power to name all those it believes necessary for the organization of each of the branches of government. All of the authorities and offices of the Republic would be obliged to assist the commission and to give it whatever information and data might be necessary. By the end of a year, all of its work would be concluded. This is the only possible way to reorganize, completely and simultaneously, all of the branches of the administration. It must be recognized that the system might not succeed in all parts from the beginning, but the experience of time will point out the problems that cannot be prevented before putting a political system into practice. At the end of two years we could revise all of it, keeping in mind the observations that had been made about each of the parts, in order to amend and rectify those things which needed change. Congress could make those changes that the course of time demanded.

‏ ‏＊§ 3 §＊

Church-State Relations in the Nineteenth Century

———— ◆◄◐►◆ ————

Fredrick B. Pike

To reform-minded liberals of nineteenth-century Latin America, the Catholic Church was an obvious target. Not only had it been closely associated with the Spanish monarchy but, in the opinion of liberals, its wealth, its corporate privileges, and its control over education made it a formidable threat to republican institutions. Here, Professor Fredrick B. Pike of the University of Notre Dame discusses the origins of the bitter conflicts that erupted between the Church and anticlerical governments in the nineteenth century. Professor Pike is also the author of Chile and the United States, 1808–1962 *(Notre Dame, Ind., 1963), and* The Modern History of Peru *(New York: Praeger, 1967).*

. . . Independence, as an accomplished fact, was . . . to present the Church with the greatest temporal challenge it had confronted in Hispanic America. During the colonial period, in spite of not infrequent clashes between representatives of royal and clerical interests, the crown consistently prevented civilian forces from striking genuinely crippling blows against the Church. On its part, the Church generally impressed upon the masses their duty to respect royal authority. At times, Inquisition officials seemed as concerned about stamping out signs of treason as extirpating heresy. There was a symbolic relationship between Church and state which worked to the advantage of both.

With the coming of independence to Spanish America, Church-state relations underwent a dramatic transformation. Gone was the crown, the great political institution and the one power that had been able to control contending administrative agencies. The Church remained. But without the backing of the crown, its position as an unassailable bastion of privilege was in jeopardy. Accordingly, the Church entered more directly into the political arena, hoping through political action

From Fredrick B. Pike (ed.), *The Conflict Between Church and State in Latin America* (New York: Knopf, 1964), pp. 12–19. Copyright © 1964 by Fredrick B. Pike. Reprinted by permission of Alfred A. Knopf, Inc. Italicized bracketed note in the text is by Helen Delpar.

to protect its customary rights and privileges. As often as not, the Church sustained defeat in its political ventures. When this occurred, civilian groups, at last able to give meaningful expression to their long pent-up hostility toward churchmen, moved quickly to strip the Church of its temporal power. Sometimes they even took advantage of the Church's political discomfiture to deprive it of the effective means to exercise its spiritual office. They proceeded to this extreme not only because of intellectual conviction, but because of the desire to stamp out any vestige of influence that the Church could conceivably find useful in staging a political comeback.

Even while Latin American revolutions for independence from Spain were still in progress, heated dispute between Church and state officials had burst forth over the issue of patronage. The insurrectionary governments claimed that they had inherited the patronage rights once exercised by the Spanish crown. Patronage, they insisted, was one of the inalienable prerogatives of sovereignty. Therefore, when new groups acquired sovereign control over areas once ruled by Spain, they gained the rights of patronage that had inhered in the Spanish crown. On the other hand, many churchmen contended that control over patronage had been bestowed upon the monarchs as a special, temporary, and revokable privilege. The loss of sovereignty by the crown, they asserted, meant that the Church should reclaim authority over religious affairs and so begin to exercise directly the powers of patronage.

Independence had scarcely been won when political leaders and churchmen began to argue over taxation. Should, for example, the national government continue the colonial tradition of collecting tithes for the Church? Invariably, this question precipitated serious disagreements. The separate Church courts, provided for by the ecclesiastical *fuero* of colonial times, also came in for attack. Gradually, they were abolished by national administrations. Much Church property was also seized and a substantial number of religious communities were suppressed, occasionally against a background of violence.

The issues of patronage, Church taxes, separate ecclesiastical courts, and Church property had already been fought out to a large degree in various European nations, beginning as early as the eleventh century, and by 1800 had been substantially resolved. Although in the process the temporal power of the Church had been weakened, in general its rights to minister to the spiritual needs of its followers had not been denied. In Latin America, vexatious problems that had concerned Europeans for centuries were resolved in the course of a few short years.

Other disputes which had erupted generations and even centuries previously in Europe, and for which certain accommodations had been arranged, appeared in Latin America only after the attainment of independence. For a variety of reasons, many political leaders in the new republics sought to limit Church control over education and charity. In several Latin American countries cemeteries were secularized so as to deprive the Church of the formidable power to deny burial in the *campo santo* (consecrated ground) to those who had incurred its displeasure. Laws were also passed to remove marriage from the control of the Church by providing for the legality, sometimes the exclusive legality, of civil marriage contracts. In addition, some republics enacted laws of religious toleration during the nineteenth century. To these measures Church authorities often replied with massive excommunications. At other times, supported by large numbers of the lay faithful, they resorted to civil insurrection.

During this period Latin Americans did not develop indigenous intellectual movements, but looked to Europe for philosophical guidance. The anticlerical aspect of nineteenth-century European liberalism found fertile ground in an environment where hostility toward the clergy had long existed. Furthermore, particularly in Mexico, Chile, and Brazil, intellectuals were influenced by the positivism of Auguste Comte. Positivism proclaimed that the laws of progress for civilizations could be discovered only by scientific, empirical investigation. Positivists equated revealed truth with superstition and maintained that formal religions must be swept away so that allegedly obscurantist, unfounded views could not stand in the way of progress based upon scientific truth.

The changes in status with which the Church was threatened during this period meant an inevitable reduction of its material and temporal strength. Churchmen, however, tended to interpret any attempt to alter the *status quo* as inimical to religion itself. They were largely justified in this alarmist viewpoint, precisely because most champions of change and reform believed that the Church, *per se,* was incompatible with modern progress. Clerical fear of novelty sprang also from the manner in which many churchmen of the previous century had indiscriminately welcomed the ideas of the Enlightenment. This movement had led to notable scientific and economic progress in Latin America, as well as to a remarkable freedom of intellectual activity. However, in Latin America the Enlightenment in its ultimate effects also spawned a lack of respect for authority, a religious relativism, and a secularism which redounded to the serious disadvantage of the Church and the values it defended. Because they had once been beguiled by what had appeared to be ideas that were useful and yet not opposed to formal religion, churchmen became hyper-cautious and consistently opposed manifestations of the new.

Church authorities and their lay partisans in the late nineteenth century insisted that the only unifying, constructive tradition from which Latin Americans could establish order and achieve progress was the Catholic tradition of colonial times. To depart from it, they contended, would produce chaos and political institutions that were distorted and unnatural because they were not rooted in the past. Diego Portales of Chile (the dominant political figure from 1830 to 1837), Gabriel García Moreno of Ecuador (sometimes the president and always the main political power from 1860 to 1875), and Rafael Núñez of Colombia (the president or president-maker from 1880 to 1894) were among those controversial statesmen who felt it necessary to preserve the traditional power and influence of the Church as a means of attaining national unity and stability. . . . On the other hand, anticlerical leaders insisted that the Catholic tradition was one of sterility and oppression. Their viewpoint is . . . manifested . . . in extreme form by a statement of the nineteenth-century Chilean journalist Domingo Arteaga Alemparte: "So deplorable has been the record of the Church in regard to political interference that it is impossible for a Catholic to be a good citizen."

The struggle between liberal, anticlerical forces and conservative, proclerical groups was violent and protracted in Guatemala, Ecuador and Colombia. The passion with which Colombians of these two respective camps assailed each other during the nineteenth century is reflected in the works of many national historians. Writing in 1938, Colombia's liberal author Jorge Espinosa Londoño referred to the origins of the Church-state dispute in the national period:

> The fanaticism of the population was the polar star for the leaders of the reactionary movement. . . . In waging their political fights, the Conservatives always associated their cause with that of the Divinity. Ultimately, they profaned the name of Christ. . . . Those people taking up the banner of religion confused, or found it expedient to seem to confuse, the purely political actions of the government with the universal principles of religion.

José Manuel Groot, a conservative intellectual of the past century, interprets events from an opposite point of view:

> Peace and harmony could have been established then [in 1830], but the uncurbed passions of the anticlerical, liberal forces did not permit this, and the unhappy consequences have continued to plague the country, bringing discord, combat, and revolution. . . . The truth is that the ecclesiastical and political life of our nation had been always so intertwined that religion was necessarily the vital element of all our civilization and progress.

It was in Mexico that the struggle between Church and state reached a peak of bitterness, doing much to shape the character of Mexican history throughout the national period. The intensity of partisan emotions which this dispute evoked is suggested by the statements of two [twentieth-century] Mexican historians. The liberal Alfonso Toro declares:

> The clergy had made of colonial society an assembly of hypocritical and subservient human beings. The priests made the Mexicans as ignorant as they were, as dirty, immoral and lazy as they were. Accordingly, the reformers have always tended to root out these vices, seeking to reduce the clergy to its proper role and to deprive it of the property it has collected and monopolized to the disadvantage of the people.[1]

At the opposite extreme Félix Navarrete maintains:

> The detractors of the Church pretend that grounds have existed for a struggle between the Church and the civil power since the earliest period of the discovery of Mexico, and that this fight has always been provoked by the Church. I say that grounds for this struggle have existed in Mexico only since 1833, the year in which Masonry provoked it so as to bring an end to the influence of the clergy and even to the clergy itself. From that time on the Church has only defended itself against attacks.[2]

.   .   .

Brazil, because it remained a monarchy for sixty-seven years after declaring its independence from Portugal, maintained intact many aspects of the administrative institutions fashioned during the colonial period. The relationship between Church and state was not altered essentially, and the battles that marked the dealings of churchmen with political leaders in the Spanish-American republics were largely absent from Brazilian development. In part, this was because Brazilian Catholicism had developed a greater flexibility and spirit of compromise than Hispanic-American Catholicism. It is notable that in 1810 a Portuguese-English treaty extended rights to the British to build a Protestant church in Rio de Janeiro, although it had to look like a private house and could not use bells to summon worshippers. The Bishop of Rio, José Caetano, strongly favored this concession to

---

[1] *La iglesia y el estado en México: estudio sobre los conflictos entre el clero católico y los gobiernos mexicanos desde la independencia hasta nuestros días* (México, D.F., 1927), p. 43.

[2] *La lucha entre el poder civil y el clero a la luz de la historia* (El Paso, Texas, 1935), p. 230.

Protestant believers. It is difficult to imagine a similar response from a Spanish prelate in the year 1810.

The remarkable figure of Fr. Diogo Antônio Feijó also imparted an unusual character to Church-state relations in the early years of Brazilian independence. Fr. Feijó, regent of Brazil from 1835 to 1837, was a pious priest and at the same time the leader of anti-clerical forces who demanded the superiority of civil over ecclesiastical authority, and the confiscation of the wealth of the religious orders. Moreover, Fr. Feijó abandoned the wearing of his clerical garb and led an unsuccessful campaign for legislation to permit the clergy to marry.

The most dramatic and consequential Church-state clash in nineteenth-century Brazil erupted in 1872, and involved the attempt of two bishops to promulgate and enforce instructions from the Vatican that had not been officially cleared by civil authorities. Although the dispute left unpleasant memories on both sides, it did not generate the sort of bitterness that prevailed in several of Brazil's sister republics of Latin America. When the monarchy was overthrown and Brazil became a republic in 1889, Church and state officials were able within a short time to reach an amicable agreement upon separation of the two powers.

⋅§ 4 §⋅

The Origins of *Caudillismo*

◆◀◉▶◆

François Chevalier

*The power vacuum created by the extinction of Spanish authority in
America is usually cited as a principal cause of the emergence in the
early nineteenth century of* caudillos *and* caciques, *who ruled arbitrarily, and sometimes brutally, over a nation or a locality. In this
selection, François Chevalier of the University of Bordeaux discusses
the origins and characteristics of* caudillismo *and* caciquismo *in Spanish America, with special reference to the nineteenth century. Professor Chevalier is best known for his analysis of* Land and Society in
Colonial Mexico: The Great Hacienda *(Berkeley: University of California Press, 1963).*

It has been observed that in many countries of Central and South
America the local and even national government has often been
monopolized by "strong men," *caudillos* and *caciques* who perpetuate
themselves in power, sometimes even under cover of constitutional or
judicial fictions. There is, also, nothing new in emphasizing the exceptional importance that "personal relations" have had in these
countries for the conduct of business affairs and the function of
institutions in general. But rarely have these two phenomena been
linked so as to delve deeply into their causes and to reveal their
mechanisms. . . .

Origins

In times or in countries where life is difficult, where man is placed
in a hostile environment constantly menaced by enemies or famine,
where a state, if it exists at all, is too weak or too far away to insure
the security of individuals, these individuals associate and naturally

From Hugh M. Hamill, Jr. (ed. and tr.), *Dictatorship in Spanish America*
(New York: Knopf, 1965), pp. 36–51. Copyright © 1965 by Hugh M. Hamill,
Jr. Reprinted by permission of the author and Alfred A. Knopf, Inc. Italicized
bracketed notes in the text are by Helen Delpar.

coalesce into firm groups: at first, into groups of relatives because the ties of blood are fundamental; then into groups of the most faithful, of clients, of friends . . . around an elder, a chief, a powerful man, around a man who has more experience, more initiative, or a man of more material means than the others. Ties of blood and personal bonds are the only ones which have a real importance in societies where written contracts, if they exist at all, play a limited role; where the typical relations of modern societies, and even of certain traditional communities, are found only in the embryonic state.

There are countless examples. In Rome itself the *gens* [*clan*] and the *clientes* [*dependents*] survived in spite of the development of a central power having a relatively complex administration and in spite of the birth of the personal property concept under Roman Law, which favors the autonomy of the individual capable of operating independently of a group. With the Germanic invasions, the *clientes* and the group reappear with new vigor, not because of a peculiarly Germanic influence . . . but because of the fact that the newcomers were simply more primitive socially. . . .

In the West during the Middle Ages, the chiefs were surrounded by relatives and retainers who lived and ate with them, who helped them in time of peace as well as in time of war. While in a large part of Europe these faithful received land, at first temporarily and later on in a hereditary manner according to the classic feudal system, in Castille, on the contrary, . . . the *criados* or retainers continued to be rewarded ordinarily by sustenance and by presents, for reasons which doubtless have something to do with the Reconquest of the Peninsula from the Moors and the possible distribution of important spoils of war.

No matter what the causes may be . . . it is noteworthy that in the sixteenth and seventeenth centuries groups of criados around powerful men and high royal functionaries persisted in Spain. They might be hidalgos and nobles; and when it was a question of men of high rank, they did not always live permanently under the same roof as their protector, all the more because they were often charged with missions of confidence, even to foreign countries. Thus Hernán Cortés was a criado of Diego Velázquez. The obligations were clear for each party: protection, help, favors, and presents from one side; of faithfulness and help from the other.

The institution went to America with the conquerors, and it found new forces in the immensity of a continent where the king of Spain had difficulty in making his authority felt in all places. In a case in Mexico in 1602, Guadalajara had only 160 households, but the president of the *Audiencia* there was surrounded by forty-six relatives and by a quantity of "dependents" who monopolized the offices and the most lucrative jobs of a huge region called New Galicia. Similar cases are by no means rare in the New World. [The Crown], however, reacted against these practices and sought to prohibit the distribution of administrative positions or other advantages to the retainers of Royal bureaucrats. . . . Above all the latter changed posts and could therefore take root in one place with difficulty.

On the other hand, there were few obstacles for the private citizens who had the means, whether Spaniard, creoles, or mestizo, to have permanently the kind of personal following that poverty, insecurity, or the hostility of the environment often rendered natural, and even necessary, in many regions of the vast Spanish Empire. . . . Incapable of extending its administration everywhere, at least before the end of the eighteenth century . . . , the government of Madrid sometimes found it advantageous to use powerful men so that order might be kept, even at the cost of abandoning to them a little of its sovereignty. Sometimes contracts of this kind were made with rich proprietors of lands or mines, who took it upon themselves to maintain private armies in exchange for honorary titles. . . . Nevertheless, in a time of monarchic centralization, the king avoided as much as possible the creation of judicial precedents lest his rights be alienated, especially if they were to be hereditarily alienated. There were, therefore, more frequently *de facto* situations, especially in dangerous areas or in troubled times.

It is clear that the mentality of the great proprietors encouraged the proliferation of personal bonds. If they received only a small income from their haciendas, which were, by the way, heavily mortgaged to the Church, they found compensation in the quasi-seignorial prestige that a crowd of men attached to their land and to their person could give to their masters. . . . Employing the authority of their military titles, they occasionally led these followers to fight nomadic Indians and bandits or, during the wars of independence, the party opposed to the one they themselves had chosen. Finally, the haciendas were often entailed estates which belonged to dynasties rather than to individuals; these family lines thus insured the importance and the primitive force of blood ties.

In fact, certain proprietors reigned on their estates somewhat in the manner of lords and seigneurs of ancient time, at least before the reforms of the eighteenth century. Sure of themselves in a world where the hierarchy seemed immutable, their psychology was simple and their authority a tradition. It would not always be so after the earthquakes of independence which seriously shook the established order.

The National Period

In renouncing the presidency of Gran Colombia, Bolívar, in a disillusioned address, foresaw the coming of cruel petty tyrants "of all races and colors" who would divide the continent among themselves. In fact, caudillos, big and small, sprang everywhere from the wars of emancipation. The disappearance of the Spanish state left a void, made larger by the retreat of the traditional aristocracy and soon that of the Church. When a precarious peace returned, the new men often kept the power which audacity and chance had given them. The most energetic—sometimes the most violent—became "the first of his village or the republic, the one who has more authority or power and who because of his pride wants to make himself feared and obeyed by all his inferiors," to employ the definition for "cacique" used by the first Spanish dictionary of the Academy published in 1729.

Where did these chiefs come from? Sometimes they emerged from the old landed aristocracy, but more often from the petite bourgeoisie or from the people. Because it is usually not in his tradition . . . that he commands others, the new man does not feel sure of himself. Therefore he is in urgent need to affirm his power, if necessary by force, and at the same time to distinguish himself from the common man. Thereby we see a new style among these dictators, these caudillos and caciques of the national era, whether they sprang directly or not from the wars of independence.

The Horsemen

In countries where "mounted barbarism" of the gauchos or of the llaneros still ruled, in rural areas of little population, these all powerful caudillos were often primitive beings whose power seemed to be tied to physical force and virility (*hombre macho*). In Argentina the Spanish state abandoned the region to these "kings of the big spurs," to use Sarmiento's expression: a Facundo "courageous almost to boldness, gifted with Herculean strength," extraordinary knight who imposed himself by violence, and even by terror; a Rosas so overflowing with energy and with life that . . . he could ride a horse almost to death . . . ; in Venezuela a Páez, who became civilized later, Monagas, Zaraza . . . exalted in the popular . . . *corrido,* and also a fictional character taken from life, like Rómulo Gallegos' Doña Bárbara, the terrible female cacique of the boundless wild llano. . . .

It would be easy to make this list of names longer, because in those regions of extensive animal raising which cover vast spaces in almost all the countries of the American continent, it is or was almost impossible to conceive of the chief as other than a man physically stronger than his rivals, a better horseman and a better shot . . . (which, however, did not always prevent him from meeting a violent death . . .).

The Military Men

In general, the easiest means for an ambitious man . . . to secure power is, naturally, through a military career. This is true whether he be a man raised by revolution or war to leadership, or whether [he] be a professional soldier, the latter being of particular value in one of the numerous countries where the army is, with the Church, one of the only two solidly organized forces. . . . In fact, almost all dictators have been military men. Those who were not so originally have usually taken the title of "general." . . .

Even in Mexico, a country which has long passed the stage of *pronunciamientos,* and where politics is entirely in the hands of civilians, it is only rather recently that a general changes posts without including in his transfer all those officers who were personally attached to him. This situation, outmoded under the government of Porfirio Díaz, was recreated by the revolution of 1910–1917. Thus in 1919 the psychology of the caudillo and the resort to purely personal ties were still expressed in a manifesto of General Obregón: "I declare myself a candidate for the presidency of the republic, backed by my own pistols without ties with any parties nor offers of any platform. My background as a soldier of the revolution is sufficient guarantee that I know how to insure the well-being of the people and the happiness of the country. He who loves me follow me!"

Other Styles

In the old days the powerful men were great landlords and sometimes captains of private armies. Some of them, who had chosen the party of independence, kept their local power. In Mexico this was reinforced by the renewed incursions of nomadic Indians and by the climate of insecurity which existed in the whole country. The land being the essential source of income and prestige, the generals, caudillos, and caciques had to own haciendas or to acquire some if they had none to start with. Later Porfirio Díaz who favored large holdings . . . integrated the proprietors into his system because they seemed to him the most able to control local governments.

During the nineteenth century, however, ideals change while pressures of the haciendas on the rural communities increase. This brings about an uneasiness among the peasants which is expressed by uprisings of Indians and of village people or peons all anxious to recuperate their land. In Mexico this tendency is clear fifty or eighty years before the agrarian revolution began in 1910–1911. . . . So it was that caudillos of the new style appeared here and there, sensitive to the aspirations of the most humble rural groups from which they sometimes came.

Thus in Mexico General Juan Álvarez emerged all-powerful in the southwest and the state of Guerrero during the decades which followed independence. He is the type of the "good cacique," who lives very simply on his hacienda, and defends the Indian communities and the poor people in these vast regions of arid sierras. . . . In a series of neglected pamphlets, "the patriarch of the south" described the misery of the natives in dramatic fashion, with precise examples, and the methods which the proprietors use in order to despoil them of their water and their lands. . . . He himself quells uprisings by extending justice to the peasants, who are very deeply attached to him at the same time that they express their defiance toward the aloof government of the capital. . . .

Quite different, certainly, was the famous Manuel Lozada, absolute ruler of Nayarit, a little further north, which he dominated through fear and terror for several decades before his death in 1873, first as a bandit chief and then as military commander supported by the conservatives. He was even decorated by order of Napoleon III! This man, once a shepherd on a hacienda and of Cora Indian origin, was a born chief who enjoyed great prestige among all the natives and who did not hesitate, on occasion, to distribute the lands of a hacienda among his soldiers. Finally taken by treason and sent to the firing squad, fifty of Lozada's principal adherents accepted invitations to a great banquet of reconciliation where, at a signal—the host raising his glass—they were all assassinated.

But the chief who wants to stay in power forever—which is the essence of *caciquismo*—must be able to count on the collaboration and unconditional support of forces which he permanently attaches to his person. The popularity, the ascendancy, and the prestige, absolutely necessary to start with, are never sufficient for a prolonged retention of power. To rule by fear or by terror does not last if it is impossible to create a stable community of interest with the men and the groups on which the chief leans. Then, how to succeed? In countries where resources are few, the *primum vivere* is an unavoidable imperative: the chief must first be able to feed his relatives, his dependents . . . and the soldiers who support him. He must be rich.

To Be Rich

For the caudillo time is pressing. If he is not rich, he must become rich as soon as possible. . . .

Sarmiento in the last century described how Facundo Quiroga, the Argentine caudillo, gathered a large fortune; the means are numerous, from the collection of the tithe to gambling, but the terror he inspires is at the base of all gain. Who would dare bid above the ridiculously small sum which Facundo offers in order to get the right to collect the tithe? Who would dare break up a card game after having won the gold of this frightful chief? It is he alone who can decide when to end the game and it is he who, having unlimited resources at his disposal, will win.

Facundo was, certainly, a kind of a barbarian. Later, in other places, the means may have been more discreet, but especially for those who have nothing to start with influence peddling is a way to acquire some early capital; after which a fortune increases more easily by itself: monopolies on imports or manufacturing, extremely lucrative contracts obtained from the state for public works, contraband . . . and above all the acquisition through intimidation of the best land . . . are but a few of the ways to wealth. . . .

For the ambitious officer or politician during the nineteenth century, all kinds of financial arrangements allowed them to take a cut from the sums borrowed from England or other countries, sums which were generally guaranteed by the income from customs. During the second half of the nineteenth century, the Venezuelan dictator Guzmán Blanco became rich in such a way. . . . Later the increasing commercial relations and the development of foreign capitalistic enterprise in a large part of the continent offered increasing possibilities to the new man thirsty for power and money, a few of whom have made huge fortunes in the twentieth century. The guarantees that the men offered to powerful financial groups were compensated by effective support, thanks to which they maintained themselves in power. . . .

There are chiefs of state who still possess large fortunes. For instance, in a country of Central America an open letter to its president has recently been published, a letter which gives in detail all his businesses and properties—evidently inherited from his low-born father who had governed the country as an absolute master. The list makes quite an impression with its fifty-one stock-raising haciendas, forty-six coffee plantations, and eight of sugar cane; thirteen industries; his daily newspaper; his shipping, aviation, trucking, and import-export companies; and finally his interests in almost everything from the monopoly of firearms to gold exports. . . .

If modern capitalism did not color such a system, one would tend to think about the retainers who served their chief, making war or working for him, in exchange for food, presents, and protection. One might even recall the ancient concept of the personal patrimonial state. . . .

The Dependents

The men whom caudillos call upon first will naturally be their relatives, because the ties of blood are the surest and the strongest. Familial solidarity often remains very strong in rural and provincial environments, and is sometimes revealed in the form of extreme "vendettas." Spontaneously the relatives, even those living far away, take the side of that member of the family who occupies an important position or who wants to occupy it, and consequently they find themselves fighting with rival factions. These family rivalries, made so famous in the old days in Italy, divided many regions of the American continent, such as the Argentine Rioja at the time of Sarmiento. . . .

The relatives of the strong man expect from him positions, favors, or simply their daily bread. This reaction is so natural that any person receiving a fixed income of any importance would usually feed at his home his cousins and supporters who render him little services in return. For example, in Spain a successful torero may see his whole familial clan move into his house, expecting him to insure their subsistence. By the same token, the caudillo cannot refuse assistance in the form of positions and favors to relatives who, after all, are his surest support. Even the most personally disinterested men sometimes practice nepotism, which seemed natural enough in the old days. Today such practices are severely censured, at least in Mexico where the governor of [Michoacán] recently had to resign under pressure of public opinion. Newspaper readers were shocked to learn that his relatives occupied all the important positions of the state, ranging from treasury and tax collection offices to that of attorney general, including along the way the director of public works, the mayor of the only important city, and the state liquor inspector.

At a much higher level, [Anastasio Somoza of Nicaragua] placed his sons or near relatives at the head of the high command of the army, of the presidential guard, of the bank of issue, and of the presidency of the national assembly. . . . Another and most typical example would be [Trujillo] whose brothers, legitimate and illegitimate sons (the latter in impressive numbers), nephews, relatives, and allies divided among themselves the principal positions of the country in such a manner as to deal with it as with a big business or as a patrimony.

One cannot help but think of the groups of relatives and dependents of ancient Europe when one sees in such Latin American countries the parades of people who accompany, surround, and assist certain chiefs of state, politicians, or important figures when they move from one place to another, or even when they are in their own homes.

To the ties of blood can be added those which create a religious relationship between the *compadres* or godfathers . . . and the relatives of the baptized as well as the child himself. These ties often remain powerful enough to oblige the partners to help each other in all circumstances. Thus [Trujillo] systematically agreed, and even used pressure to become the godfather of thousands of children, obviously in order to create a tie of fidelity toward him with a large number of families, belonging by the way to all social classes including the most humble. There is no doubt that this practice gained [Trujillo] the support of a considerable part of the population, who became thus linked to him as if by a blood relationship. . . .

The local caciques lean so much on these *compadrazgos* that the word itself often takes on a political shade. Among the rural people, the mestizos, and the more advanced Indians, the extraordinary proliferation of these religious relationships even appears, in a spontaneous fashion, to replace and to recreate personal bonds . . . where solidarity among the clan has softened or lost its control. It has been noted that in Maya communities where ancient clannish organizations exist there are neither compadres nor *comadres*. Everywhere else, however, compadrazgo plays an essential role which is perhaps similar to that of the religious brotherhoods of Spain in creating reciprocal obligations of assistance which were, and still are, sometimes necessary in isolated regions where law has little influence and where the individual lacks personal guarantees. Furthermore, the ties of compadrazgo multiply even outside baptism: in some villages this occurs through the acquisition of a religious image to which sponsors or "godfathers" are assigned or through an important event in the life of a child . . . and in other places because all the ancestors and descendants of compadres assume the same title. . . .

The word *amigo* itself implies, especially in the countryside, a solidarity and reciprocal duties which are not evoked to the same degree by the word "friend." . . .

Personality Cults

In the political and military phase of the conquest of power, the caudillo lived in a state of quasi-permanent alert. [An Argentine chief] "always had a harnessed horse ready at the door for fighting or for flight at the least sign of attack from his domestic enemies." For the caudillo who has taken power and who retains it for profit, the state of alert, like that of war, leads to a double state of insecurity—first physical, because of the enemy whom he has not been able to eliminate or who rekindles the ambitions of faithless partners, and second, because of that internal sense of insecurity of someone who needs to justify to others, perhaps even to his own kin, the exercise of an unlimited power which has neither the social prestige nor the legitimacy, and certainly not the majesty, of an ancient absolute monarchy. Consciously or not, the new chief of state seeks, therefore, to provide a moral and intellectual base for the loyalty of his subjects, for he is well aware that without traditional foundations for fidelity he cannot depend solely on either economic interests or on coercive force.

From this stems the caudillo's propensity to exalt and magnify his personality beyond all limits, especially if his humble origin and total absence of family tradition make him believe in the necessity of convincing others of the transcendental and exceptional character of his own person. From this, also, comes the taste for all which can strike the popular imagination: the theatrical gesture, the sumptuous uniform, the impressive monument, the spectacular performance . . . to engrave the ideal of a superman in the minds of the citizens.

In the Mexico of the first half of the last century a president, Santa Anna, showed such inclinations when he organized the solemn burial of his leg shot away by a cannon ball, or when, after having arranged that he be made dictator for life, he organized a whole etiquette according to which his ministers had the obligation to travel in yellow coaches with valets in green livery, while His Most Serene Highness—himself—was escorted by lancers in red uniforms and plumed hats.

Here too it would be easy to give more examples, from the regional cacique who gives the name of his father, of his mother, of himself to markets, to schools, or to avenues of the *pueblos* which he dominates, to the dictator or president with overly ornate and bemedaled uniforms whom it has become such a pleasure to caricature in Mexican newspapers and elsewhere. . . .

The Caudillo as Unifier

If the power of the national dictator is of the same nature as that of the local cacique and they both use similar means, then between them the only difference is one of station; on the other hand, the two authorities may sometimes be at odds, and even at war. According to circumstances and his personal temperament, the caudillo either will want to destroy the provincial caciques who limit his power, or else he will cooperate with them by drawing them into his system of government.

In this regard the Mexican economist Germán Parra sees in certain Latin American dictatorships a state of social development comparable to that which the emergence of absolute monarchy in Europe represents. In fact, certain chiefs of state have succeeded in centralizing the government and in unifying under their authority badly organized nations which were being exploited to different degrees by local caciques. Thus in Argentina Facundo Quiroga broke the spirit of independence in eight provinces which he dominated as a semibarbaric gaucho. He and other tyrants were in turn destroyed by one of their own, the "federalist" caudillo Rosas, who by violence and trickery succeeded in what the "unitarian" parliamentary governments of Buenos Aires had not been able to obtain: the fusion of the entire country into one compact unit. . . .

In the same way that the railroad, in replacing the horse, widened and strengthened the sphere of influence of the provincial chief, so too the national dictator tends to replace the local cacique. But because the roots of personal power were so deep in some more or less isolated rural areas, it could not be destroyed in a complete and definitive fashion with one blow. In short, other caudillos who were not able or who did not want to choose military means as brutal as those of Rosas tried to integrate into their system of government those caciques judged useful and assimilable. Such was the approach of Porfirio Díaz in Mexico. . . .

What General Díaz did was to counteract existing threats to centralized power and to reinforce the authority and prestige of the state everywhere, which before him had only little influence beyond the central plateau except for a small portion of the Atlantic coast. In most other places "the supreme law was the will of one man—a cacique." [As Luis Chávez Orozco has written,] "in order to centralize this power absolutely General Díaz did not destroy caciquismo, because this would have been impossible even if he had wanted to. What he did, was to give to caciquismo more vigor by placing it under official protection. The result was that all the caciques recognized him as the supreme political authority (the Great Cacique) in exchange for certain economic advantages which he deigned to let them enjoy."

Perhaps geographical reasons obliged Díaz to compromise with certain caciques instead of trying to suppress them. The topography of Mexico presented obstacles to the unification of the country which did not exist in the Argentine pampa: it is only during the last twenty-five or thirty years that the influence of the Mexican capital has been able to penetrate everywhere through the many sierras. This has been due to an important road system, completing on a large scale the work of centralization begun by the Porfirian railways. Moreover, Díaz did not support himself with the army, which never was very large, and he never tried to enrich himself personally.

In a large country with complex structures such as Mexico, no amount of money, distributed as presents, would have been sufficient to win over enough dependents and friends to form solid bases for personal power, which was, as we know, so often managed in isolated provinces or countries with rudimentary economies . . . elsewhere on the American continent. But Díaz let the caciques, governors, and *jefes políticos* get rich under his protective wing, while keeping public opinion opposed to possible rivals and convinced of the advantages and prestige resulting from personal honesty.

This system, carefully perfected over more than thirty years of rule, left neither perspective nor room for political parties, because everything rested on personal power from the top to the bottom of the ladder. But Díaz felt the need to give to his government the ideological bases which it lacked.

Quite naturally he found these bases in Auguste Comte's Positivism which had been adapted by Mexican thinkers and educators of the second half of the nineteenth century. From a political standpoint, the ideals suited the Porfirian system admirably because they advocated the establishment of an authoritarian regime to fight against any tendency toward anarchy or disintegration, and to maintain social unity at all costs during the transitional phase when theological beliefs were fast disappearing yet before the doctrine of Positivism had definitely triumphed in the minds of the people. This "Order" closely linked as it was to economic "Progress" also represented the goal of the *"Científicos,"* those technocratic friends of Porfirio Díaz. The Científicos and Díaz, however, did not know how to add "Love" for the peasants who had been despoiled of their land, as Comte had finally done. It was this failure which was a fundamental cause of the powerful social revolution of 1910–1911 that caused his downfall.

Especially since the beginning of the century, the influence of powerful economic interests has been and often still is important. Large private companies, most of them foreign, which exploit or sell oil, tropical fruits, sugar, and other export products, are proprietors of large enterprises and huge estates with enormous incomes. Naturally they have feared the demands of their employees, the requests for land from the peasants, the nationalistic and xenophobic tendencies of the mob, and they have also feared popular troubles which might compromise the success of their businesses. Thus their representatives have sometimes shown certain preferences for authoritarian government which seemed to them more capable of insuring order and better disposed to support their interests in exchange for financial and even political support.

The importance of personal and familial ties as a caudillo's means of government may now be somewhat archaic. But as with other American institutions, caudillismo and caciquismo still bear the marks of a long history: the prestige of physical force, of the proud horseman, of the best shot; the semipatriarchal authority of the landed proprietors, once lord and master of extensive domains; the prowess of the military man who encounters no obstacles . . . ; the ostentation of the new man, who is not quite sure of himself; and finally, the power of the businessman who succeeds in controlling the principal means of production.

Today this boss or that dictator may be maintained and propelled by economic interests in an environment where money retains all the strength and vitality of youth. At the same time he is more and more questioned and threatened; he is often eliminated by societies which have achieved self-awareness and no longer allow themselves to be guided blindly as once they were. However, when the strong man learns how to adapt himself to this new situation, when, instead of representing personal interests and of leaning on clans or families, he becomes the representative of the rural people and the "leader" of masses, then he still may enjoy a long career.

<§ 5 ße

Facundo in Power

---◆-◄■►-◆---

Domingo F. Sarmiento

The classic nineteenth-century study of caudillismo *is* Civilization and
Barbarism, The Life of Juan Facundo Quiroga *(1845) by the Argentine
educator and statesman Domingo F. Sarmiento (1811–1888), who wrote
it while in exile in Chile. Ostensibly a biography of the ruthless caudillo of La Rioja province, Juan Facundo Quiroga, the book was also
an attack on Juan Manuel de Rosas, who was master of Argentina
from 1829 to 1852, as well as an indictment of the crude gaucho culture in which Facundo Quiroga and Rosas flourished and which
Sarmiento equated with barbarism. This selection vividly illustrates
Sarmiento's admiration for "civilization," especially of the European
variety, and his contempt for the rapacity and ignorance of the un-
couth Facundo.*

The English translation of Facundo *from which the selection is
taken was made by Mary Mann, wife of the noted American educator
Horace Mann, who was a good friend of Sarmiento.*

. . . That day of evil omen [when Facundo Quiroga seized power
in La Rioja] corresponds to April of 1835 in the history of Buenos
Ayres—when its country commandant, its desert hero [Juan Manuel
de Rosas], made himself master of the city.

I ought not to omit, since it is to Quiroga's honor, a curious fact
which occurred at this time (1823). The feeblest gleam of light is not
to be disregarded in the blackness of that night.

Facundo, upon his triumphant entry into La Rioja, stopped the
ringing of the bells, and after sending a message of condolence to the
widow of the slain General, directed his ashes to be honored with a
stately funeral. He appointed for governor one Blanco, a Spaniard of

---

From Domingo F. Sarmiento, *Life in the Argentine Republic in the Days
of the Tyrants: or Civilization and Barbarism,* translated by Mrs. Horace
Mann (New York: Hurd and Houghton, 1868), pp. 101–111. This article appears
as reprinted in Hugh M. Hamill, Jr. (ed.), *Dictatorship in Spanish America*
(New York: Knopf, 1965), pp. 95–103. Deletions in the text are by Hugh M.
Hamill, Jr. and Helen Delpar.

low rank, and with him began the new order of affairs which was to realize the best ideal of government, as conceived by Facundo Quiroga; for, in his long career among the various cities which he conquered, he never took upon himself the charge of organizing governments; he always left that task to others.

The moment of the grasp of power over the destinies of a commonwealth by a vigorous hand is ever an important one and deserves attention. Old institutions are strengthened, or give place to others, newer and more productive of good results, or better adapted to prevailing ideas. From such a focus often diverge the threads which, as time weaves them together, change the web of history.

It is otherwise when the prevailing force is one foreign to civilization,—when an Attila obtains possession of Rome, or a Tamerlane traverses the plains of Asia; old forms remain, but the hand of philosophy would afterwards vainly remove them with the view of finding beneath them plants which had gained vigor from the human blood given them for nourishment. Facundo, a man imbued with the genius of barbarism, gets control of his country; the traditions of government disappear, established forms deteriorate, the law is a plaything in vile hands; and nothing is maintained, nothing established, amid the destruction thus accomplished by the trampling feet of horses. Freedom from restraint, occupation, and care, is the supreme good of the gaucho. If La Rioja had contained statues, as it contained doctors, they would have had horses tied to them, but they would have served no other purpose.

Facundo wanted to have means at his command, and, as he was incapable of creating a revenue system, he resorted to the ordinary proceeding of dull or weak governments; but in this case the monopoly bears the stamp of South American pastoral life, spoliation, and violence. The tithes of La Rioja were at this time farmed out at ten thousand piastres a year; this was the average rate. Facundo made his appearance at the board, and his presence overawed the shepherds. "I offer two thousand piastres a year," said he, "and one more than the best bid." The committee repeated the proposal three times; no one made a bid; all present left, one by one, reading in Quiroga's sinister glance that it was the last one he would allow. The next year he contented himself with sending to the board the following note:—

"I give two thousand dollars and one more than the best bid.
                                                "*Facundo Quiroga.*"

The third year the ceremony of adjudication was omitted, and in 1831, Quiroga again sent to La Rioja the sum of two thousand dollars, his estimate for the tithes.

But to make his tithes bring in a hundred for one, another step was required, and, after the second year, Facundo refused to receive the tribute of animals otherwise than by giving his mark among the proprietors, so that they might brand with it the animals set apart for the tithe and keep them on the place until he called for them. The creatures multiplied, their number was constantly augmented by new tithes, and, after ten years, it might be reckoned that half the stock of a whole pastoral province belonged to the commanding general of the forces, and bore his mark.

It was the immemorial custom in La Rioja that the *estrays,* or the animals that were not marked at a certain age, should become the lawful property of the treasury, which sent its agents to collect these gleanings, and derived no contemptible revenue from them, but the annoyance to the proprietors was intolerable. Facundo demanded the adjudication to himself of these animals, to meet the expenses he had incurred for the invasion of the city; expenses which were reducible to the summons of irregular forces, who assembled, mounted on horses of their own, and lived constantly on what came in their way. Already the proprietor of herds which brought him six thousand bullocks a year, he sent his agents to supply the city markets, and woe to any competitor who should appear! This business of supplying meat for the markets was one which he carried on wherever he ruled, in San Juan, Mendoza, or Tucumán; and he was always careful to secure the monopoly of it by proclamation or simple notification. It is with shame and disgust that I mention these disgraceful transactions, but the truth must be told.

The general's first order, after a bloody battle which had laid a city open to him, was that no one should supply the markets with meat! In Tucumán he learned that a resident of the place was killing cattle in his house, in spite of this order. The general of the army of the Andes, the conqueror of the Citadel, thought the investigation of so dreadful a crime should be entrusted only to himself. He went in person, and knocked lustily at the door of the house, which refused to yield, and which the inmates, taken by surprise, did not open. A kick from the illustrious general broke it in, and exposed to his view a dead ox, whose hide was in process of removal by the master of the house, who also fell dead in his turn at the terrible sight of the offended general.

I do not intentionally dwell upon these things. How many I omit! How many misdeeds I pass over in silence which are fully proved and known to all! But I am writing the history of government by barbarians, and I am forced to state its methods.

Mehemet Ali, who became master of Egypt by means identical with those of Facundo, delivers himself up to a rapacity unexampled even in Turkey; he establishes monopolies in every occupation and turns them to his own profit; but Mehemet Ali, though he springs from a barbarous nation, rises above his condition so far as to wish to acquire European civilization for himself and for the people he oppresses. Facundo, on the contrary, not only rejects all recognized civilization, but destroys and disorganizes. Facundo, who does not govern, because any government implies labour for others' good, gives himself up to the instincts of an immoderate and unscrupulous avarice. Selfishness is the foundation of almost all the great characters of history; selfishness is the chief spring of all great deeds. Quiroga had this political gift in an eminent degree and made everything around him contribute to his advantage; wealth, power, authority, all centered in him; whatever he could not acquire,—polish, learning, true respectability,—he hated and persecuted in all those who possessed them.

His hostility to the respectable classes and to the refinement of the cities was every day more perceptible, and the governor of La Rioja, whom he had himself appointed, finally was forced, by daily annoyances, to resign his place. One day, Quiroga, feeling inclined to pleasantry, was amusing himself with a young man as a cat sports with a frightened mouse; he liked to play at killing; the terror of the victim was so ludicrous, that the executioner was highly diverted, and laughed immoderately, contrary to his habit. He must have sympathy in his mirth, and he at once ordered the *general*[1] to be beat throughout the city of Rioja, which called out the citizens under arms. Facundo, who had given the summons for diversion's sake, drew up the inhabitants in the principal square at eleven o'clock at night, dismissed the populace and retained only the well-to-do householders and the young men who still had some appearance of culture. All night he kept them marching and countermarching, halting, forming line, marching by front or by flank. It was like a drill-sergeant teaching recruits, and the sergeant's stick travelled over the heads of the stupid, and the chests of those who were out of line; "What would you have? this is the way to teach!" Morning came, and the pallor, weariness, and exhaustion of the recruits showed what a night they had passed. Their instructor finally sent them to rest, and extended his generosity to the purchase and distribution of pastry, each recipient made in haste to eat his share, for that was part of the sport.

Lessons of such a kind are not lost upon cities, and the skillful politician who has raised similar proceedings to a system in Buenos Ayres, has refined upon them and made them wonderfully effective. For example: during the periods between 1835 and 1840 almost the whole population of Buenos Ayres has passed through the prisons.

---

[1] A certain call to arms. [Tr.]

Sometimes a hundred and fifty citizens would be imprisoned for two or three months, to be then replaced by two hundred who would be kept, perhaps half the year. Wherefore? What had they done? What had they said? Idiots! Do you not see that this is good discipline for the city? Do you not remember the saying of Rosas to Quiroga, that no republic could be established because the people were not prepared for it! This is his way of teaching the city how to obey; he will finish his work, and in 1844, he will be able to show the world a people with but one thought, one opinion, one voice, and that a boundless enthusiasm for the person and will of Rosas! Then, indeed, they will be ready for a republic!

But we will return to La Rioja. A feverish excitement on the subject of investments in the mines of the new States of Spanish America had arisen in England; powerful companies were proposing to draw profit from those of Mexico and Peru; and Rivadavia, who was then residing in London, urged speculators to invest their capital in the Argentine Republic. The mines of Famatina offered an opening for a great enterprise. At the same time, speculators from Buenos Ayres obtained the exclusive right to work those mines, meaning to sell it for an enormous sum to the English companies. These two speculations, one started in England and the other in Buenos Ayres, conflicted with each other, and were irreconcilable. Finally, a bargain was made with another English house, which was to supply funds, and in fact, sent out English superintendents and miners. Later, a speculation was got up to establish a bank at La Rioja, which was to be sold at a high price to the national government when it should be organized. On being solicited, Facundo took a large number of shares, making payment with the Jesuits' College, which had been assigned to him, on his demand, in payment of his salary as general. A party of Buenos Ayres stockholders came to La Rioja to carry out the project, and soon asked to be presented to Quiroga, whose name had begun to exercise everywhere a mysterious and terrific power. Facundo received them in his lodgings, in very fine silk stockings, ill-made pantaloons, and a common linen poncho.

The grotesque appearance of this figure was not provocative of any smiles from the elegant citizens of Buenos Ayres. They were too sagacious not to read the riddle. The man before them meant to humiliate his polished guests, and show them what account he made of their European dresses.

The administrative system established in his province was finally completed by exorbitant duties on the exportation of cattle which did not belong to him. But in addition to these direct methods of acquiring wealth, he had one which embraced his whole public career, —gambling! He had a rage for play as some men have for strong drink, and others for tobacco. His mind, though a powerful one, had not the capacity of embracing a large sphere of ideas, and stood in need of this factitious occupation, in which a passion of the soul is in constant exercise, as it is crossed, appeased, provoked, excited, and kept upon the rack. I have always thought that the passion for gambling was some useful faculty that organized society has perverted or left in inaction. The will, self-control, and steadfastness which it requires, are the same which advance the fortunes of the enterprising merchant, the banker, and the conqueror who plays for empires with battles. Facundo had habitually gambled since his childhood; play had been the only pleasure, the only relaxation of his life. But what an agreeable partner he must be who controls the terrors and the lives of the whole party! No one can conceive such a state of things without having had it before his eyes for twenty years. Facundo played unfairly, say his enemies. I do not believe the charge, for cheating at play was unnecessary in his case, and he had been known to pursue to the death, others who were guilty of it. But he played with unlimited means; he never let any one carry from the table the money he used for stakes; the game could not be stopped till he chose; he would play forty hours or more at a time; he feared no one, and if his fellow gamblers annoyed him, he could have them whipped or shot at pleasure. This was the secret of his good luck. Few men ever won much money from him, although, at some periods of the game, heaps of coin lost by him lay upon the table; the game would go on, for the winner did not dare to rise, and in the end he would have nothing but the glory of reckoning that his winnings, afterwards lost, had once been so large.

Gambling, then, was to Quiroga a system of plunder as well as a favorite amusement. No one in La Rioja received money from him, no one possessed any, without being at once invited to a game, or, in other words, to leave his funds in the chieftain's hands. Most of the tradesmen of La Rioja failed and vanished, their money having taken up its quarters in the general's purse; and it was not for want of lessons in prudence from him. A young hand had won four thousand dollars from Facundo, and Facundo declined to play longer. His opponent thought that a snare was in readiness for him, and that his life was in danger. Facundo repeated that he had finished playing; the stupid fellow insisted on another game, and Facundo, complying with the demand, won the four thousand dollars from the other, who then received two hundred lashes for his uncivil pertinacity.

. . .

What consequences to La Rioja were occasioned by the destruction of all civil order? Reasonings and discussions are here out of place. A visit to the scene of these occurrences will be sufficient to answer the query. The Llanos of La Rioja are now deserted; their population has emigrated to San Juan; the cisterns are dry which once gave drink to thousands of flocks. Those Llanos which fed those flocks twenty years ago, are now the home of the tiger who has reconquered his former empire, and of a few families of beggars who live upon the fruit of the carob-tree. This is the retribution the Llanos have suffered for the evils which they let loose upon the Republic. "Woe to ye, Bethsaida and Chorazin! Verily I say unto you, that the lot of Sodom and Gomorrah was more tolerable than that which was reserved for you!"

❦ 6 ❧

Peru in the Guano Age

Jonathan V. Levin

During the nineteenth century Latin America retained its traditional role as a supplier of agricultural commodities and other raw materials to Europe and the United States. However, new export products, such as coffee, were developed, and foreign capital, technology, and managerial skills often contributed to an expanded volume of trade. All too often profits from increased exports served primarily to enrich the foreign investor and entrepreneur and a small local elite, as Jonathan V. Levin, a senior economist with the International Monetary Fund, shows in this reading. Levin analyzes the domestic impact of Peruvian exports of guano (bird droppings accumulated on uninhabited offshore islands), which was prized as a fertilizer in the mid-nineteenth century.

. . .

Guano-Income Receivers

Peru's guano age had lasted forty years, from the first export contract to Chilean occupation of the islands in the War of the Pacific. During this period more than 10,800,000 tons of guano were exported, bringing over $600,000,000 on the retail market. Who received this money? What did they do with it and what effect did it have upon the Peruvian economy?

Because neither labor, nor capital, nor entrepreneurship was present in 1840 Peru in quantities sufficient to operate the guano industry, the industry was in large part operated by factors of production that came in from abroad. Part of the guano-trade proceeds went abroad to pay for these factors. The Chinese coolies [*imported as laborers*] probably did not remit any significant quantity of earnings to China but the $400 a head paid for the coolies at Callao dockside was distributed among ship captains and others engaged in the coolie trade between

From Jonathan V. Levin, *The Export Economies: Their Pattern of Development in Historical Perspective* (Cambridge, Mass.: Harvard University Press, 1960), pp. 112–123. Copyright, 1960, by the President and Fellows of Harvard College. Reprinted by permission of the publishers. Footnotes deleted. Italicized bracketed note in the text is by Helen Delpar.

Macao and Callao. Foreign entrepreneurs and their capital were of great importance in the guano trade, as consignment contractors holding virtually all the exclusive country sales contracts before Peruvians were able to amass enough capital to take on contracts themselves in the 1850's and 1860's, and quite often as partners to Peruvians later on.[1] The foreign consignment contractors' shares of guano-trade profit were the foundation of many a fortune in Europe, and particularly in Great Britain.

The desire of some Peruvians to share in this guano income going to foreign contractors led the Peruvian congress to grant preference to Peruvian contractors in 1849. Because capital and entrepreneurship were rather scarce in Peru in the 1850's—and because the Peruvian consignment contractors were able to perpetuate their hold on the guano trade through a system which kept the government constantly in their debt and dependent upon their fresh credits—the guano contracts were in the hands of a relatively small group of Peruvians and an important share of the guano-contract profits, particularly in the late 1850's and 1860's, went to them.

The most important share of the guano-trade receipts—perhaps as much as half of the total—went to the government, which at the first sign of the profits ahead had sought to reserve the greatest possible portion for itself. A part of the guano proceeds the government lost to the contractors because of its inability to devise a guano sales system which would induce the contractors to work for the maximization of the government's guano earnings. Yet the government's guano income was vast and through its disbursement the government became the most important generator of income in the exchange sector of the Peruvian economy.

As might be expected, the government's disbursement of its guano income followed the political situation of the time. Some of the guano receipts were used to promote specific political objectives—to redeem the slaves, make the church more dependent on the state, wage several small wars, and pay off the Independence War debt to the foreign bondholders. Another portion of the guano revenues was used to wipe out the tax system and thus increase by the amount of the abolished taxes the retained income of most of the population. The greater part of its guano income before 1868, however, the government

---

[1] Starting in the 1840s, exclusive rights to sell guano, which was declared a national monopoly, in specified areas were granted by the Peruvian government to consignment contractors, at first foreign corporations and later Peruvians as well. Since the government regularly borrowed funds from the contractors, to be repaid from its revenue from future sales of guano, it was constantly in their debt. [H. D.]

devoted to promoting the narrower interests of those in control. Political power in guano-age Peru rested not on a broad base of popular support, but on a small, mostly European-descended group, centered in Lima. Accordingly it was to the benefit of this small group, rather than to the promotion of nation-wide welfare, that the government's guano-income expenditures before 1868 were dedicated. Through the consolidation operation,[2] corruption, and the maintenance of a huge military, civil, and pensioned bureaucracy, the government guano funds were disbursed to the politically significant segment of the populace.

With seemingly unlimited guano funds pouring into the government's coffers, the bureaucratic traditions of Lima's Spanish colonial days came into full flower, and an "empleomania" seemed to grip the city. The swollen army, bureaucracy and pension lists created a class whose continued financial support was of increasing importance for both the political stability of the government and the economic stability of the small exchange economy. Politically, the life of the government rested to a great extent on the continued welfare of this military and civilian group, as the Roman emperor's had rested on the pretorian guards. Economically, though Peruvian guano contractors enjoyed an income from guano exports, and sugar exports had also risen to some significance, the government had become the most important generator of income in Peru's exchange economy. Stability of government expenditures, therefore, was of vital concern both to those holding political power and to the entire exchange economy.

This stability of government expenditures depended, of course, upon the maintenance of stability in the government's guano income. Yet, oddly enough, in all of the vast literature of controversy and debate over the merits of various guano-export systems, the problem of avoiding fluctuations in the government's guano proceeds found no place. This was not due to any absence of fluctuations in guano exports; a graph of annual guano export tonnage shows marked irregularity. The reason for this lack of a fluctuation problem lies rather in the fact that the government's guano receipts in any one year bore no relation to that year's guano exports or sales. By obtaining almost all of its guano revenues in loans and advances against future sales the government had divorced its guano income completely from the current level of sales. Though this stabilization through credit added considerably to the interest charges the government paid, it insulated the

---

[2] A consolidation of the internal debt during the administration of José Rufino Echenique (1851–1854), which permitted speculators to reap large profits. [H. D.]

government effectively from any fluctuations in guano income so long as the government could borrow.

These then were the people who—before the government embarked on its railroad-building program in 1868—shared the guano-export proceeds: the foreign contractors, the Peruvian contractors who succeeded many of them, the coolie traders supplying the laborers from China to Callao, the Chinese coolies on the islands, and—through the government's treasury—the influential Peruvians who benefited from the consolidated debts, the mass of Peruvians relieved of their tax burden, the soldiers, the bureaucrats, and the pensioners. Among them in unequal portions the guano proceeds were divided.

How these guano-income receivers spent their money, and where, determined to a large extent what effect the guano trade was to have on the economic development of Peru.

Guano-Income Expenditures

The foreign contractors' expenditures—principally for consumption or investment in their home countries—could have little effect on the Peruvian economy. Similarly the funds paid to non-Peruvian coolie traders for the guano-islands labor supply were expended outside the country. Among those expending guano-trade proceeds within Peru, the coolies on the islands could do little more than cover their bare necessities with the meager earnings they received. The Peruvian taxpayers, relieved of almost all taxes, consumed a little more than previously. The soldiers, bureaucrats, and pensioners supported by the government's guano proceeds devoted virtually all of their rising income to a marked increase in their style of living, with little left for saving and investment. It was the small class of Lima capitalists that through consignment contracts and other transactions with the government received the most important share of guano proceeds in Peru, and it was this group's expenditures that held the greatest significance for the country's economic development. This was a high-living extravagant class, however, which very early acquired expensive tastes and directed the greatest part of its income—and of Peru's guano-trade proceeds—to the consumption of luxuries. Residing in Lima, this new wealthy class summered in the nearby resort of Chorillos, imported fashionable drawing rooms and costly European manufactures, and set the style for Lima society. Most of the products this group sought to consume were not available in Peru, since the small exchange sector, containing about 40 per cent of the country's total population of two million, made domestic manufacture rarely profitable. "The lack, or rather the complete absence of [domestic] manufactures and factories," wrote a Peruvian author in 1858, "makes necessary the importation of almost everything required for the comforts of life. . . ." This absence of domestic manufactures continued despite the growth of Peruvian guano income because a large portion of this income was concentrated in the hands of the small group of guano-enriched Lima residents—who presented too small a potential market to encourage profitable domestic manufacture and were in any case acquiring European tastes. With their large share of guano incomes, therefore, the new class of Lima wealthy drove up the volume of Peruvian imports. In 1859, with only about 5 per cent of the nation's population, the Lima area was importing 63 per cent of all Peruvian imports.

Guano-Income Investment

Not all of the guano income received by Peruvians went into consumption. Some saving and investment did take place and, indeed, the guano age witnessed a great increase in Peruvian enterprises. By 1871 there were in Lima 9 banks, 23 consignment houses, 94 importers, 81 *negociantes de capitales,* and more than 2,000 commercial establishments.

What direction did Peruvian enterprise and the investment of guano income take? As might be expected, it gravitated toward those activities in which the greatest profit could be made—primarily the guano trade and other export industries producing for the profitable foreign market with which Peruvians were now becoming acquainted. The attraction of high profits in areas connected with the guano trade is well illustrated by the early career of William Russell Grace, founder of W. R. Grace and Company. As a young man in 1850 Peru, Grace went into the marine supplies business in Callao. To get ahead of his competitors he towed a barge of supplies out to the Chincha Islands where he did a brisk business selling to the dozens of ships waiting to take on guano. Thus a great deal of guano-age enterprise and a large part of the investment funds derived from guano income went into some branch of the guano trade or its various connected areas.

Other guano-derived funds went into other export industries. With the disruption of United States cotton production during the Civil War, the cultivation of cotton was greatly expanded for a few years on the Peruvian coastal estates with Chinese coolie labor. Guano-derived capital was probably at work too in the development of the nitrate industry in the southern Peruvian desert before that area and the industry were lost to Chile. Probably the most important field of investment, outside of the guano industry itself, for Peruvian guano-income savings, however, was the Peruvian sugar industry, which enjoyed a period of great prosperity between 1861 and 1875. Having flourished in Spanish colonial days with African slave labor, the coastal sugar industry declined after independence from a shortage of labor and the closing of the Chilean market as the result of a high duty. The industry regained some importance after the initiation of shipments to European markets by the Gibbs Company in the 1830's, but it was not until the reopening of the Chinese coolie trade in 1861 and the mobilization of guano-derived capital by the new banks after 1862 that it entered into a new era of expansion. Owners of sugar lands by the score converted their properties into large plantations as they obtained all the Chinese coolies they needed and all the equipment for the installation of mills on credit extended by the new mortgage banks at 8 per cent interest per annum, repayable in twenty years. Working capital came from Peruvian and foreign commercial houses against the pledge that the next sugar crop would be consigned to them for sale. On this base of borrowed guano-derived capital and imported coolie labor the Peruvian sugar industry expanded production to over 100,000 tons a year during 1870–73. By 1875 the industry was in debt by about 30 million soles, including about 17.5 million to the banks and 4.5 million to foreign commercial houses. The end of the sugar boom soon appeared, however, as the closing of the coolie trade in 1874 withdrew the industry's labor supply, and the Peruvian financial crisis of 1875 dried up its sources of credit. The overworked sugar lands began to show signs of exhaustion and the price of sugar was declining on world markets. By the time the War of the Pacific and Chilean occupation had ended, Peruvian sugar production had been reduced by more than 50 per cent.

After the war the rehabilitation of the sugar industry was undertaken, with an increase in mechanization to save on labor costs and the merger of estates to save on management and allow the use of larger, more modern mills. Peruvian capital was no longer available, however, as the guano trade had ended and many banks had failed during the war. A great many of Peru's sugar estates therefore passed into the hands of foreign corporations—British, German, Italian, American, etc.—possessing enough capital to rebuild and operate the estates along more modern lines.

While various amounts of guano-derived capital were devoted to the guano trade and other export industries, very little was invested in industries producing for the domestic market. This, as noted, was due to the small size of the Peruvian market and the fact that so large a portion of the guano income was concentrated in the hands of too few consumers to make domestic manufacture profitable. A few small industrial establishments did exist—such as several iron foundries, woodworking plants, ice factories, and plants for the manufacture of copper stills—but these were of little significance and virtually all of the manufactured products consumed in Peru continued to be imported. Attracted by the greater profits to be made in the guano trade and in other export industries, the investment of private.capital derived from the guano trade left production in the rest of the Peruvian economy—outside the cotton and sugar estates and the southern nitrate desert—much the same as it had found it. The consumption of Peru's guano income on the other hand was concentrated in the hands of a small group ot wealthy Lima residents. For the country outside the export industries and the Lima consumers, there was little economic development indeed when the new government of young Nicolás de Piérola ushered in the railroad-building era in 1868.

The Railroads

It was as a reaction against this pattern of development—and against the corrupted system of guano consignment—that the Peruvian government withdrew the guano trade from the domestic contractors, placed it in the hands of the Dreyfus Company of France, and proceeded to invest its newly increased income in the building of more than 750 miles of railroads. By diverting to itself through the Dreyfus Contract the excessive profits the domestic consignment contractors had received, the government hoped to obtain enough funds to pay for the building of the railroads. These funds were far from sufficient, however, for the government's reaction against the old pattern of guano expenditures had been incomplete. Though the guano contractors' high profits were discontinued, the flow of guano income to the large body of soldiers, bureaucrats, and pensioners was allowed to continue, and too little of the guano proceeds remained to pay for the railroads. To a large extent, therefore, the railroads were built with borrowed foreign funds, and when the income from guano ceased to cover the charges on these loans the railroads had eventually to be transferred to the foreign bondholders' ownership.

Though they might have been better planned and perhaps more cheaply built, the railroads constituted an important addition to the Peruvian economy. Dissected into small pockets by some of the most difficult mountain terrain in the world, Peru must depend upon good transportation for its political and economic organization. The railroads did not unite Peru as the north-south Inca roads had, but rather formed feeder lines connecting its various cities, valleys, and mountain centers with the sea. Where profitable production of sugar, cotton, or mineral products could take place the railroads facilitated their transport to the sea and to the world markets beyond. The railroad whistle did not wake the mountain Indian from his centuries of lethargy, as some of its planners had hoped; obstacles other than distance remained to block his departure from the self-contained native world. The railroads formed the basis, however, for the revival of the Peruvian mining industry and the twentieth-century expansion of cotton and sugar production.

By the 1890's, when the war and the debt settlement were over, Peru had a system of foreign-held railroads, a coastal sugar industry, a poorer but temporarily more entrepreneurial urban class, a demolished tax system, and an inflated supply of paper money. The guano age was over, but elsewhere in the overseas world new export economies were to flower. In Chile, to the south, the nitrate age had already begun.

⌘ 7 ⌘

The Anglo-Argentine Connection in the Nineteenth Century

———◆◀◆▶◆———

H. S. Ferns

Nowhere was the imprint of foreign enterprise in Latin America more visible than in Argentina, where between 1870 and 1914 British capital financed railroad construction, meat-packing plants, and public works projects that helped transform the nation into one of the world's leading exporters of beef and cereals. Some Argentines have argued that the size and nature of the British stake in the Argentine economy converted their country into a colonial dependency of Great Britain. In this selection, however, Professor H. S. Ferns of the University of Manchester denies that the Anglo-Argentine relationship in the years before World War I was an imperialistic one, pointing out that it was initiated and controlled by the dominant economic interests of Argentina.

. . . These prosperous years [1900–1914] witnessed a considerable relaxation of political tension within Argentina. The armed forces as a factor in politics appeared to be fading out and the institutions and political habits of representative democracy to be gaining in strength. There was little direct political tension between Britain and Argentina, but indirectly Argentina eyed Britain with suspicion. The pressure of the financial interests to use force in the collection of debts and other claims, which Salisbury had resisted during the Baring Crisis,[1] was successful in 1902 in the case of Venezuela, and Britain joined with Germany and Italy in blockading Venezuelan ports. Argentina reacted sharply to this unwise proceeding. The Drago

From H. S. Ferns, *Britain and Argentina in the Nineteenth Century* (Oxford: The Clarendon Press, 1960), pp. 486–491. Reprinted by permission of The Clarendon Press, Oxford. This article appears as reprinted in Marvin D. Bernstein (ed.), *Foreign Investment in Latin America* (New York: Knopf, 1966), pp. 121–128. Italicized bracketed notes in the text are by Helen Delpar.

[1] In 1890 the English banking house of Baring Brothers collapsed as a result of Argentine economic difficulties. Lord Salisbury was prime minister and foreign secretary of England at the time of the Baring Crisis. [H. D.]

Doctrine [*see Article 8*] was given to the world by the Argentine Foreign Minister. For the first time since the brief romance of 1846 the United States and Argentina found themselves effectively on the same side politically. But even the Venezuelan *contretemps* was obliterated from the public conscience by the flood of prosperity.

The long-standing ambivalence of the Argentine community to foreign enterprise was not effaced by an age of abundance nor by favorable terms of trade. Professor Eteocle Lorini, in his study of the Argentine public debt, voiced a very common view: "All the industrial, commercial, agricultural, and mining companies which furnish our Argentine statistics bear the foreign mark *limited;* so that one ends by getting the impression that one is studying a purely English colony, for one finds *limited* upon all species of manufactures; *limited* after the statement of capitals; all undertakings are *limited;* insurance is *limited;* the circulation and distribution of Argentine wealth is *limited.*" [2] Lorini acknowledged that capital investment increased employment, raised land values, and increased production, but he advised his countrymen to save and invest on their own account in order to create a "national capital" which would reduce dependence upon international finance. Thoughts of this kind take us back to the 1850's when the business men and politicians of Buenos Aires Province were projecting a development based on their own accumulation and forward to the 1950's when Perón was seeking to emancipate Argentina from foreign influences. Were they worth uttering then and are they worth examining now?

Speculation on the subject of British enterprise in Argentina carries us to the heart of Anglo-Argentine relationship, both as it has existed historically and as it exists at the present time. The term "imperialism" is widely used in Argentina and elsewhere in discussing the connection between the two countries. Argentina has never belonged to the British Empire, of course; but Argentina is, or was, part of Britain's informal empire. Argentina is within a British sphere of influence. Britain exercises great influence in Argentina. Britain exploits Argentina. So the argument runs, and the argument is widely believed, and attitudes affecting action derive from it.

There is a case for the large British investment in Argentina, and there is one against it. The evidence suggests, however, that neither case has been sufficiently related to the facts.

Can the term imperialism be applied to Anglo-Argentine relations? If we accept the proposition that imperialism embraces the fact of control through the use of political power, then the verdict for Britain

---

[2] Quoted in Albert B. Martínez and Maurice Lewandowski, *The Argentine in the Twentieth Century* (London, 1911), p. 359.

is unquestionably "Not Guilty." The only complete attempt made by Britain to establish political power in the River Plate failed, and out of that failure developed a policy which specifically recognized that political power exercised in and over Argentina or any other country in South America was an ineffective means of achieving the British objective of a beneficial commercial and financial relationship. The Anglo-Argentine political equation, which recognized Britain and Argentina as independent variables, was not derived from the liberal idealism of Canning, but from the material facts learned on the field of battle and discernible to anyone familiar with the character of the terrain and people of Argentina. During the nineteenth century there was no alteration in the Anglo-Argentine equation, and there is no reason for supposing it is any different today than it was a century and a half ago.

This political equation is the equation from which all equations in the sphere of economics have been derived. The Argentine Government has always possessed the power to forbid, to encourage, or to shape the economic relations of Argentina with other communities, including the British community. The British Government has never had the power to oblige Argentina to pay a debt, to pay a dividend, or to export or import any commodity whatever. The only occasion when the British Government went beyond talk in dealing with Argentina, during the troubled time of General [*Juan Manuel de*] Rosas [*Argentine strong man, 1829–1852*], they were defeated and they formally admitted that they were defeated. When powerful financial interests urged the use of political power to influence Argentine economic policy in 1891, the British Foreign Secretary privately and publicly repudiated such a suggestion. Every crisis in the economic and financial relations of Britain and Argentina has been resolved in economic and financial terms—by a weighing of advantages and disadvantages by both parties—and not by the intrusion of political power. Of course, British commercial and financial interests have exercised great influence in Argentina; but so have Argentine interests exercised great influence in Britain. Any agricultural landlord or farmer in Britain between the years 1890 and 1939 could argue that Argentina was a factor in their fate, and a very adverse one. Derelict fields in Cambridgeshire existed in part because fields in the Argentine Republic were heavy with cheap cereals, and Argentine *estancieros* have wintered on the Riviera while herdsmen in Shropshire went bankrupt. These are facts which make nonsense of myths about British imperialism and Argentina as a semi-colony of a great and powerful state.

One may deplore the consequences for Argentina, and likewise the consequences for Britain, of the kind of relationship worked out by the Argentine landed and commercial interests in conjunction with the financial, industrial, and commercial interests of Great Britain, but when one starts deploring let no one blame an abstraction called Britain or another one called Argentina. If, over a long span of time, Argentina has possessed a weak and narrowly based industrial structure compared with that of the United States or even Canada, this has been due to the concentration of effort in Argentina upon agricultural and pastoral enterprise and upon the production of pastoral and agricultural commodities. Political power and/or decisive influence upon policy in Argentina has belonged until recent times to the interests with most to gain by such a concentration.

The dominant interests in Argentina sought out the foreign capitalists in the first instance; the foreign capitalists did not invade Argentina, and in the beginning and for many years after the investment process commenced European investors were reluctant to supply Argentina with as much purchasing power as the Argentine Government required. That the European investors invested anything depended partly upon the guarantees given by the Argentine authorities, partly upon the direct responsibility for payment undertaken by the state, and partly upon the existence in Argentina of a British business community capable of organizing in a practical way enterprises like railways and meat-freezing plants. Contrary to common belief the British investor received help and protection from the Argentine Government, not the British Government. When the British Government finally felt obliged to assist British investors in Argentina, it did so not by sending an expeditionary force to the River Plate, but by underwriting the Bank of England, which in turn underwrote the private and joint-stock banks, which in their turn underwrote the firm of Baring Brothers.

There is still much work to be done before any convincing answer can be given to the question: who benefited most from economic development in Argentina? The evidence in hand, however, suggests some tentative answers. Some foreign interests benefited greatly; for example, the shareholders of some of the banks; some railway shareholders and investors in meat-processing and cold-storage enterprises and some mercantile establishments. But the overall profits of British investors were sufficiently low to prompt the hypothesis that the great interests of Argentina did not dominate the fields occupied so largely by British enterprise because the returns were greater in the fields dominated by Argentinos. The appreciation of land values and the profits of pastoral enterprise, commercial agriculture, and sharecropping seem to have been the best sources of wealth in the years from 1860 to 1914. The political power, the social knowledge, the entrenched position of native Argentinos gave them a tremendous advantage in this field. The system of education, handicapped in its scope by niggardly state expenditure and in its content by the influence of the Roman Catholic Church, further ordained that native Argentinos were ill equipped to take control of enterprises requiring great technical knowledge and habits of exact application to managerial responsibilities. Thus foreigners, and particularly the British, dominated in the less rewarding and more demanding fields of endeavor.

There seems to be considerable evidence during the period we have studied that the permanent wage worker both urban and rural benefited least from the developments we have described. If this is so, why was immigration so abundant? Economic opportunities, not wage rates, seem to be the predominant inducement to immigrants. Argentine wages in the long run seem to have been rather better than wages in Italy and Spain, from whence the majority of immigrants came, but much inferior to wage rates in the United States, Canada, or Australia. But economic opportunities seem to have been roughly alike. Indeed, in Argentina the prizes open to people possessed of peasant shrewdness in buying and selling were, perhaps, greater than elsewhere. For a man with only a strong back and a willingness to work, Argentina was, perhaps, a slight improvement on his homeland, but not a place of rich rewards.

Among the beneficiaries of Argentine expansion before 1914 we must not neglect mention of the English wage working class. Some benefited from employment opportunities created by manufacturing for the Argentine market. A much wider mass benefited as consumers from the cheap food products flowing in increasing flood from the River Plate. If the Englishman of that age was the biggest meat eater in Europe it was partly due to the fact that Argentina was the cheapest producer of beef in the world.

The Anglo-Argentine connection, with the benefits and disadvantages which we have described as they existed in the years between the Boer War and World War I, was a phase in the life of growing communities and not a system which can be recreated. The passage of time and the changing social composition of the Argentine community revealed weaknesses and altered the objectives of economic activity. One of the leading staples of Argentine international trade—cereals—was marketed under conditions of nearly perfect competition. So long as the overall factors in the world market kept up cereal prices in relation to the prices of manufactured goods, the Argentine economy functioned without crippling frustrations. When the overall factors in the world market began to alter this relationship between cereal prices and the prices of manufactured goods, Argentina began to discover the limitations and defects of concentration on food production.

8

The Drago Doctrine

―――◆◗●◖◆―――

Luis M. Drago

During the nineteenth century foreign investments in Latin America were frequently the motive for European diplomatic or military intervention in Latin America, especially for the purpose of collecting unpaid debts from a defaulting government. One of the best-known instances of such intervention was the joint British, German, and Italian blockade of Venezuelan ports in 1902–1903. The blockade led the Argentine minister of foreign affairs, Luis M. Drago (1859–1921), to enunciate the principles which have since been incorporated into the international law of the Western Hemisphere as the Drago Doctrine. It is interesting to note that Drago invoked the Monroe Doctrine to support his rejection of the use of armed force to collect debts from Latin American governments. Only two years later, partly as a result of the Venezuelan crisis, President Theodore Roosevelt reinterpreted the Monroe Doctrine in such a manner as to permit unilateral American intervention in Latin America to coerce nations guilty of "chronic wrongdoing, or an impotence which results in a general loosening of the ties of civilized society."

Buenos Aires, December 29, 1902

MR. MINISTER:

I have received your excellency's telegram of the 20th instant concerning the events that have lately taken place between the government of the Republic of Venezuela and the Governments of Great Britain and Germany. According to your excellency's information the origin of the disagreement is, in part, the damages suffered by subjects of the claimant nations during the revolutions and wars that have recently occurred within the borders of the Republic mentioned, and in part

From Luis M. Drago, "Señor Luis M. Drago, Minister of Foreign Relations of the Argentine Republic, to Señor Martín García Mérou, Minister of the Argentine Republic to the United States, December 29, 1902," in *Foreign Relations of the United States*, 1903, pp. 1–5. This selection is printed as it appears in C. Neale Ronning (ed.), *Intervention in Latin America* (New York: Knopf, 1970), pp. 142–149.

also the fact that certain payments on the external debt of the nation have not been met at the proper time.

Leaving out of consideration the first class of claims the adequate adjustment of which it would be necessary to consult the laws of the several countries, this Government has deemed it expedient to transmit to your excellency some considerations with reference to the forcible collection of the public debt suggested by the events that have taken place.

At the outset it is to be noted in this connection that the capitalist who lends his money to a foreign state always takes into account the resources of the country and the probability, greater or less, that the obligations contracted will be fulfilled without delay.

All governments thus enjoy different credit according to their degree of civilization and culture and their conduct in business transactions; and these conditions are measured and weighed before making any loan, the terms being made more or less onerous in accordance with the precise data concerning them which bankers always have on record.

In the first place the lender knows that he is entering into a contract with a sovereign entity, and it is an inherent qualification of all sovereignty that no proceedings for the execution of a judgment may be instituted or carried out against it, since this manner of collection would compromise its very existence and cause the independence and freedom of action of the respective government to disappear.

Among the fundamental principles of public international law which humanity has consecrated, one of the most precious is that which decrees that all states, whatever be the force at their disposal, are entities in law, perfectly equal one to another, and mutually entitled by virtue thereof to the same consideration and respect.

The acknowledgment of the debt, the payment of it in its entirety, can and must be made by the nation without diminution of its inherent rights as a sovereign entity, but the summary and immediate collection at a given moment, by means of force, would occasion nothing less than the ruin of the weakest nations, and the absorption of their governments, together with all the functions inherent in them, by the mighty of the earth. The principles proclaimed on this continent of America are otherwise. "Contracts between a nation and private individuals are obligatory according to the conscience of the sovereign, and may not be the object of compelling force," said the illustrious Hamilton. "They confer no right of action contrary to the sovereign will."

The United States has gone very far in this direction. The eleventh amendment to its Constitution provided in effect, with the unanimous assent of the people, that the judicial power of the nation should not be extended to any suit in law or equity prosecuted against one of the United States by citizens of another State, or by citizens or subjects of any foreign State. The Argentine Government has made its provinces indictable, and has even adopted the principle that the nation itself may be brought to trial before the supreme court on contracts which it enters into with individuals.

What has not been established, what could in no wise be admitted, is that, once the amount for which it may be indebted has been determined by legal judgment, it should be deprived of the right to choose the manner and the time of payment, in which it has as much interest as the creditor himself, or more, since its credit and its national honor are involved therein.

This is in no wise a defense for bad faith, disorder, and deliberate and voluntary insolvency. It is intended merely to preserve the dignity of the public international entity which may not thus be dragged into war with detriment to those high ends which determine the existence and liberty of nations.

The fact that collection can not be accomplished by means of violence does not, on the other hand, render valueless the acknowledgment of the public debt, the definite obligation of paying it.

The State continues to exist in its capacity as such, and sooner or later the gloomy situations are cleared up, resources increase, common aspirations of equity and justice prevail, and the most neglected promises are kept.

The decision, then, which declares the obligation to pay a debt, whether it be given by the tribunals of the country or by those of international arbitration, which manifest the abiding zeal for justice as the basis of the political relations and nations, constitutes an indisputable title which can not be compared to the uncertain right of one whose claims are not recognized and who sees himself driven to appeal to force in order that they may be satisfied.

As these are the sentiments of justice, loyalty, and honor which animate the Argentine people and have always inspired its policy, your excellency will understand that it has felt alarmed at the knowledge that the failure of Venezuela to meet the payments of its public debt is given as one of the determining causes of the capture of its fleet, the bombardment of one of its ports, and the establishment of a rigorous blockade along its shores. If such proceedings were to be definitely adopted they would establish a precedent dangerous to the security and the peace of the nations of this part of America.

The collection of loans by military means implies territorial occupation to make them effective, and territorial occupation signifies the suppression or subordination of the governments of the countries on which it is imposed.

Such a situation seems obviously at variance with the principles many times proclaimed by the nations of America, and particularly with the Monroe doctrine, sustained and defended with so much zeal on all occasions by the United States, a doctrine to which the Argentine Republic has heretofore solemnly adhered.

Among the principles which the memorable message of December 2, 1823, enunciates, there are two great declarations which particularly refer to these republics, viz., "The American continents are henceforth not to be considered as subjects for colonization by any European powers," and ". . . with the governments . . . whose independence we have . . . acknowledged, we could not view any interposition for the purpose of oppressing them or controlling in any other manner their destiny by any European power in any other light than as the manifestation of an unfriendly disposition toward the United States."

The right to forbid new colonial dominions within the limits of this continent has been many times admitted by the public men of England. To her sympathy is due, it may be said, the great success which the Monroe doctrine achieved immediately on its publication. But in very recent times there has been observed a marked tendency among the publicists and in the various expressions of European opinion to call attention to these countries as a suitable field for future territorial expansion. Thinkers of the highest order have pointed out the desirability of turning in this direction the great efforts which the principal powers of Europe have exerted for the conquest of sterile regions with trying climates and in remote regions of the earth. The European writers are already many who point to the territory of South America, with its great riches, its sunny sky, and its climate propitious for all products, as, of necessity, the stage on which the great powers, who have their arms and implements of conquest already prepared, are to struggle for the supremacy in the course of this century.

The human tendency to expansion, thus inflamed by the suggestions of public opinion and the press, may, at any moment, take an aggressive direction, even against the will of the present governing classes. And it will not be denied that the simplest way to the setting aside and easy ejectment of the rightful authorities by European governments is just this way of financial interventions—as might be shown by many examples. We in no wise pretend that the South American nations are, from any point of view, exempt from the responsibilities of all sorts which violations of international law impose on civilized peoples. We do not nor can we pretend that these countries occupy an exceptional position in their relations with European powers, which have the indubitable right to protect their subjects as completely as in any other part of the world against the persecutions and injustices of which they may be the victims. The only principle which the Argentine Republic maintains and which it would, with great satisfaction, see adopted, in view of the events in Venezuela, by a nation that enjoys such great authority and prestige as does the United States, is the principle, already accepted, that there can be no territorial expansion in America on the part of Europe, nor any oppression of the peoples of this continent, because an unfortunate financial situation may compel some one of them to postpone the fulfillment of its promises. In a word, the principle which she would like to see recognized is: that the public debt can not occasion armed intervention nor even the actual occupation of the territory of American nations by a European power.

The loss of prestige and credit experienced by States which fail to satisfy the rightful claims of their lawful creditors brings with it difficulties of such magnitude as to render it unnecessary for foreign intervention to aggravate with its oppression the temporary misfortunes of insolvency.

The Argentine Government could cite its own example to demonstrate the needlessness of armed intervention in these cases.

The payment of the English debt of 1824 was spontaneously resumed by her after an interruption of thirty years, occasioned by the anarchy and the disturbances which seriously affected the country during this period, and all the back payments and all the interest payments were scrupulously made without any steps to this end having been taken by the creditors.

Later on a series of financial happenings and reverses completely beyond the control of her authorities compelled her for the moment to suspend the payment of the foreign debt. She had, however, the firm and fixed intention of resuming the payments as soon as circumstances should permit, and she did so actually some time afterwards, at the cost of great sacrifices, but of her own free will and without the interference or the threats of any foreign power. And it has been because of her perfectly scrupulous, regular, and honest proceedings, because of her high sentiment of equity and justice so fully demonstrated, that the difficulties undergone, instead of diminishing, have increased her credit in the markets of Europe. It may be affirmed with entire certainty that so flattering a result would not have been obtained had the creditors deemed it expedient to intervene with violence at the critical financial period, which was thus passed through successfully. We do not nor can we fear that such circumstances will be repeated.

At this time, then, no selfish feeling animates us, nor do we seek our own advantage in manifesting our desire that the public debt of States should not serve as a reason for an armed attack on such States. Quite as little do we harbor any sentiment of hostility with regard to the nations of Europe. On the contrary, we have maintained with all of them since our emancipation the most friendly relations, especially with England, to whom we have recently given the best proof of the confidence which her justice and equanimity inspire in us by intrusting to her decision the most important of our international questions, which she has just decided, fixing our limits with Chile after a controversy of more than seventy years.

We know that where England goes civilization accompanies her, and the benefits of political and civil liberty are extended. Therefore we esteem her, but this does not mean that we should adhere with equal sympathy to her policy in the improbable case of her attempting to oppress the nationalities of this continent which are struggling for their own progress, which have already overcome the greatest difficulties and will surely triumph—to the honor of democratic institutions. Long, perhaps, is the road that the South American nations still have to travel. But they have faith enough and energy and worth sufficient to bring them to their final development with mutual support.

And it is because of this sentiment of continental brotherhood and because of the force which is always derived from the moral support of a whole people that I address you, in pursuance of instructions from His Excellency the President of the Republic, that you may communicate to the Government of the United States our point of view regarding the events in the further development of which that Government is to take so important a part, in order that it may have it in mind as the sincere expression of the sentiments of a nation that has faith in its destiny and in that of this whole continent, at whose head march the United States, realizing our ideals and affording us examples.

Please accept, etc.,

Luis M. Drago

9

The Need for Agrarian Reform in Brazil

A. P. Figueiredo

During the nineteenth century the pattern of large landholdings which had developed in Latin America during the colonial period encountered no serious challenge and in fact was aggravated in some areas. To be sure, voices were raised on occasion to denounce the evils of the latifundium *and to propose measures for its elimination or control, but they had little effect. One such voice was that of Antonio Pedro Figueiredo, editor of the review* O Progreso, *published in the Northeastern city of Recife. In 1846–1847 Figueiredo eloquently stated the need for agrarian reform in the sugar-growing zone of Northeast Brazil in a series of articles in* O Progreso, *which are printed below.*

I

In our coastal plains, in the areas about our great population centers, there are vast expanses of land, most of it fertile, of which only a tenth, and frequently a hundredth, is cultivated. In these lands internal colonization should be put into effect. They should be put at the disposition of the workers. But these areas were alienated many years ago; they are in the possession of legitimate owners, and their location with respect to commercial facilities for exportation gives them a high market value. The government is far from being able to buy them. Therefore, it is necessary to take recourse to some other means. What is this means? That which is indicated to us, in a very evident manner, by a quick survey of the way in which the turbulent class of our population was formed, and which, impelled by necessity, becomes the effective cause of our other policies and even of our many other ills.

Among us, as among all other young countries, the population goes on increasing and the fecundity of unions is fantastic, in cities and towns as well as in the country, and above all in the large cities such

From T. Lynn Smith (ed.), *Agrarian Reform in Latin America* (New York: Knopf, Inc. 1965), pp. 67–79. Copyright © 1965 by T. Lynn Smith. Reprinted by permission of Alfred A. Knopf, Inc.

as the one in which we live. Let us examine what comes from this increase of population, first here in Recife and then in the interior. We shall not speak of the rich families because they are few and, furthermore, they are becoming impoverished generation after generation through the subdivision of property by inheritance; instead we are concerned with those in moderate circumstances and the poor. The daughters overburden these families, creating for them new necessities which in commerce result in many bankruptcies and also give rise to an insatiable thirst for public employment; among the poor this leads to results still more deplorable for public morals. The boys, if the parents have the means, go to school and then seek employment; if the parents are poor, they learn a trade and in this manner increase the number, already excessive, of tailors, shoemakers, masons, carpenters, etc., and bring about a ruinous competition among themselves, and often they are without work. Some go to establish themselves in the interior, but in small numbers. Because of this, we ask what destiny has the continued increase of population in the interior? Will they come to be employed in agriculture? No! The best elements will come here to Recife to seek their fortunes, to solicit a ridiculous employment; and the remainder will move to the towns and other population centers to pass lives of misery because we have no industry to offer steady work and regular pay to the free worker.

This is the source of those masses of men who lack secure means of existence and who in certain spheres feed the politics of the parties and in the lower strata of society practice robbery in all its varieties.

Why is it that the offspring of the families of some means, instead of entering the precarious paths of public employment, do not engage in commercial activities, or, what would be even better, why do they not engage in agriculture? Why, instead of learning to be tailors, masons, and carpenters, do not the sons of families slightly favored by fortune return to the interior; and why do they not become agriculturists? Why, unless forced to do so, do not the inhabitants of the forested zones cultivate the soil? Why do their children seek out the towns? For all of these questions there is only one answer, and unfortunately it is fully complete.

In the social state in which we live, the means of subsistence of the father of a family do not increase in proportion to the number of his children, with the result that in general the children are poorer than their parents and possess less capital. At present agriculture and commerce, and especially agriculture, are encircled by a barrier that cannot be surmounted by the man of slight means, for all of those who do not possess a considerable amount of wealth. . . . Agriculture, the productive function par excellence, the mother (alma mater) of nations, is where the vital interests of our country reside; and since it is encircled by a barrier, it is necessary that this barrier be torn down, let it cost what it may.

And what is this barrier? It is the large landed estate. This terrible entity has ruined and depopulated Ireland, the plains of Rome, and many other countries.

The culture in which our population should be occupied and which one day will give us a middle class and establish the validity of our representative system, as we have already demonstrated, is not that on a large scale, which demands large amounts of capital, and which here is carried on by slaves; it is culture on a small scale, which can be performed by the father of a family and his sons, aided at the most by a few hired workers during the periods of planting and harvest. But the lands which are most advantageous for small-scale farming, because of the nature of the soil, the availability of springs and creeks, and the nearness to centers of consumption and exportation, are not those of far-distant *sertões,* nor those of the rolling, sunburned plains (*catingas*) which have been reduced almost to sterility by the imprudent activities of the cotton planters. The lands [most suited for family-sized farms] are those near the seacoast; in our provinces they are in the region occupied by the *engenhos* [sugar-cane plantations]. This region, which extends along the entire coast of our province and to a depth of 10, 12, and even 15 and 18 leagues, is, as is well known, divided into plantations or estates whose dimensions vary from one fourth of a square league to 2, 3, and even 4 or 5 square leagues. Here, because the culture of the sugar cane requires a special type of soil which is not found in all parts of the area, it follows that in addition to the cane fields, the necessary woods and the lands needed for the cattle and for the fields of mandioca, indispensable for the feeding of the slaves, the majority of the engenhos contain huge extensions of unused lands, lands that would be eminently suited for small farming, and which, if they were cultivated, would suffice to supply an abundance of mandioca flour, beans, and corn for the entire population of the province, for the neighboring provinces, and even for export.

But the owners refuse to sell these lands, or even to rent them. If one is wealthy, then he can buy an engenho; but if his means are slight and he wishes to buy or rent a few acres of land, he will not find them! This is what creates the unproductive population of the cities, the class of those seeking public employment, which increases daily. This is what causes the crimes against property to become more frequent and what daily impoverishes the country, since the number of consumers is growing, whereas that of the producers either remains constant or at least increases more slowly. But, say the large landowners, we are far from refusing poor people the land they need to cultivate; let them come and for a modest charge, or even gratis, we will give them not merely land to plant but also timber with which to construct their homes. This is true, but these favors which you landowners bestow upon them only continue at your pleasure. At any moment you may, either because of your own capriciousness or because they refuse to vote for your candidates in an election or because they fail to carry out any order you may give them, eject them without recourse. How can you ask them to plant, if they have no certainty of being able to harvest? What incentive is there in this for them to improve the land from which they may be expelled at any moment? On your lands they enjoy no political rights, because their opinions must perforce be in accord with your own; for them you are the police, the courts, the administration—in a word, everything; and, except for the right and the possibility of leaving you, these unhappy beings are in no way different from the serfs of the Middle Ages.

The power of the great landowners of the interior (and this power is great) is based upon the number of these obedient vassals that they maintain on their estates. Thus, because of the weakness of the government in comparison with these powerful individuals, it is impossible for a respect for the law to be extended to the interior. Under these circumstances each proprietor is obliged, as best he can, to maintain a kind of private militia so as to avoid being tyrannized by his neighbors or political adversaries, transformed into police authorities. In order that he can dispense with part of his lands, and consequently with a part of the influence of his armed forces, it is necessary for his neighbors to do the same and for the government to become sufficiently strong that it can protect all of them against possible aggressions.

But there is only one effective means for obtaining a result of this kind: to restrain all of them, simultaneously, by an external force; and we find this force in the direct taxation which is authorized in our Constitution and in the general property tax. . . . If it were gradually extended throughout the province this land tax would force the large landowners to get rid of the lands which are of no use to them. These lands, subdivided among numerous individuals, would be the source of a middle class of small farmers who would augment the production of the nation on a large scale and contribute greatly to the government with respect to the maintenance of public order. Then, with all of its sons occupied productively and advantageously, Brazil could issue a call for the excess of the industrious populations of Europe to whom it could offer work and secure means of existence. Other than this, any attempts at colonization are absurd.

II

Here we shall be concerned only with the measures that should be taken to replace with a regular government the despotic oligarchy that oppresses us. This despotism, here in our land of Pernambuco, is no exotic fruit; it was not invented by the Cavalcanti family, nor by the presidents that have succeeded one another since the date of our independence. Nor does it come from the greater or lesser degree of morality in the government; it results logically and inevitably from the fact that the political form of the government is not in harmony with the state of social organization, with the actual distribution of wealth and of the instruments of production.

The nature of a constitutional government consists in giving the individual security against the possible despotism of the social author- ity, which is always supposed to be very much more powerful than the separate individuals who make up the nations; this is the case in Europe where the authority has the support, to aid it in the admin- istration of the laws, of the disinterested mass of citizens.

But with us, the authority and the individuals are in totally different circumstances. The major part of the land in our province is divided into great estates, remains of the ancient *sesmarias* of which very few have been subdivided. The proprietor or the renter occupies a part of them and abandons, for a small payment, the right to live on and cultivate the other portions to 100, 200, and sometimes up to 400 families of free mulattoes or blacks, of whom he becomes the protector but from whom he demands absolute obedience and over whom he exercises the most complete despotism. As a result of this the guarantees of the law are not for these unfortunates, who make up the large majority of the population of the province, but are for the landowners of whom three or four, united by ties of blood, friendship, or ambi- tion, are sufficient to obliterate, in vast expanses of territory, the power and influence of the government. Thus these modern feudal barons, when their estates are located far from the provincial capital, live in an almost complete independence, administering justice with their own hands, arming their vassals for open warfare with one another, in disobedience to the orders of the government and the decrees of the judges: this is what goes on in the interior of the province. For such a state of affairs there are only two effective remedies: the first is a return to the old forms of absolute government, which invests the central power with extraordinary control; the second is to create im- mediately, at the expense of current feudalism, a middle class which will permit the constitutional government to proceed normally, in the interest of all, supported by public opinion and by material force that is independent of individual intrigues and much greater than the opposing coalitions of personal interests.

Now the first of these alternatives is nothing but a step backward; and we would never recommend, in order to correct a temporary problem, the restoration of these ancient obstacles, whose destruction has cost rivers of blood of all civilized peoples. Therefore, it is necessary to resort to the second alternative, which is the creation of a middle class. Now there are only three sources from which a middle class may be derived: commerce, industry, and agriculture. At present commerce actually occupies and makes unproductive a much larger number of individuals than are needed for the exchange of our products. Large-scale industry, in a country as poor as ours in capital and scientific knowledge, and where the interest rate is so high, can only be created by placing a terribly high tax upon the consumers; as for small industry, it is already overburdened and complains of the competition. Hence, only agriculture remains. Now in order that agriculture may make possible the rapid creation of a middle class it is essential that people of slight means be able to obtain lands and cultivate them with the certainty of enjoying the products. These conditions do not exist today, because the owners of sugar-cane plantations or the *fazendas* obstinately refuse to sell any portion of their lands, source and guarantee of their feudal power, and because the unfortunate occupant who takes the risk of planting remains at the mercy of the proprietor, who may expel him from the land within twenty-four hours.

III

How does it happen that with us agriculture is out of reach of all those who do not possess considerable wealth? All of you know, gentlemen, that it comes from the manner in which our land is subdivided; it is the necessary result of the large landed estate. The same effects that the celebrated economist Sismondi de Sismondi identified in the Roman countryside, and in unfortunate Ireland, we see reproduced here today, on a lesser scale with respect to the feeding of the masses because of the vast extension of our territory, but on a larger scale in its political aspects, because of the relative weakness of the government.

You know, gentlemen, that our province is divided naturally into three regions. The first is occupied in sugar making, and it extends from the seashore for 15 or 20 leagues to the interior. The second extends to the upper limits of the basins of the Capibaribe, the Ipojuca, and the Una. Finally, the third includes the affluents of the São

Francisco. The absolute lack of roads places the latter region entirely outside the movement of production and exportation of the province. The central region, ruined by the destruction of the forests, and by the droughts produced by it, cannot be counted upon for a fixed production and, in addition to this, it is far from Recife, our center of consumption and exchange. There remains, then, the region of the littoral, in which is concentrated three fourths of the population of the province; it is the only one capable, under present conditions, of producing in abundance and of finding buyers for its products. But this region, except for some sandy, unhealthful stretches along the coast which are unsuited for most crops, is divided into great landed estates, fragments of the ancient *sesmarias* [huge land grants].

From the Abiay River to the Persenunga River, if you lack the means to buy or rent a sugar-cane plantation or other huge property, you will not find an inch of cultivatable land to buy or rent; even so, nine tenths of the land in the area is unused. They will offer lands for you to cultivate, but without any guarantee whatsoever, reserving to themselves the right to expel you any day that it suits their pleasure. Wherever man has no assurance of enjoying the fruits of his labor, he will not work; for this reason, the occupant of the sugar-cane plantation plants hardly anything in the clearing surrounding his hut, and, fearful each moment of being ejected, lives by transporting the sugar cane of the landowners. Thus, instead of the countryside offering a place for the excess population of the cities and towns, quite to the contrary, it is adding to the excess of all those who seek to get away from such a precarious and dependent mode of life. Whose fault is this, gentlemen? Is it that of the large landowners? No; they are obeying the law of necessity. The obedient vassals, who, under the name of *moradores,* are maintained on his lands by each of the large landowners, are needed by the latter to defend themselves against usurpations and aggressions, from which the Government is much too weak to protect them.

There is in this, gentlemen, on a small scale, something analogous to the question of general disarmament that is agitating Europe. In order for one nation to be able to diminish its power to make war it is necessary that all the others do likewise; here, in order for one *senhor de engenho* to be able, without placing himself in danger, to sell or rent a part of his lands and in this way diminish the number of his vassals, it is necessary that his neighbors do the same. Because of this, gentlemen, it is essential that all of them simultaneously be exposed to a superior force. This force, gentlemen, is not to be found except in the direct imposition, promised by our Constitution, of the tax upon land. The establishment of this tax in proportion to the area possessed, and if necessary making it weigh more heavily upon unused

lands than upon those that are cultivated, will force the large landowners to sell or lease those immense tracts of fertile lands which
today are lost to agriculture and give work to only a small number of
hands; then (or at least so I believe) not only will we be able to
employ all of our people usefully, but also to invite the industrious
populations of Europe, a thing which today would be gross insanity.

I understand, gentlemen, that many years will be required to extend
the land tax over the immense area of our province. But even these
delays are necessary and useful. The twenty or thirty years that must
pass before it is possible to terminate the scientific work needed in
order to extend this impost to our most remote areas will be advantageous; it will allow time for the construction of the roads that are
needed to put the provinces in easy communication with the coast; and
it will avoid the flagrant injustice of imposing the same burden upon
the lands in the coastal districts, which are the areas of export crops
and for this reason have a high value, and upon those in the interior
which, for the lack of means of communication, attract very few buyers.

Gentlemen, the party of the opposition promises you that it will
make use of all its power to put into effect this land tax which the
Constitution promises us, and which today falls within the jurisdiction
of our provincial assembly. These doors of agriculture and commerce,
today closed to our fellow citizens, shutting them out from benefits of
fortune, it promises you will be opened; and in this endeavor it counts
upon your unanimous support.

Time is too short, gentlemen, to demonstrate to you how rich in
beneficial results such a measure will be for our province. But the
great landowners will have no more vassals, and the present moradores
will be transformed into thousands of small landowners who will
sustain public order and be a guarantee against the despotism of the
authorities. Production will double; justice will be extended without
difficulty to all parts; and elections, which today in the interior are
merely a parody upon the constitutional system, will change their
character and will shortly come to represent the opinion of the
country.

This done, gentlemen, that which is legitimate in the popular
hatred of the oligarchy and of foreigners will be satisfied without any
disruption of justice and with great advantages for our country. Commerce and agriculture, today closed to our poor compatriots, will be
opened to them. Our population will find abundant means of existence
and we will not be forced to say, as we are today, that Brazil is overpopulated.

10

The Italian Immigrant in São Paulo

Pierre Denis

If foreign capital made undoubted contributions to the economic de-velopment of Latin America in the nineteenth century, so did the large numbers of Europeans who migrated to Argentina and Brazil after 1870. Of the 2,752,395 immigrants entering Brazil between 1884 and 1913, nearly half were Italians. Many became laborers on the coffee plantations of São Paulo, which became Brazil's principal coffee-produc-ing region in the last decades of the nineteenth century. The life of the immigrant coffee worker in São Paulo is described in this reading by Pierre Denis, French financier and geographer, who traveled in Latin America as a young man.

The immigrants rarely arrive alone. The planter engages not isolated individuals, but families. The Government has always endeavoured to reduce to a minimum the proportion of single men among those introduced at the public expense. The stability of the colonist is to a great extent ensured by the presence of his family; it makes him less of a nomad. If he has a family one is not so likely to see him re-em-igrate at the slightest whim. San Paolo [*São Paulo*] attaches all the more importance to the introduction of emigrant families, because its Government does not give them holdings, so that the problem of their establishment on the soil is not decided beforehand.

Let us follow the colonists from the *hospedaria* of San Paolo—an immense hotel where for eight days they are in receipt of official hospitality—to the *fazenda*.

After landing at Santos the *hospedaria* marks the first stage of their journey. It is there that they contract for their first engagement. Until a recent period the procedure was as follows: the planters in search of labourers used themselves to visit the new arrivals, or send repre-sentatives speaking their language. The *hospedaria* was the market for labour; prices rose when the demand was heavy and the planters com-

From Pierre Denis, *Brazil,* translated by Bernard Miall (London: T. Fisher Unwin, Ltd., 1911), pp. 196–208. Reprinted by permission. Italicized bracketed notes are by Helen Delpar.

peted among themselves; in the contrary case they fell. The market being public, the colonists could compare the offers among themselves. They are, by the way, less ignorant than is usually supposed; they know the customs of the country and the average rate of wages, either from experience gained upon previous visits, or from information given by friends or relatives. The contract is never signed for more than a year. Sometimes it is written at the beginning of the wages book in which the mutual accounts between the planter and the labourer are kept; more often it is made by word of mouth.

In 1906 the Government of San Paolo, wishing to give the immigrants some form of guarantee, created the Agency of Colonisation and Labour. Its duties are to supervise the labour market of the *hospedaria*. It sees that the contracts made are honestly and punctually executed. It serves as an intermediary between the planter and the labourer, and constitutes a national bureau of employment. The planter is required to advise the agency beforehand of the number of colonists he wishes to recruit, and the terms he is willing to offer. He is then allowed to bargain freely with the immigrants, and, the bargain once struck, the contract is officially registered by the agency, which keeps the original text and sends a copy to each new colonist. The agency also serves as an arbitration court in the event of difficulties arising between planter and colonist having reference to the application of the contract. It wields a terrible weapon against any planter convicted of abusing his authority, for it may forbid him access to the *hospedaria,* thus putting him into a position in which he cannot renew his staff of labourers.

All the contracts drawn up under the supervision of the agency are drafted according to the same model; the text is printed beforehand, and blank spaces are left for the figures. This does not mean that the agency is seeking artificially to standardise the colonising system of San Paolo. The model contract adopted has not been created arbitrarily; it is in conformity with the contracts in general use, and is merely drafted with an attempt at greater precision. Before the agency intervened in any way the other forms of contract—that of *métayage* [*sharecropping*], for instance, which is preferred in Minas— were already spontaneously becoming extinct in San Paolo. The official text as drafted by the agency will therefore give us an exact idea of the usual contracts. Here I translate the essential articles:

Article 1. The proprietor will gratuitously furnish the colonist with the means of transport for himself, his family, and his baggage, from the railway station nearest the *fazenda* (the Government paying the railway fare); the proprietor will also provide a dwelling-house, pasture for one or more animals, and land on which to plant alimentary crops.

Article 2. The colonist must attend to the coffee-lines, so as to keep them always tidy; must replace missing trees, remove harmful weeds . . . in the manner and at the moment indicated by the proprietor.

Article 3. The proprietor will make no advances except such as are strictly necessary for the board of colonists recently arrived, or in case of illness. . . .

Article 5. If the colonist neglects any of the duties enumerated in Article 2, the proprietor may have the work performed by whomsoever he pleases, and cause the colonist to pay the expenses. . . .

Article 9. The proprietor who wishes to discharge a colonist must give him thirty days' warning, in default of which the contract will be considered as renewed.

Article 10. The colonist who wishes to leave the *fazenda* is under a like obligation.

Article 11. The colonist's cattle and crops are the guarantee of his debt to the proprietor. . . .

Article 13. The colonist may buy what provisions he may require where he pleases. . . .

Article 15. The proprietor undertakes to pay the colonist, per 1,000 stems of coffee attended to, the sum of . . . . ; per 50 litres (11 gallons) of coffee picked, the sum of . . . . ; per day's labour (in addition to work on the coffee plantation), the sum of . . . .

Article 18. The last article determines the crops which the colonist will be permitted to grow for his own profit.

An account of the colonist's life on the *fazenda* will serve as commentary upon this contract. Just as the contracts are uniform, so the *fazendas* are alike. I visited a great many during my stay in San Paolo; and the same observations would be true of nearly all. There is scarcely any difference: a more or less perfect equipment in the way of plant, a more or less expensive installation of drying machines and storehouses; but the same picturesque aspect, the same terraces, like great stairs, in the hard-beaten red earth; the same labouring population in clothes smeared with red (the livery of the red soil); the same methods of work, the same gestures, the same cares, the same enjoyments.

The houses of the colonists are not as a rule scattered among the coffee-shrubs; they form, according to the importance of the *fazenda,* a hamlet or village of regular construction, having nothing of the disorder of a European village. To be precise, it is really only a small city of labourers, just as the colonist is only a rural proletariat.[1] The house is of bricks or mud, often whitewashed, and only moderately comfortable, but the climate of San Paolo is extremely mild, and life is passed almost entirely in the open air. As for diet, it is sufficient. Bread is

---

[1] Some of the largest *fazendas* employ from 1,000 to 8,000 colonists. [Tr.]

rare, for neither wheat nor rye is a usual crop, but they are replaced by meal prepared from boiled maize, polenta, manioc, and black beans.

Each *fazenda* constitutes a little isolated world, which is all but self-sufficient, and from which the colonists rarely issue; the life is laborious. The coffee is planted in long regular lines in the red soil, abundantly watered by the rains, on which a constant struggle must be maintained against the invasion of noxious weeds. The weeding of the plantation is really the chief labour of the colonist. It is repeated six times a year. Directly after the harvest, if you ride on horseback along the lines of shrubs, which begin, as early as September, to show signs of their brilliant flowering season, you will find the colonists, men and women, leaning on their hoes, while the sun, already hot, is drying behind them the heaps of weeds they have uprooted.

Each family is given as many trees as it can look after; the number varies with the size of the family. Large families will tend as many as eight or ten thousand trees; while a single worker cannot manage much more than two thousand.

Like the vine, coffee requires a large number of labourers in proportion to the area under cultivation; it supports a relatively dense population. The two thousand trees which one colonist will receive will not cover, as a matter of fact, more than five to seven acres; yet the coffee supports other labourers who work on the *fazenda,* in addition to the labourers proper, or colonists. Pruning, for instance, which so far is not universally practised, is never done by the colonists, but by gangs of practised workmen, who travel about the State and hire themselves for the task. The colonist is only a labourer; if he were allowed to prune the shrubs he would kill them. Heaven knows, the pruners to whom the task is confided ill-treat the trees sufficiently already! They use pruning-hook and axe with a brutality that makes one shudder.

When the coffee ripens, towards the end of June, the picking of the crop commences. Sometimes, in a good year, the crop is not all picked until November. The great advantage enjoyed by San Paolo, to which it owes its rank as a coffee-producing country, is that the whole crop arrives at maturity almost at the same moment. The crop may thus be harvested in its entirety at one picking; the harvester may pick all the berries upon each tree at once, instead of selecting the ripe berries, and making two or three harvests, as is necessary in Costa Rica or Guatamala. This entails a great reduction in the cost of production and of labour. San Paolo owes this advantage to the climate, which is not quite tropical, and to the sequence of well-defined seasons and their effect upon the vegetation.

At the time of picking the colonists are gathered into gangs. They confine themselves to loading the berries on carts, which other labourers drive to the *fazenda*; there the coffee is soaked, husked, dried, and selected, and then dispatched to Santos, the great export market. All these operations the colonists perform under the supervision of the manager of the *fazenda*. A bell announces the hour for going to work; another the hour of rest; another the end of the day; the labourers have no illusions of independence. In the morning the gangs scatter through the plantation; in the evening they gradually collect on the paths of the *fazenda*, and go home in family groups, tired after the day's work, saving of words, saluting one another by gestures. On Sunday work is interrupted; games are arranged; parties are made up to play *mora* [*an Italian game*], or Italian card games, with *denari* and *bastoni* [*suits in an Italian pack of cards*]. Women hold interminable palavers. Sometimes, on an indifferent nag, borrowed at second or third hand from a neighbour, the colonist will ride as far as the nearest town, to see his relations, exercise his tongue, and pit himself against such hazards of fortune as the world outside the *fazenda* may offer.

What are the annual earnings of the agricultural worker? The conditions vary in different localities, but we may estimate that the colonist receives about 60 or 80 milreis—£4 to £5 7s. at the present rate of exchange—per 1,000 stems of coffee. This is a certain resource; a sort of fixed minimum wage. To this we must add the price of several days' labour at about 2 milreis, or 2s. 8d. A still more irregular element in the profits of a colonist's family is the amount it receives for the harvest. By consulting the books of several *fazendas* I was able to realise the extent of this irregularity. Sometimes the wage paid for the harvest is insignificant, while sometimes it is greater by itself than all the other sources of income put together. It is calculated at so much per measure of berries given in by the colonist. When the branches are heavily laden, not only is the total quantity greater, but the labour is performed more rapidly, and each day is more productive. Years of good harvest are for the colonist, as for the planter, years of plenty. With this important element essentially variable, how can we estimate the annual earnings of the colonist?

His expenses, again, cannot be estimated with any exactitude. An economic family will reduce them to practically nothing, if it has the good fortune to escape all sickness, and so dispense with the doctor, the chemist, and the priest.

What really enables the colonists to make both ends meet is the crops they have the right to raise on their own account, sometimes on allotments reserved for the purpose set apart from the coffee, and sometimes between the rows of the coffee-trees. They often think more of the clauses in their contract which relate to these crops than to those which determine their wages in currency. A planter told me that he had learned that a party of colonists intended to leave him after the harvest. We met some of them on the road, and I questioned them. "Is it true that you are engaged to work on Senhor B——'s *fazenda* for the coming year?" —"Yes."—"What reason have you for changing your *fazenda*? Will you be better paid there? Don't you get over £6 a thousand trees here?"—"Yes."—"How much do they offer you over there?"—"Only £4."—"Then why do you go?"—"Because there we can plant our maize among the coffee."

The culture of coffee is thus combined with that of alimentary crops. Almost all the world over the important industrial crops have to make room in the neighbourhood for food crops. Every agricultural country is forced to produce, at any rate to some extent, its own food, and to live upon itself if it wishes to live at all. In Brazil the dispersion of food crops is extreme, on account of the difficulties of transport; it is hardly less in San Paolo, in spite of the development of the railway system. Each *fazenda* is a little food-producing centre, the chief crops being maize, manioc, and black beans, of which the national dish, the *feijoade*, is made.

It even happens at times that the colonists produce more maize than they consume. They can then sell a few sacks at the nearest market, and add the price to their other resources. In this way crops which are in theory destined solely for their nourishment take on a different aspect from their point of view, yielding them a revenue which is not always to be despised.

The colonists make their purchases in the nearest town, or, more often, if the *fazenda* is of any importance, there is a shop or store— what the Brazilians call a *negocio*—in the neighbourhood of the colonists' houses. Its inventory would defy enumeration; it sells at the same time cotton prints and cooking-salt, agricultural implements and petroleum. An examination of the stock will show one just what the little economic unit called a *fazenda* really is. Although the colonists are to-day almost always free to make their purchases where they please, the trade of shopkeeper on a *fazenda* is still extremely profitable. He enjoys a virtual monopoly; the *fazendeiro* sees that no competitor sets up shop in the neighbourhood. The shop is the planter's property; he lets it, and usually at a high rent, which represents not only the value of the premises, but also the commercial privilege which goes with it. It is a sort of indirect commercial tariff levied by the planter on the colonists; a sign of the ever so slightly feudal quality of the organisation of property in San Paolo. The custom that used to obtain, of the planter himself keeping shop for the profit, or rather at the expense of his colonists, has generally disappeared.

One of the most serious of the planter's anxieties is the maintenance of the internal discipline of the *fazenda*. This is a task demanding ability and energy. One must not be too ready to accuse the planters of governing as absolute sovereigns. I myself have never observed any abuse of power on their part, nor have I seen unjustifiable fines imposed. The *fazendeiro* has a double task to perform. He employs his authority not only to ensure regularity in the work accomplished, but also to maintain peace and order among the heterogeneous population over which he rules. He plays the part of a policeman. The public police service cannot ensure the respect of civil law, of the person, or of property. How could the police intervene on the plantation, which is neither village nor commune, but a private estate? It falls to the planter to see that the rights of all are protected. Many colonists have a preference for plantations on which the discipline is severe; they are sure of finding justice then. The severity of the planter is not always to the detriment of the colonist.

Individually the colonists are often turbulent and sometimes violent; collectively they have hitherto shown a remarkable docility. On some *fazendas,* however, there have been labour troubles, and actual strikes; but they have always been abortive. The strikes have not lasted, and have never spread. One of the means by which the planters maintain their authority and prevent the colonists from becoming conscious of their strength is the prohibition of all societies or associations. They have had little trouble in making this prohibition respected. Among an uneducated group of labourers, of various tongues and nationalities, the spirit of combination does not exist. We have seen the development of workingmen's societies, of socialistic tendencies, in the cities of San Paolo, but nowhere in the country. An incoherent immigrant population, but lightly attached to the land, is not a favourable soil for the growth of a party with a socialistic platform. One must not look for agricultural trades-unions in San Paolo. The contract between the planter and his labourers is never a collective but always an individual contract.

Accounts are settled every two months. It often happens, even to-day, that the colonist is in the planter's debt. The planter has kept up the custom of making advances, and every family newly established in the country is, as a general rule, in debt. But the advances are always small, the colonist possessing so little in the way of securities; he has few animals and next to nothing in the way of furniture. His indebtedness towards the planter is not enough, as it used to be, to tie him down to the plantation; that many of them continue to leave by stealth is due to their desire to save their few personal possessions, which the planter might seize to cover his advances. At the last payment of the year all the colonists are free; their contract comes to an end after the harvest. Proletarians, whom nothing binds to the soil on which they have dwelt for a year, they do not resume their contracts if they have heard of more advantageous conditions elsewhere, or if their adventurous temperament urges them to try their luck further on.

The end of the harvest sees a general migration of the agricultural labourers. The colonists are true nomads. All the planters live in constant dread of seeing their hands leave them in September. Even the most generous *fazendeiros* experience the same difficulty. According to the Director of Colonisation, 40 per cent. to 60 per cent. of the colonists leave their *fazendas* annually. It is difficult to confirm this statement; but at least it is no exaggeration to say that a third of the families employed on the plantations leave their places from year to year. Towards September one meets them on the roads, most often travelling afoot; the man carrying a few household goods and the woman a newly-born child, like the city labourers at the end of the season. One can imagine what a serious annoyance this instability of labour must be to the coffee-planter. Long before the harvest the planter is planning to fill up the gaps that will appear in the colony directly after the harvest. He secretly sends out hired recruiting agents to the neighbouring *fazendas* or to the nearest town; he employs for this purpose some of the shrewder colonists, to whom he pays a commission for every family engaged. Finally, at the end of his resources, if he no longer has any hope of finding workmen in the neighbourhood who are experienced in plantation work, he decides to apply to the colonisation agent in San Paolo, and resigns himself to the employment of an untrained staff, whom he will have to spend several months in training.

.   .   .

The agricultural workers of San Paolo are for the most part of Italian nationality. It is Italy that has furnished the greatest proportion of immigrants. Many *fazendas* are peopled entirely by Italians, and in some municipalities they surpass in number the Brazilians and the immigrants of all other nationalities together. From 1891 to 1897 the Italians formed three-fourths or four-fifths of the total immigration, according to the year.

What is the number of Italians to-day residing in San Paolo? It is impossible to say precisely. In 1901, according to a report published in the "Bulletin of Italian Emigration," they should have numbered from 650,000 to 700,000. The Italian Consul, turning his attention to the matter in 1905, declared that the latter figure was notoriously insufficient. According to the statistics of the Secretary of Agriculture in San Paolo, up to the year 1901, 568,000 more Italians had arrived in the country than had left it. To these we must add the Italians who had entered the State by land, crossing the boundary between Minas and San Paolo. We may also count as Italians the children of Italian families born in San Paolo, but in exclusively Italian surroundings, such as most of the colonies afford. Italian families are as prolific in San Paolo as in Italy, and the Italian population has notably increased by the excess of the birth-rate over the death-rate. We may therefore conclude that the Italians in San Paolo number scarcely less than a million. They form there one of the largest and most compact Italian populations that immigration has created overseas.

BIBLIOGRAPHY

Charles E. Chapman, "The Age of the Caudillo: A Chapter in Hispanic American History," *Hispanic American Historical Review,* 12 (1932), 281–300 is an early but still useful attempt to characterize *caudillismo.* Also of interest are George S. Wise, *Caudillo: A Portrait of Antonio Guzmán Blanco* (New York: Columbia University Press, 1951); Roger M. Haigh, "The Creation and Control of a Caudillo," *Hispanic American Historical Review,* 44 (1964), 481–490; and R. A. Humphreys, "Latin America: The Caudillo Tradition," in Michael Howard (ed.), *Soldiers and Governments: Nine Studies in Civil-Military Relations* (Bloomington: Indiana University Press, 1959). Hugh M. Hamill, Jr. (ed.), *Dictatorship in Spanish America* (New York: Knopf, 1965) contains several selections dealing with the nineteenth century as well as a comprehensive bibliography. Allison W. Bunkley, *The Life of Sarmiento* (Princeton, N.J.: Princeton University Press, 1952) is a biography of the author of *Facundo,* which sees him as becoming representative of a new *caudillismo* after 1852. José Luis Romero, *A History of Argentine Political Thought* (Stanford, Cal.: Stanford University Press, 1963) places both Sarmiento and Juan Facundo Quiroga in the context of Argentine intellectual history.

The ideas of liberal and conservative thinkers in nineteenth-century Latin America can be examined in William Rex Crawford, *A Century of Latin American Thought,* rev. ed. (Cambridge, Mass.: Harvard University Press, 1961). The evolution of liberalism and conservatism in Mexico can be traced in Charles A. Hale, *Mexican Liberalism in the Age of Mora, 1821–1853* (New Haven, Conn.: Yale University Press, 1968) and in two books by W. H. Callcott: *Church and State in Mexico, 1822–1857* (Durham, N.C.: Duke University Press, 1926) and *Liberalism in Mexico, 1857–1929* (Stanford, Cal.: Stanford University Press, 1931). Conflict between Church and state in nineteenth-century Latin America, which can be viewed as an aspect of the liberal-conservative struggle, has been studied in a number of works including J. Lloyd Mecham, *Church and State in Latin America,* rev. ed. (Chapel Hill: University of North Carolina Press, 1966); Francis M. Stanger, "Church and State in Peru," *Hispanic American Historical Review,* 7 (1927), 410–437; Fredrick B. Pike, "Church and State in Peru and Chile Since 1840: A Study in Contrasts," *American Historical Review,* 73 (1967), 30–50; Carey Shaw, Jr., "Church and State in Colombia as Observed by American Diplomats, 1834–1906," *Hispanic American Historical Review*, 21 (1941), 577–613; Mary Watters, *A History of the Church in Venezuela, 1810–1930* (Chapel Hill: University of North Carolina Press, 1933); Mary P. Holleran, *Church and State in Guatemala* (New York: Columbia University Press, 1949); and Sister Mary Crescentia Thornton, *The Church and Freemasonry in Brazil, 1872–1875* (Washington, D.C.: Catholic University of America, 1948).

Several of the readings in Marvin D. Bernstein (ed.), *Foreign Investment in Latin America: Cases and Attitudes* (New York: Knopf, 1966), focus on the nineteenth century, which is also well represented in the bibliography. R. A. Humphreys, *Liberation in South America, 1806–1827: The Career of James Paroissien* (London: Athlone Press, 1952) illustrates the travail often experienced by foreign investors and entrepreneurs in Latin America in the years immediately following independence. Watt Stewart, *Henry Meiggs, Yankee Pizarro* (Durham, N.C.: Duke University Press, 1946) and *Keith and Costa Rica* (Albuquerque: University of New Mexico Press, 1964) also deal with individual entrepreneurs, the former a controversial railroad builder in Chile and Peru, the latter one of the founders of the United Fruit Company. Also relevant to the topic of foreign investment in nineteenth-century Latin America are Sanford Mosk, "Latin America and the World Economy, 1850–1914," *Inter-American Economic Affairs*, 2 (Winter, 1948), 53–82; J. Fred Rippy, *British Investments in Latin America, 1822–1949* (Minneapolis: University of Minnesota Press, 1959); and Richard Graham, *Britain and the Onset of Modernization in Brazil, 1850–1914* (Cambridge, Eng.: Cambridge University Press, 1968). On the Drago Doctrine see H. E. Nettles, "The Drago Doctrine in International Law and Politics," *Hispanic American Historical Review*, 8 (1928), 204–223.

A convenient summary of immigration to Brazil, especially from 1887 to 1934, can be found in T. Lynn Smith, *Brazil: People and Institutions*, rev. ed. (Baton Rouge: Louisiana State University Press, 1963), pp. 118–143. Stanley J. Stein, *Vassouras: A Brazilian Coffee County, 1850–1900* (Cambridge, Mass.: Harvard University Press, 1957) is an analysis of a county in the Parahyba Valley, center of Brazilian coffee production until after the 1880s when leadership passed to São Paulo. On the development of the city of São Paulo see Richard M. Morse, *From Community to Metropolis: A Biography of São Paulo, Brazil* (Gainesville: University of Florida Press, 1958); and on the roots of *Paulista* enterprise see Warren Dean, "The Planter as Entrepreneur: The Case of São Paulo," *Hispanic American Historical Review*, 46 (1966), 138–152.

~§ TWO §~

THE TWENTIETH CENTURY

Since the early years of the twentieth century, and with greater frequency since World War II, the republics of Latin America have experienced a series of political, economic, social, and intellectual changes that have seriously undermined the bases of the relatively static and traditional societies of the previous century. Of the many forces that have encouraged and legitimized change perhaps the most pervasive is nationalism. Although the concept of nationalism is a many-faceted one which resists definition and can be manipulated by groups with diverse and occasionally conflicting interests, its most widespread and powerful form in the twentieth century has undoubtedly been economic nationalism. The exponents of economic nationalism see the Latin American republics as victims of neocolonial exploitation by the more highly developed nations of western Europe and the United States and are likely to believe that economic independence and social justice can best be achieved by rapid industrialization and by limiting or eliminating foreign participation in the economy, especially in the extractive industries.

Stimulated in part by economic nationalism and in part by the impact of international events, such as the two world wars, industry has made impressive strides in the major Latin American countries since 1914. One of the consequences of industrial growth has been the rise of a native entrepreneurial elite and the expansion of the middle class. Both groups now wield much of the political power formerly monopolized by landowners and merchants, but it is by no means clear that the erosion of the latter's influence has been accompanied by increased democracy in political or social life.

Certainly, the champions of political democracy cannot be much cheered by the course of Latin American politics since World War II. In fact, the very desirability of liberal constitutionalism has been questioned by those who argue that in Latin America the machinery of democratic government has been utilized by conservatives and reactionaries to block needed reform. Although the composition and training of the armed forces have changed significantly since the nineteenth century, military domination of government still remains a prominent feature of Latin American politics. A relatively recent development is the appearance of "military populism," exemplified by the nationalist and leftist military governments established in Peru in 1968 and in Bolivia in 1970.

If the Latin American armed forces can no longer be regarded as automatic allies of the conservative right, the same can be said of the Roman Catholic clergy. This was clearly demonstrated at the epochal meeting of the Latin American Bishops Council (CELAM) in Medellín, Colombia, in 1968. The 236-page document adopted at the Medellín meeting condemned both Marxism and capitalism as systems destructive of human dignity and committed the Church to the quest for social justice.[1] Although many of the conservative bishops who signed the report will undoubtedly ignore its recommendations, the very fact of its adoption bears witness to the heightened social consciousness of an increasing number of Catholic clergymen.

---

[1] Harvey Rosenhouse, "La Iglesia: Lucha por el cambio," *Visión* (May 8, 1970), 25–26.

◈ 11 ◈

The True Peruvian Nation

———◆◀◉▶◆———

Víctor Raúl Haya de la Torre

A prominent feature of twentieth-century nationalism in Latin America has been the development of a sense of national identity which often portrays the Indian or the mestizo as its human foundation. In this reading, Víctor Raúl Haya de la Torre (1895–) identifies Peru with the Indian, whom he depicts as the victim of exploitation by the native elite, and rejects this elite's appropriation of the mantle of nationalism. The selection, which is taken from a letter written in London in 1925, also illustrates the reevaluation of the aboriginal past and its relevance to contemporary Latin America which was undertaken in Peru by José Carlos Mariátegui (1895–1930) and in Mexico as a result of the revolution of 1910. Haya de la Torre, exiled from Peru in 1923 by dictator Augusto Leguia, was the founder of APRA (Alianza Popular Revolucionaria Americana), an international political movement which called for the unification of Indo-America (as Haya de la Torre renamed Latin America), nationalization of land and industry, and inter-American control of the Panama Canal.

In the same way that Peru and Mexico were the centers of Indian America, they were also centers of colonial America. But colonial Mexico was different from colonial Peru. In Mexico there was an attempt to create a culture. To Peru, the Spaniards have left nothing. You have seen colonial Lima; it is a city of adobe that subsists because it does not rain. Mexico is a magnificent city of stone, and each one of its great centers—Puebla, Guadalajara, San Luis, Querétaro, and so on—offers monumental remains—incomparably superior to ours—of an era which if it was characterized by slavery and brutal exploitation, it was also characterized by a constructive spirit, by discipline, and by vitality. I believe that the conquest of America was a repugnant event for us. I believe, furthermore, that our advanced Indian empires

From Samuel L. Baily (ed.), *Nationalism in Latin America* (New York: Knopf, 1971), pp. 123–128. Copyright © 1970 by Samuel L. Baily. Reprinted by permission of Alfred A. Knopf, Inc. Deletions in the text are by Samuel L. Baily. Italicized bracketed note in the text is by Helen Delpar.

would have been able to perfect themselves within Western Civilization; like Japan, they would have been able to take advantage of it and to grow stronger while retaining their traditional systems. But it is not the time to dwell on this point. We lament the conquest, convinced that the Spaniards were ferocious in bringing it about. Nevertheless, I prefer Cortés to Pizarro, and I believe that Mexico was more fortunate with her enslavement than was Peru.

I have gone so far back in time because the Spanish conquistador, the enslaver, the oppressor, the cold egotist devoid of humanity and piety, is still in our midst. In Mexico the races have amalgamated and the new capital has been erected in the same spot where the old one used to be. The city of Mexico and the other great cities are in the heart of the country, in the mountains, in the high plains crowned by volcanoes. The tropical Mexican coast provides communication with the sea. The Mexican conquistador united with the Indian in the heartland of the mountains and forged a race which, although not properly a race in the strict sense of the word, is in fact so by the homogeneity of its customs, by the trend toward a definitive fusion of blood, and by its continuity—without violent disruption—of national life. In Peru, that did not happen. The Peruvian sierra was Indian; the real Peru remained the western Andes. The old national cities—Cuzco, Cajamarca, etc.—were banished. New Spanish cities were founded in the tropical coast where it never rains, where there are no changes of temperature, where it was possible to develop that sensual Andalusian atmosphere of our happy and submissive capital.

Mountainous Peru declined. It was a field for exploitation, a place of slavery. Spanish feudalism became the order of the day, destroying a nearly perfect system of socialism. The Indian who had lived in the great community of his Empire was suddenly converted into a slave. Millions of these beings died in the mines extracting gold for their insatiable masters. The colony did not take pity on them; it insulted them, robbed them and murdered them. There was no attempt to forge any race. When it was found impossible to make the Indian of the sierra work on the coast under the implacable sun of the deep valleys, the Negro was imported. But the Indian continued to be the white man's slave, and what is unique in Peru is that that slavery continued.

Independence was for us a deceptive movement. Our real heroes of liberty were the Tupac Amarus, the Pumacahuas because they are the precursors of the liberty of the Indian. The Indian has continued before and after the political independence without any change in status. He was always the slave, the cannon fodder. He was dragged to the War of Independence, to the civil wars, and to the slaughter of the war with Chile. But the Indian, who for the most part does not speak Spanish, obeys out of terror. Ricardo Palma [*nineteenth-century Peruvian writer noted for his sketches of Peruvian life called* tradiciones] has said that during the war of '79 [the Indian] repeated that he was going to kill the "señor of Chile." During the Colonial period as during the time of the Republic, the Indian's desire for liberty has been the same. The Indian loves a meaningful liberty. The Indian wants the restoration of his land. For four centuries he has risen up, he has rebelled, he has let himself be killed by the hundreds, fighting in the name of hunger and of his tradition against the feudal lord who oppressed him. That is his patriotism, because that is his justice.

. . . There are no ideological or class differences among the leaders of the different ruling groups: Leguía, Pardo, Riva Agüero, Prado, Benavides, Villarán, Miró Quesada, they are all wolves of the same pack. Catholics, *gamonales* [bosses of the Indians], capitalists, bourgeois, absolutely bourgeois, there are no differences. Moreover, all have acted together, and all are united, directly or indirectly, by family and economic ties. In their various struggles, they all use more or less violent means, essentially they all represent the conservative caste, the class of the great exploiters, the neo-Spanish foreign nobility, disdainful of our reality, disposed to continue the exploitation and liquidation of the population that supports them. On fundamental questions such as the chauvinistic agitation against Chile, they are at one in their position. Each one of them struggles to be more "patriotic" than the other. The groups of intellectuals or journalists that surround each of these *caciques* also shout their hatred toward Chile, and between Leguía and the rest of them there is but one word of insult and agitation: "Chilean." Leguía calls them "Chileans" and vice-versa.

In social questions they are all reactionaries. They are all great feudal lords, or capitalists, or subjects of one or the other. The fundamental problems of the nation—those of the Indian, the land and, at the same time, that of our economic base—have never been dealt with. There has not been a single ruler who has been moved by the horror of the Indian's situation. *Gamonalismo* [bossism] is in Peru an organized and legalized crime. I have lived eight months in Cuzco, I am familiar with Cajamarca, Apurimac and other places in the Peruvian sierra. You cannot imagine the horrors that are committed there. I have seen Indians' flesh torn open by the steel bar with which they are punished. In an article published by the European and Asiatic Library of Switzerland, I made a report of what I have seen in the Peruvian sierra. The *gamonales* call the whip *hualpacaldo* (chicken soup). With it they destroy the flesh of those unfortunate beings. They kill, they rob, they burn the huts, they rape the women and the daughters with unparalleled coldness. But the *gamonal* is the deputy, the senator, the minister, the president. When I passed by Tumbes, I heard that in the coastal estate of Plateros, of which Leguía is the owner, the workers were punished by being tied up naked with their backs to the sun. Tumbes is in the tropics. These tortures are well known on the coast and in the sierra of Peru.

All of this is not new. It is the kind of terror that has prevailed for a long time. The massacres of Indians and workers have taken place in Peru under all governments, since that clown Nicolás de Piérola [President, 1895–1899], who had himself cynically called "the protector of the Indian race." For this we are exiled, because we have cried out against so much horror. We have not been exiled because of the intrigues of coteries. Our generation has awakened from its dream and from its patriotic stupor and from frivolity to look clearly into the entrails of our reality. . . . Peru is now searching for its own path. Leguía is in power, above all, because the instinct of the people tells them to remain with one tyrant rather than replace him with another. There are no other men on the political stage of the dominant class. All are old, all are evil, all are hungry for power; their vision extends no farther than their appetites. The country is waiting for a profound change. Peru is preparing to redeem itself definitively. To redeem itself not only from the tyrant, but also from the class that he represents; to redeem itself from oppression and to bring about justice for four million slaves.

For this reason it does not matter that Señor Leguía might have told Leopoldo Lugones, his agent in Buenos Aires, that the dissemination of our revolutionary doctrines will signify the destruction of the Peruvian nationality and a struggle between the races. For Leguía the nationality is the elite who accept the horror of the present situation. This position of Leguía is the same as that of all of the "distinguished" men of Peru. You will see that on the day when the hour of liberation of the people, of redemption of the Indians, of the true and just revolution rings in Peru, the bitter rivals of today will automatically unite. Señor Leguía, if he is still alive, will be the common leader. "The nationality is in danger," will be the hypocritical shout of all the groups that make up the elite. Then there will be no more subterfuge; the struggle will clearly be between the minuscule group of families that exploits the Peruvian people and that forms the dominating class, and the people who fight for liberty. Then the Pardos, the Aspillagas, the Prados, the Benavides, the Riva Agüeros, and so on will form one block; it will be the block of the bourgeois of the great landowners, of reaction in alliance with Yankee imperialism.

Our struggle, therefore, is not only against Leguía; our struggle is against the class that, divided or not, oppresses the Peruvian people and sells them to the foreigner. For this reason they have exiled those of us who have headed up or initiated that social movement, and they have done so with the blessing of all the conservative sectors, even of those that are at the present time in temporary opposition. But although the enemy is strong, we shall always continue to advance. It is true that because of the long terror a great part of the Peruvian people is lulled, intimidated, and indifferent, but this does not mean that it does not suffer, or comprehend, or that it does not desire justice. . . .

❧ 12 ❧

The Economic Development of Latin America

Raúl Prebisch

In the years following World War II one of the most influential advocates of the industrialization of Latin America was the Argentine economist Raúl Prebisch (1901–), who served as executive secretary of the United Nations Economic Commission for Latin America from 1948 to 1962. In this selection, Prebisch sets forth the thesis that the concept of the international division of labor has worked to the disadvantage of the countries on the economic periphery, which includes Latin America, because they have not benefited from increased productivity to the same extent as the nations of the economic center, which includes the United States. Prebisch urges industrialization as the best means available to Latin America "of obtaining a share of the benefits of technical progress and of progressively raising the standard of living of its masses."

In Latin America, reality is undermining the out-dated schema of the international division of labour, which achieved great importance in the nineteenth century and, as a theoretical concept, continued to exert considerable influence until very recently.

Under that schema, the specific task that fell to Latin America, as part of the periphery of the world economic system, was that of producing food and raw materials for the great industrial centres.

There was no place within it for the industrialization of the new countries. It is nevertheless being forced upon them by events. Two world wars in a single generation and a great economic crisis between them have shown the Latin-American countries their opportunities, clearly pointing the way to industrial activity.

The academic discussion, however, is far from ended. In economics, ideologies usually tend either to lag behind events or to outlive them.

From Raúl Prebisch, *The Economic Development of Latin America and Its Principal Problems* (United Nations: Department of Economic Affairs, 1950), pp. 1–7. This article appears as reprinted in Samuel L. Baily (ed.), *Nationalism in Latin America* (New York: Knopf, 1971), pp. 153–161. Deletion in the text is by Samuel L. Baily.

It is true that the reasoning on the economic advantages of the international division of labour is theoretically sound, but it is usually forgotten that it is based upon an assumption which has been conclusively proved false by facts. According to this assumption, the benefits of technical progress tend to be distributed alike over the whole community, either by the lowering of prices or the corresponding raising of incomes. The countries producing raw materials obtain their share of these benefits through international exchange, and therefore have no need to industrialize. If they were to do so, their lesser efficiency would result in their losing the conventional advantages of such exchange.

The flaw in this assumption is that of generalizing from the particular. If by "the community" only the great industrial countries are meant, it is indeed true that the benefits of technical progress are gradually distributed among all social groups and classes. If, however, the concept of the community is extended to include the periphery of the world economy, a serious error is implicit in the generalization. The enormous benefits that derive from increased productivity have not reached the periphery in a measure comparable to that obtained by the peoples of the great industrial countries. Hence, the outstanding differences between the standards of living of the masses of the former and the latter and the manifest discrepancies between their respective abilities to accumulate capital, since the margin of saving depends primarily on increased productivity.

Thus there exists an obvious disequilibrium, a fact which, whatever its explanation or justification, destroys the basic premise underlying the schema of the international division of labour.

Hence, the fundamental significance of the industrialization of the new countries. Industrialization is not an end in itself, but the principal means at the disposal of those countries of obtaining a share of the benefits of technical progress and of progressively raising the standard of living of the masses. . . .

The industrialization of Latin America is not incompatible with the efficient development of primary production. On the contrary, the availability of the best capital equipment and the prompt adoption of new techniques are essential if the development of industry is to fulfil the social objective of raising the standard of living. The same is true of the mechanization of agriculture. Primary products must be exported to allow for the importation of the considerable quantity of capital goods needed.

The more active Latin America's foreign trade, the greater the possibility of increasing productivity by means of intensive capital formation. The solution does not lie in growth at the expense of foreign trade, but in knowing how to extract, from continually growing foreign trade, the elements that will promote economic development.

If reasoning does not suffice to convince us of the close tie between economic development and foreign trade, a few facts relating to the situation today will make it evident. The economic activity and level of employment in the majority of the Latin-American countries are considerably higher than before the war. This high level of employment entails increased imports of consumer goods, both nondurable and durable, besides those of raw materials and capital goods, and very often exports are insufficient to provide for them.

This is evident in the case of imports and other items payable in dollars. There are already well-known cases of scarcity of that currency in certain countries, despite the fact that the amount of dollars supplied by the United States to the rest of the world in payment of its own imports was considerable. In relation to its national income, however, the import coefficient of the United States has, after a persistent decline, arrived at a very low level (not over 3 percent). It is, therefore, not surprising that, notwithstanding the high income level of the United States, the dollar resources thus made available to the Latin-American countries seem insufficient to pay for the imports needed for their intensive development.

It is true that as European economy recovers, trade with that continent can profitably be increased, but Europe will not supply Latin America with more dollars unless the United States increases its import coefficient for European goods.

This, then, is the core of the problem. It is obvious that if the above-mentioned coefficient is not raised, Latin America will be compelled to divert its purchases from the United States to those countries which provide the exchange to pay for them. Such a solution is certainly very dubious, since it often means the purchase of more expensive or unsuitable goods.

It would be deplorable to fall back on measures of that kind when a basic solution might be found. It is sometimes thought that, by reason of the enormous productive capacity of the United States, that country could not increase its import coefficient for the purpose of providing the basic solution to this world problem. Such a conclusion cannot be substantiated without a prior analysis of the factors that have caused the United States steadily to reduce its import coefficient. These factors are aggravated by unemployment, but can be overcome when it does not exist. One can understand that it is of vital importance, both to Latin America and the rest of the world, that the United States achieve its aim of maintaining a high level of employment.

It cannot be denied that the economic development of certain Latin-American countries and their rapid assimilation of modern technology, in so far as they can utilize it, depend to a very large extent upon foreign investment. The implications involved render the problem far from simple. The negative factors include the failure to meet foreign financial commitments during the great depression of the nineteen thirties, a failure which, it is generally agreed, must not be allowed to happen again. Fundamentally the problem is the same as that referred to in the preceding paragraph. The servicing of these foreign investments, unless new investments are made, must be paid for by means of exports in the same currency and, if these do not show a corresponding increase, in time the same difficulties will arise again. They will be the greater if exports fall violently. The question thus arises whether, pending that basic solution, it would not be wiser to direct investments toward such productive activities as would, through direct or indirect reduction of dollar imports, permit the regular servicing of foreign obligations.

Here one must beware of dogmatic generalizations. To assume that the meeting of foreign commitments and the proper functioning of the monetary system depend upon nothing more than a decision to obey certain rules of the game is to fall into an error involving serious consequences. Even when the gold standard was in operation in the great centres, the countries of the Latin-American periphery had great difficulty in maintaining it, and their monetary troubles frequently provoked condemnation from abroad. The more recent experiences of the large countries have brought a better understanding of some aspects of the situation. Great Britain, between the two wars, encountered difficulties somewhat similar to those which arose and continue to arise in the Latin-American countries, which have never taken kindly to the rigidity of the gold standard. That experience doubtless helps to bring about a better understanding of the phenomena of the periphery.

The gold standard has ceased to function, as in the past, and the management of currency has become even more complex in the periphery. Can all these complications be overcome by a strict application of sound rules of monetary behaviour? Sound rules for these countries are still in the making. Here there arises another vital problem; that of utilizing individual and collective experience to find a means of harmoniously fitting monetary action into a policy of regular and intensive economic development.

Let this not be interpreted as meaning that the classic teachings are of no value. If they do not provide positive rules, they at least show what cannot be done without impairing the stability of the currency. The extremes to which inflation has gone in Latin America show that monetary policy was not based upon these teachings, since some of the larger Latin-American countries increased circulation to a greater extent than did those countries which had to meet enormous war expenditure.

These facts must be taken into account in an objective analysis of the effects of the inflationary increase on the process of capitalization. It must, however, be admitted that, in most of the Latin-American countries, voluntary savings are not sufficient to cover the most urgent capital needs. In any case, monetary expansion does not bring about an increase in the foreign exchange reserves necessary for the importation of capital goods; it merely redistributes income. It must now be determined whether it has led to a more active capital formation.

The point is a decisive one. The raising of the standard of living of the masses ultimately depends on the existence of a considerable amount of capital per man employed in industry, transport and primary production, and on the ability to use it well.

Consequently, the Latin-American countries need to accumulate an enormous amount of capital. Several have already shown their capacity to save to the extent of being able to finance a large part of their industrial investments through their own efforts. Even in this case, which is exceptional, capital formation has to overcome a strong tendency towards certain types of consumption which are often incompatible with intensive capitalization.

Nevertheless, it does not appear essential to restrict the individual consumption of the bulk of the population, which, on the whole, is too low, in order to accumulate the capital required for industrialization and for the technical improvement of agriculture. An immediate increase in productivity per man could be brought about by well-directed foreign investments added to present savings. Once this initial improvement has been accomplished, a considerable part of the increased production can be devoted to capital formation rather than to inopportune consumption.

How are sufficient increases in productivity to be achieved? The experience of recent years is instructive. With some exceptions, the rise in employment necessitated by industrial development was made possible by the use of men whom technical progress had displaced from primary production and other occupations, especially certain comparatively poorly paid types of personal services, and by the employment of women. The industrial employment of the unemployed, or ill-employed, has thus meant a considerable improvement in productivity and, consequently, where other factors have not brought about a general lowering of productive efficiency, a net increase in national income.

The great scope for technical progress in the field of primary production, even in those countries where it has already been considerable, together with the perfecting of existing industries, could contribute, to national income, a net increase that would provide an ever-increasing margin of saving.

All this, however, especially in so far as it is desired to reduce the need for foreign investments, presupposes a far greater initial capitalization than is usually possible with the type of consumption of certain sectors of the community, or the high proportion of national income absorbed, in some countries, by fiscal expenditure, which makes no direct or indirect contribution to national productivity.

It is, in fact, a demonstration of the latent conflict existing in these countries between the desire to assimilate, quickly, ways of life which the technically more advanced countries adopted step by step as their productivity increased, and the need for capitalization without which this increase in productivity could not be achieved.

For the very reason that capital is scarce, and the need for it great, its use should be subjected to a strict standard of efficacy which has not been easy to maintain, especially where industries have developed to meet an emergency. There is, however, still time to correct certain deviations and, above all, to avoid them in the future.

In order to achieve this, the purpose of industrialization must be clearly defined. If industrialization is considered to be the means of attaining an autarchic ideal in which economic considerations are of secondary importance, any industry that can produce substitutes for imports is justifiable. If, however, the aim is to increase the measurable well-being of the masses, the limits beyond which more intensive industrialization might mean a decrease in productivity must be borne in mind.

Formerly, before the great depression, development in the Latin-American countries was stimulated from abroad by the constant increase of exports. There is no reason to suppose, at least at present, that this will again occur to the same extent, except under very exceptional circumstances. These countries no longer have an alternative between vigorous growth along those lines and internal expansion through industrialization. Industrialization has become the most important means of expansion.

This does not mean, however, that primary exports must be sacrificed to further industrial development. Exports not only provide the foreign exchange with which to buy the imports necessary for economic development, but their value usually includes a high proportion of land rent, which does not involve any collective cost. If productivity in agriculture can be increased by technical progress and if, at the same time, real wages can be raised by industrialization and adequate social legislation, the disequilibrium between incomes at the centres and the periphery can gradually be corrected without detriment to that essential economic activity.

This is one of the limits of industrialization which must be carefully considered in plans of development. Another concerns the optimum size of industrial enterprises. It is generally found in Latin-American countries that the same industries are being attempted on both sides of the same frontier. This tends to diminish productive efficiency and so militates against fulfilling the social task to be accomplished. The defect is a serious one, which the nineteenth century was able to attenuate considerably. When Great Britain proved, with facts, the advantages of industry, other countries followed suit. Industrial development, however, spurred by active competition, tended towards certain characteristic types of specialization which encouraged profitable trade between the various countries. Specialization furthered technical progress and the latter made possible higher incomes. Here, unlike the case of industrial countries by comparison with those producing primary products, the classic advantages of the division of labour between countries that are equal, or nearly so, followed.

The possibility of losing a considerable proportion of the benefits of technical progress through an excessive division of markets thus constitutes another factor limiting the industrial expansion of these countries. Far from being unsurmountable, however, it is a factor which could be removed with mutual benefit by a wise policy of economic interdependence.

Anti-cyclical policies must be included in any programmes of economic development if there is to be an attempt, from a social point of view, to raise real income. The spread of the cyclical fluctuations of the large centres to the Latin-American periphery means a considerable loss of income to these countries. If this could be avoided, it would simplify the problem of capital formation. Attempts have been made to evolve an anti-cyclical policy, but it must be admitted that, as yet, but little light has been thrown on this subject. Furthermore, the present dwindling of metallic reserves of several countries means that, in the event of a recession originating abroad, they would not only be without a plan of defense but would lack means of their own to carry out the measures demanded by the circumstances.

13

American Capital and Brazilian Nationalism

Werner Baer
and
Mario Henrique Simonsen

*In the years since World War II the position of foreign investors in
Latin America has become increasingly precarious, and it is likely
that in the future Latin American governments will impose even
more severe restrictions on private foreign capital. The reasons for
Brazilian distrust of foreign, particularly American, capital are discussed here by Professor Werner Baer of Vanderbilt University and
Brazilian economist Mario Henrique Simonsen, who also suggest steps
that might be taken to mitigate this distrust. Although the selection
has special reference to Brazil, its generalizations can be applied to
any Latin American country with a large foreign stake in its economy.*

Many North Americans can hardly believe how much Latin American
nationalists dislike and distrust foreign capital. North Americans
know that wherever industrialization has taken place in Latin America,
foreign capital has played a major role. In Brazil, for instance, it was
foreign capital that built the first railroads, the communication and
light systems, the automobile industry, the new consumer durable
industry, and the capital goods industry. The North American sees
all this as an occasion for gratitude, but the Brazilian nationalist sees
it as exploitation. He argues that, far from really adding to the national well-being, foreign capital (by which he usually means United
States capital, though in fact investors from many other countries
have participated in financing Brazil's new industries) has been bleed-
ing the country, that it has taken more money out than it has brought
in. He claims that, far from helping the country to industrialize, it

From Werner Baer and Mario Henrique Simonsen, "American Capital and
Brazilian Nationalism," *The Yale Review,* 53 (Winter 1964, December 1963),
192–198. Copyright Yale University. Reprinted by permission of the publisher.
This article appears as reprinted in Marvin D. Bernstein (ed.), *Foreign Investment in Latin America* (New York: Knopf, 1966), pp. 273–282.

has distorted investment to such an extent as to postpone "real" industrialization.

The arguments against foreign capital all center on the subject of exploitation. Nationalists claim that foreign capital has come to Brazil only because it has seen there the possibility of earning exorbitant profits, profits many times greater than it could earn at home. This attitude was unforgettably presented to the Brazilian people in the late President Vargas's widely publicized suicide letter, where the despairing president dramatically accused foreign firms of making profits as high as five hundred per cent a year. The figure, needless to say, was based on erroneous calculations, but it has been firmly imprinted in the minds of countless Brazilians. Another claim is that direct foreign investment often consists of obsolete machinery, already fully depreciated for tax purposes in the country of origin, which enters at an overvalued price. (This charge has been most often made against the automobile industry.) Nationalists further maintain that the outflow of profits to investors is many times as great as the inflow of new capital, with the result that the country is bled of its resources. They argue that foreign concerns actually bring in relatively small amounts of capital and, whenever possible, use local sources of credit, that is, the savings of Brazilians. Resentment against foreign banks operating in Brazil is particularly strong. Nationalists see the chief function of such banks as capturing the deposits of Brazilians in order to lend them to foreign enterprises, and thus direct domestic savings away from Brazilian investors. Finally, nationalists maintain that foreign capital has concentrated on industries producing "superfluous" goods—television, Coca-Cola, automobiles, and so on. This argument goes beyond the purely economic by suggesting that there has been a conspiracy to create tastes for the frivolous products of light industry so that the development of heavy industry, which would make Brazil more economically independent, will actually be delayed.

With some exceptions, these arguments do not find much support in the facts. Foreign banks do not siphon off Brazilian savings into enterprises controlled from abroad; the largest proportion of their deposits comes from those very enterprises. The majority of foreign enterprises do not produce "superfluous" goods; for example, only one American company produces passenger cars, while the other two produce only utility vehicles and tractors. The outflow of profit is not greater than the inflow of capital. In the years 1955 to 1961, a period when there were no restrictions on the movements of capital or its earnings, the inflow was much greater than the remittance of earnings. When nationalists reply that a large part of the profit remittances do not appear in the balance of payments because they are hidden in such items as payments for royalties and technical assistance or in the form of overvaluation of imports and undervaluation of exports, the figures still do not support them.

The one economic argument that finds support in the facts is that foreign capital will not go to Brazil (or to other underdeveloped countries) unless it can expect a larger profit than it makes at home. The expectation of higher profits is necessary not only because of the greater trouble of setting up an enterprise abroad, but also because of the greater risks, real or alleged, of carrying on business in uncertain political conditions such as most investors believe prevail in Brazil and elsewhere in the underdeveloped world. The investor thinks that he has to earn his money back fast, because nobody knows what will happen in a few years. To an American businessman all this makes perfect sense, but many Brazilians cannot understand why Americans expect to earn higher profits in a poor country like Brazil than in a rich country like the one they come from; they cannot understand why foreign investors have to earn their money back with such speed when it means that the foreign resources introduced into Brazil will be quickly offset by the fast withdrawal of resources when earnings and the original investment are repatriated.

These objections are probably unanswerable, until and unless Brazilians achieve a far greater sophistication in economic understanding than they now have. Objections to the high profits made by North American investors may be in some measure met by the steps currently being taken by the United States to offer better insurance against the hazards of investing in underdeveloped countries. A good deal of the responsibility for Brazilian misconceptions of the actual operation of foreign capital in their country lies with the foreign firms themselves. They simply do not make any effort to get their side of the story before the Brazilian people. The advertising of United States firms in Brazil is limited to the direct selling of products; the kind of institutional advertising that has been so successful in selling business, in getting its aims and problems before the public, is unknown. One never sees in Brazil advertisements showing what a company does for its workers, what community programs it has developed, etc. This lack could be easily remedied.

There are other changes that could be made with no great trouble or expense to create a friendlier atmosphere. For example, a great many foreign enterprises use the untranslated name of the parent company, a daily reminder to a sensitive people of foreign economic domination. Everywhere the consumer turns he is faced by foreign, especially North American names—Palmolive, Willys, Esso, Shell, Gillette, Crush, Spray, General Electric, and on and on. The foreign name is often localized by adding "do Brazil" to the name of the parent company, but that does little good, especially when *Brasil* is spelled with a foreign z, which is galling to many people. Sometimes, of course, the foreign name should be retained; when it designates a famous brand, the name increases sales and thus creates jobs for Brazilians. But some of the companies can make no such claim for the names they use. Light for the city of Rio de Janeiro, for instance, is furnished by a company that calls itself "Rio Light." Brazilians who object may be oversensitive, but many New Yorkers would dislike it if in 1963 they paid their light bills to the Allgemeine Lichtgesellschaft von Neu Jork.

Another thing that could be done with some ease would be a planned effort to improve the integration of North American businessmen in Brazilian society. Brazilians, like the residents of other underdeveloped countries, resent the fact that outsiders come to their country to make money but otherwise isolate themselves from it. United States executives and their families do not expect to settle there permanently; often the man sees his period of work in Latin America as simply one rung in a ladder of success most of which is to be climbed elsewhere, and his family are not necessarily the most willing camp followers. They do not learn Portuguese, the children do not attend local schools, the parents keep to their own clubs and social activities. Back in the United States these same families might keep to their own clubs and social activities, and the Brazilian businessman may sometimes be just as exclusive socially, but the fact remains that the isolationism practiced by the American business community gives a most unfavorable impression of colonialism. The government of the United States, working discreetly through the trade associations, could have considerable influence in persuading companies with substantial interests overseas to establish training programs for their personnel going abroad similar to the training programs for foreign service officers.

Some changes need to be made that are more significant economically. North American firms should not have Brazilian technicians working side by side with colleagues from the United States at a third the salary, yet one often hears of such situations. The subsidiaries of North American firms in Brazil should open their capital to Brazilians. Many are now closed companies, or offer only nonvoting stock to Brazilian investors. If they were to open up and spread their shares among the rising middle classes, they would automatically receive widespread support by an influential section of society. Wherever the shares of a company are commonly traded on the Brazilian Stock Exchanges, such as Belgo-Mineira (Benelux), Souza Cruz (British), Mannesmann (German), and Willys (United States), that company is never singled out for criticism by nationalist groups. The usual argument against opening the companies to Brazilian investment is that, in an inflationary atmosphere like Brazil's, the reinvestment of profits necessary for expansion would be impossible if a large portion of the profits had to be distributed to shareholders. It is well known, however, that most Brazilian corporations distribute a very small proportion of their earnings and that the growth-conscious Brazilian investor is quite happy with a very low dividend to stock value ratio in companies with a high growth potential.

Foreign firms also need to be more respectable in their use of money to secure economic advantage. Bribery is frequently charged against outside enterprises by Brazilian nationalists, and in some instances the charge is accurate. Newspapers receive financial rewards for favoring policies friendly to foreign enterprises; a few years ago a prominent United States-dominated public utilities company was reported to have bribed a substantial number of representatives in a local legislature to get a favorable vote on a rate increase. Other companies, especially mining, cold storage production, and the pharmaceutical industry, have been accused of bribing officials. The fact that bribery cannot exist unless there are bribable officials, or that Brazilian firms use bribery too, does not refute the charge; it only increases the odiousness of foreign capitalists who exploit weaknesses in the local society to their own advantage.

A more general problem is sometimes involved here. In the United States businesses think it is only natural and right to attempt to influence legislation, and in a pluralistic society they are right, so long as they recognize and observe proper limits for such activities. But when American businessmen abroad try to put pressure on influential politicians or buy up or finance newspapers favorable to their interests, quite a different interpretation will be put on their efforts— they will be seen as illegitimate interference by foreigners in domestic affairs.

The record, then, of foreign capital in Brazil is not all favorable. Its economic effects have been undoubtedly beneficial, but its social side-effects have been sometimes unfortunate. Yet even these social side-effects are hardly sufficient to account for the bitterness of nationalist resentments and their great popular acceptance, so apparent to anyone who has lived in Brazil. There are increasing numbers of "nationalists" in the Brazilian Congress, recently severe profit remittance laws have been passed, currently there is a wave of sentiment for nationalizing public utilities.

The North American is likely to look for Communism behind all this, and in fact the anti-foreign capital arguments of the nationalists agree perfectly with the Communist line, and there is a distinct possibility that Communists have played an active part in formulating, elaborating, and propagating those arguments. But Communism fails to explain their popularity. There are very few Brazilian Communists and very many Brazilians who believe in the villainy of foreign capital. Other explanations must be sought.

One explanation lies in the need for a scapegoat, so marked in many underdeveloped countries. Poor people with no training in economics need an emotionally satisfying explanation of their plight, and opportunistic politicians throw them the foreign capitalist for the purpose. Soon perfectly sincere politicians echo the explanation, and soon it has countless believers.

Brazilian industrialists concerned about foreign competition contribute to the support of nationalist, anti-foreign groups. They are much given to the argument that foreign capital is monopolistic, that it uses its resources to eliminate competition from local producers and thus control the domestic market. This argument, which was recently successful in keeping out foreign competition in aluminum, textiles, and metallurgy, has some basis: there are some prominent instances of monopolistic practices by foreign firms. But the Brazilian industrialists are really trying to maintain or regain the monopolistic positions they enjoyed before the arrival of foreign competition.

The fact that Brazilian nationalism so often finds its target in North American business may seem puzzling, since Germans, Japanese, and Italians have substantial investments in Brazil. But there is more capital from the United States in Brazil than from any other nation, and besides the United States today happens to be the major power in the world, with all the conspicuousness that comes with size. Furthermore, there are many Brazilian immigrants from Germany, Japan, and Italy, so that capital and its accompanying management are less suspect when they come from those countries. The American businessman is nearly always a temporary resident; he sees Brazil as a place to make money but rarely as a place worth settling in.

The United States government seems to be confronted by a dilemma. On the one hand, it seeks to encourage private capital to go to underdeveloped countries and help them develop; one of the objectives of the Alliance for Progress is to encourage private investment in Latin America. On the other hand, private capital will inevitably create some, if not all, of the kinds of problems that have been described here. But the facts are the facts. If private capital had not flowed into Brazil in the last fifteen years, the economy of the country might have grown at a much slower rate, and the resulting social tensions might have been a good deal more severe than the tensions created by the presence of private capital from the United States.

14

The Latin American Entrepreneur

Frank Brandenburg

The attention focused on the foreign investor in Latin America often tends to obscure the emergence of a dynamic class of native entrepreneurs, especially in Mexico, Brazil, and Colombia, which has spearheaded the drive for industrialization. The characteristics and problems of the Latin American businessman are discussed in this reading by political scientist Frank Brandenburg, author of The Making of Modern Mexico *(Englewood Cliffs, N.J.: Prentice-Hall, 1964). Brandenburg bases his conclusions on a survey of 506 entrepreneurs in Argentina, Brazil, Chile, Colombia, Mexico, Peru, and Venezuela.*

Origins of Wealth

Venture capital behind the promotion of domestic industry in Latin America has come from numerous sources. Investment funds have been acquired by raising cacao, coffee, cotton, fruits, nuts, palm, sisal, sugar, timber, tobacco, and wheat; in mining gold, silver, coal, copper, lead, zinc, and other minerals; and in cattle, sheep, and other varieties of ranching. Legitimate trading, importing, shipping, and merchandising have built up capital reserves subsequently employed in industry. Breweries and smelters; textile, sugar, and flour mills; and factories making wood, leather, and metal products have also produced capital for other investments.

Urban real estate and land speculation in general have been a source of investment funds. Local private and public financial institutions have provided resources. The independent moneylender has shifted capital into promoting his own industrial ventures. Foreclosure of mortgages on industrial properties has led to reorganization and launching of new industries.

Immigrants, particularly those of Italian origin in Argentina, Brazil,

From Frank Brandenburg, *The Development of Latin American Private Enterprise.* (Washington: National Planning Association, Planning Pamphlet No. 121, 1964), pp. 29–47. Reprinted by permission of the publisher. Footnotes deleted.

and Venezuela, have arrived bringing capital which they later invested in setting up new companies. Foreign financial institutions and flight capital and other speculative capital from abroad have helped start local enterprises. Present-day industrialists also include a group of nationals that worked abroad, in capacities ranging from scientist to migratory farm laborer, and placed their savings in industry when they returned home. Income from professional careers (law, medicine, accounting, etc.) has been another source of savings.

Government employment and intermediary roles between government and private activities have accounted for numerous take-offs into capital accumulation. Among those who have accumulated industrial investments of their own are former presidents, governors, cabinet ministers, state bank officials, state industry managers, military personnel, customs officials, and diplomats. Politicians, labor bosses, and local "strong men" have manipulated funds to permit the opening of their own private manufacturing concerns. Other sources of investment funds have included devaluation, inflation, public works contracts, sales contracts, smuggling, lotteries, and betting.

A majority of Latin American entrepreneurs probably come from middle-class families of small industrialists, merchants, ranchers, civil servants, professionals, soldiers, teachers, and politicians, as well as unemployed middle-class elements living off relatively modest inheritance or other savings. This phenomenon is consistent with the generally accepted premise that family, friends, and speculators provide the preponderant source of venture capital for small and medium industries.

Nonetheless, many skilled workmen of humble origins have set up small industrial firms of their own in Córdoba, Maracaibo, Mexico City, São Paulo, and elsewhere. Some of the truly wealthy entrepreneurs of today started from very humble origins. The late William Jenkins in Mexico, who amassed a personal fortune estimated at above $100 million, once worked as a traveling salesman. In Honduras, there is Boris Goldstein and his brother who once peddled shoes in Guatemala. Gabriel Ángel in Colombia once drove his father's mule teams between Medellín and the Magdalena River.

In contrast, some family industrial fortunes stem from previous or concomitant wealth in agriculture and ranching. Probably the highest incidence of this occurs in Argentina, where old family fortunes in farming, ranching, and shipping are conspicuous in big industrial ownership. Prominent Venezuelan, Brazilian, and Mexican industrialists also stem from landed gentry.

Private industry in the Medellín region of Colombia may be taken as an example of the multiple origins of industrial wealth and the complexity of ownership in Latin America. The first Colombian efforts to promote modern industry on a large scale date from the early

1920s. Relatively modest personal savings convinced one youthful group that a collective venture was the best form of acquiring sufficient investment capital to enter industry. They centered their activities on Medellín, undertaking a variety of industrial, commercial, and financial ventures. The "Group of the 1920s" was composed of men whose backgrounds ranged from mule driver, coffee merchant, printer, engineer, small local industrialist, and middle-class rancher to moneylender and big farmer. Sound finance, integrity, and a spirit of association attained early business stature for the Medellín group, and soon attracted financing from other Colombians and from Germans and British.

Their innovating and industrious qualities helped to earn for Medellín the title of "The Industrial City of Colombia." Among the principal businesses promoted by the group were some of today's largest private enterprises: COLTEJER and FABRICATO (Colombia's two largest textile mills), Compañía Colombiana de Tabaco (Colombia's largest maker of tobacco products), Cervecería Libertad (merged later with Cervecería Antioqueño to become Cervecería Unión, the nation's no. 2 brewery), Compañía Nacional de Chocolates (the nation's largest candy and chocolate factory), Banco Alemán Antioqueño (a bank in partnership with German capital, later liquidated), and Cine Colombiano (Colombia's largest motion picture distribution and exhibition company). Through an intensive commercial battle, the group also participated in the consolidation of Bavaria brewery, the largest domestic, privately owned industry in Colombia today. While suffering business setbacks from time to time, every enterprise was nurtured responsibly and each grew into a relatively large corporation; all are listed today on the Colombian stock exchange.

Other entrepreneurs in the Medellín area worked independently of the 1920s group. The Saldarriaga family founded a modest paint factory which evolved into Colombia's largest paint manufacturer, Pintuco. The same family promoted a retail food store into the large chain of Mercados Candelaria. The Steuer family, immigrants with part of their business in Argentina, opened the first store of the nationwide chain of TIA department stores in Medellín. Luis Eduardo Yepes similarly built a nationwide chain of LEY five-and-ten stores. Mercados Candelaria, LEY, and TIA manufacture some of the merchandise sold in their respective chains. Posada Tobón established a soft-drink bottling firm which later became the country's largest. A Medellín branch of the Restrepo family, led today by Juan Gonzalo Restrepo, centered its entrepreneurial talents in the Galletas NOEL cookie factory.

After World War II, a series of new industries and supporting businesses promoted by Colombians sprang up in Medellín. Members of the 1920s group, their children, and other investors promoted the

Banco Industrial, Compañía Suramericana de Seguros, Cementos Argos, Cementos Valle (in Cali), Cementos del Caribe (in Barranquilla), and Siderúrgica, S.A. FABRICATO entered a profitable joint venture with Burlington Mills in the enterprise Textiles Panamericanos (PAN-TEX). The Vásquez brothers founded a radio-phonograph assembly plant. Alberto Vásquez and Gabriel Ángel initiated Industrias Metal-úrgicas Apolo to make cement mixers, block pipe, and agricultural and sugar mill equipment. Small factories producing all manner of goods appeared on the Medellín scene.

Perhaps the most dynamic potential for further industrial entrepreneurship in the Medellín region today resides in the private industrial and commercial development bank (*financiera*) established in Medellín by 80 individual investors in 1960. The International Finance Corporation has made a stock option loan to the *financiera,* and foreign private financial institutions also hold equity in it.

Ethnic, Religious, and Other Characteristics

Ethnic Origins

All races can be observed among Latin America's native entrepreneurs. While the skin color of industrialists tends to darken from large to small industrialists, there appear to be no formal color bars. Racial tolerance is perhaps a natural development in countries like Brazil and Mexico where many, perhaps most, inhabitants are uncertain of their racial origins. There are few nonwhite industrialists in Argentina. But Negro, Indian, and *mestizo* industrialists are encountered in Brazil, Colombia, Mexico, Peru, and Venezuela.

The ethnic origins of entrepreneurs not accountable to Indian or Negroid racial strains are largely Spanish and Portuguese, although many and possibly a majority of the entrepreneurs in Argentina come from Italian stock. Immigrants from the Iberian Peninsula have varied from the original *conquistadores* to refugees from the Franco and Salazar regimes and recent arrivals seeking to finance a return home in style. Despite the continued existence of Spanish and Portuguese social colonies in Latin America, the cultural assimilation of Spaniards and Portuguese has been great. Spanish colonies and Portuguese colonies are by no means unified ethnic groups, either. Some Brazilian Portuguese boast of descent from the aristocracy that accompanied the Portuguese royal family to Brazil during Napoleonic times; other Brazilian Portuguese deprecate such ancestry. Refugees from Republican Spain encounter bitter enemies in local Spanish colonies supporting Franco. Further splits are based on descent from different

Spanish provinces, such as Asturias, Catalonia, or Galicia. Some industrialists born of families resident for generations in Latin America still claim that they are Spaniards or Portuguese instead of Argentine, Brazilian, Colombian, or Mexican. A few seem to claim to be more Spanish and Portuguese than aristocratic families living in the Iberian Peninsula itself. These same persons are found to be among the least desirable industrialists in terms of innovation, risk taking, and civic consciousness.

Many refugees of the post-World War II epoch now in Colombia, Mexico, and Venezuela have also exhibited relatively little confidence in the future of their adopted countries, for they have shown a high proclivity to convert industrial earnings into foreign currencies.

Local entrepreneurs of non-Iberian ethnic background are also present on the Latin American industrial scene. These include permanently resident U.S. citizens, some born in this country and others born in Latin America, as well as children of mixed U.S.-Latin American marriages. Enterprising families descended from U.S. stock include Sanborn and Wright in Mexico, Byington and Marvin in Brazil, Phelps in Venezuela. A large number of industrialists are of Italian origin, particularly small industrialists in Argentina, Brazil, and Venezuela. Truly large industrial complexes in Argentina, Brazil, and Mexico have also been established by entrepreneurs of Italian origin, men such as Matarazzo and Pignatari in Brazil, DiTella in Argentina, and Pagliai in Mexico. Industrialists of British and German descent, who are most conspicuous in Argentina, Brazil, and Chile, are found everywhere in Latin America. Highly successful in the German entrepreneurial group are Frederico Schmidt and the Renner family (Brazil), Gustavo Vollmer (Venezuela), the Lenz brothers (Mexico), and the Kopp family (Colombia). The British group includes the Fraser (Argentina), Edwards (Chile), and Boulton (Venezuela) families. A French colony of entrepreneurs is very strong in Mexico, centering on the Banco Nacional de México, on Carlos Trouyet, the Braniff family, and families originating in the small French town of Barcelonette. Local entrepreneurs of French descent are also present in Argentina, Brazil, Chile, Colombia, and Venezuela. A few local industrialists claim Belgian, Canadian, Chinese, Dutch, Irish, Polish, and Scandinavian descent. Many others, concentrated in southern Brazil, come from Japanese ancestry.

Another ethnic group is the "Turcos," who are not necessarily Turks, but Lebanese, Syrians, and generally anyone from the Levant, including Christians, Jews, and Moslems. They are usually exceptionally energetic entrepreneurs who tackle obstacles that frequently overwhelm and discourage business leaders of other ethnic origins. Concentrated in Chile (where they are often called "Arabs"), in Central

America, and in Mexico, the Turcos have succeeded in becoming important in textiles (Khalil in Brazil, Yarur in Chile, Aboumrad in Mexico) and related industries.

Assimilation of immigrants is generally high, except in some instances for the Turcos and World War II refugees. The crusading drive toward assimilation by many recent Italian immigrants in Argentina, Brazil, and Venezuela leads older industrialist families to accuse them of trying to be more Argentine, more Brazilian, or more Venezuelan than citizens of local origin.

Religion

Statistically, Latin American industrialists are predominantly Catholic. But their Catholicism, according to Jesuit sociologist Rev. Joseph P. Fitzpatrick, ranges from an "intensity of practice and devotion that is heroic, to an indifference that is difficult to conceive." Many industrialists are baptized, given first communion, and married in the Church, only to become practicing Freemasons until returning to the Church for extreme unction rites. For the census taker, these "Catholic Freemasons" are simply Catholics. Some Catholic industrialists trace their family trees to Sephardic and other Jewish stock, giving rise to instances of allegiance to both Catholicism and Judaism. While the Catholic hierarchy across the continent shares universality and oneness with Rome, religious content and organizational privileges vary decidedly between and within Latin American nations. For example, small industrialists in Central America and Mexico tend to accept the dark-skinned Virgin of Guadalupe as the primordial religious symbol. In contrast, big industrialists everywhere and small and medium industrialists outside Middle America usually have little if any room in their religious beliefs for the Guadalupana.

It is common to attribute the slowness of economic progress in Latin America to religious causes. According to this argument, Catholicism has placed less emphasis on material progress than major Protestant denominations. Hence, the more Protestant nations, such as the United States, Great Britain, West Germany, and the Scandinavian countries, enjoy higher per capita incomes than traditionally Catholic nations, such as Ireland, Italy, Portugal, and Spain. However, restraints on entrepreneurship are also imposed by the influences of traditional socio-economic patterning in agricultural life, authoritarian political institutions, and military dominance. The relation between these and religion in Latin America is not always clear.

Catholic industrialists typically manifest greater concern for change in this life than do Catholic owners of *estancias, fazendas,* or *haciendas.* This should not imply that every Catholic industrialist is an enlightened, progressive business leader, dedicated to social welfare. Some industrialists interviewed for this survey subscribe to *Opus Dei,* with its emphasis on the virtues of charity and of self-denial by the labor force. In contrast, many industrialists are evidently applying the social teachings of Pope Leo XIII and Pope John XXIII on labor relations and community life. Such industrialists are found as leaders of Catholic social action and Christian democracy groups throughout Latin America. U.S. college history texts stereotyping the Catholics of Latin America as conservative, authoritarian, or paternalistic, as holding to a uniform creed, or as obstacles to progressive economic development are in need of modification.

Nor is industrial entrepreneurship in Latin America confined solely to Catholics. Many entrepreneurs are Freemasons, Jews, Protestants, Mohammedans, agnostics, atheists, and followers of oriental religions. Freemasonry is strongest in Mexico and Chile. It is considerably weaker, in declining order, in Venezuela, Brazil, Colombia, and Argentina. It binds industrialists of varying Catholic faith with those of Protestant, Jewish, and oriental creeds. In some communities, it sets the pace for socially progressive private enterprise. Masonic lodges—the one place in the nation where the Catholic, Protestant, and Jewish businessman, soldier, and politician met during the turbulent days of 1910–20— were instrumental in giving ideological content to the Mexican Revolution.

In relating Latin American entrepreneurship to religion, it is clear that various Christian and non-Christian religions provide nominal ethical standards for industrialists. The extent to which Roman Catholicism affects entrepreneurship can be determined only through consideration of its numerous mutations in Latin America and by appropriate attention to non-Catholic creeds and institutions. This applies particularly to Freemasonry, for schisms have long characterized its symbolical and philosophical orders within and between Latin American countries. Latin America is no exception to the rule that religious beliefs and institutions are modified by environment.

Family and Social Life

The family firm constitutes the prevailing form of industrial enterprise in Latin America. Because the family often encompasses as many as a dozen or more actual heads of households, the industrialist shoulders heavy financial responsibilities for the general welfare of his relatives. Family fortunes rise and fall with the successes and setbacks of the favorite son directing the family's concern or complex of enterprises.

The industrialist typically wants his wife to observe the Latin

American tradition that keeps women apart from business affairs. He wants his friends to be selected from outside the circle of his business suppliers and clients, and he designs his social life for nonbusiness purposes. He customarily draws sharp distinctions between business acquaintances and associates on the one hand, and relatives, friends, and social companions on the other. The expression of these preferences appears to be stronger among small industrialists, the older big industrialists, native-born industrialists, and provincial manufacturers. It is weaker among the new big industrialists, heads of joint capital ventures, industrialists of recent immigrant origin, and business leaders of large metropolitan centers.

The typical Latin American business leader concurs with his U.S. counterpart on what he desires *for* his family but not on what he expects and ordinarily receives *from* his family. He desires for his family good health, education, religious training, automobiles, friends, wealth, a large home, vacations, and good marriages. He also seeks sufficient domestic help, exclusive club memberships, resort homes or a ranch, and, possibly, riding horses, yachts, or insurance policies. In return he expects love, loyalty, obedience, respect, and discipline. He discourages his children from taking jobs after school hours, on weekends, or at vacation time, and from performing menial domestic chores traditionally assigned to servants. Above all, he demands the privilege of unaccountability for his private life outside the home. He wishes not only to be master of his business and family life but also to be free to express his masculinity unfettered by marriage and family.

.   .   .

Business Problems

On Profits

The true level of profits in Latin American business is cloaked in myth and haphazard bookkeeping procedures. The native entrepreneur says that he anticipates a higher rate of return than that generally prevailing in Europe and the United States because he feels his risk is much greater and the capital markets in which he operates much weaker. In Colombia, Mexico, and Venezuela, large industrialists uniformly say they expect a rate of return above 15 percent; medium industrialists, above 25 percent; and small industrialists, above 35 percent. Small, medium, and large industrialists in the inflated economies of Argentina and Chile persistently mention the need for returns above 30 percent. In the hyperinflated economy of Brazil, profit expectation now exceeds 60 percent.

But profit expectation may be far from reality. What does a profit of 60 percent mean in a country such as Brazil, experiencing an annual inflation in excess of 50 percent? If profits were exceptionally attractive in real terms, would Latin American businessmen who regularly engage in capital flights resort to this practice to the extent that they do? We hear of the big fortunes accumulated in Latin America, but nobody has undertaken a serious assessment of the number of business failures or of the level of profits of a nation's total industrial plant. Of 113 securities registered on the Bogotá Stock Exchange on December 13, 1962, only 95 paid a dividend during the preceding year. This means that 16 percent paid no dividend. Business failures probably are more common in Latin America than they are in the United States.

Just as U.S. investors are discovering that net after-tax profits are higher from European and even from domestic ventures than from Latin American investment, thousands of small and medium-size Latin American industrialists are learning that they have been operating for years believing that profits are much higher than they actually are. Confronted by growing competition, labor union demands, and regulations of and taxes on business, native industrialists are finding that presumed high profits result partly from inadequate provisions for amortization, depreciation, and reserves. They are experiencing the additional impediments to higher profits raised by the relative non-liquidity of their investment, the absence of active stock exchanges and strong capital markets, and the consequent difficulty in converting their investment to marketable securities. Devaluation and inflation can catch them off guard. Their raw material supply is frequently subject to sudden tariff changes. Small industrialists, in particular, lack the strong, continuous ties with established financial institutions that are enjoyed by large industrialists.

. . .

On Efficiency and Competition

Until recently, competition rarely transcended the bounds of gentlemen's agreements made among a few families in each of the several branches of industry. Private industries tended to be family owned, with each family concerned about protecting its particular investments against encroachments by outsiders. Professional business administrators who were not members of the family were also regarded as outsiders. Placing confidence in managers outside closed family circles was looked upon as a retreat from a desirable way of life and a danger to traditional patterns. In such circumstances, inefficiency and low risk were commonplace.

In the most populous Latin American nations, there are a growing number of socially progressive entrepreneurs who have established or who operate relatively efficient, low-cost industries. Their modern technical, managerial, and merchandising achievements are increasingly exerting pressure on traditional business practices. Family management, with or without competence, is still prevalent in all sizes of industrial enterprise. But competition from new quarters is no longer easy to meet through circuitous political devices. Improvements in product and plant efficiency are the outcome.

The average Latin American industrialist still tends to embrace notions antithetical to competition, his exhortations in defense of private enterprise notwithstanding. His usual expression of distaste for monopolies, cartels, and trusts requires examination. He readily reveals an antipathy for foreign subsidiaries, which he may charge with monopolistic practices regardless of the facts; yet monopolies and oligopolies dominated by domestic business interests are evident. At the top level of Mexican industry, for example, a group of professional bureaucrats and politicians manages formerly foreign-owned monopolies along with other state enterprises. Beside them is a group of nine giant private financial-commercial-industrial complexes exercising monopolies and oligopolies over much of the nonpublic sector of big industry. Ricardo Lagos, in the latest edition of his study on the theory and reality of economic concentration in Chile, records that "eleven financial groups, or really three (Sud American, Chile, and Edwards) because they are so intertwined with the other groups, dominate 70.6 percent of all Chilean capital invested in business corporations." Tomás Fillol, in his prize-winning study done at M.I.T., reports similar patterning in Argentina. Monopolistic practices also characterize industrial activities in other nations of Latin America. Of course, monopoly is difficult to avoid as long as existing markets fail to expand appreciably.

Lack of competition at the top has by no means eliminated the rigors of stiff competition for tens of thousands of small and medium industrialists, and for some large industrialists in Argentina, Brazil, and Mexico. The attitudes of this group on profit expectations are shaped and reshaped by growing competition, excess installed capacity, and cost differentials. Lush public works contracts in Argentina, Mexico, and Venezuela, which gave birth to thousands of small and medium industries, are less freely available now. Nor is another impetus on the scale of Brasília immediately in the Brazilian offing. Many tax concessions favoring new industries in Argentina, Chile, and Mexico have expired, reducing profit margins. At the same time, the evolution of an industrial way of life, with its demand for quality control, exerts increasing pressure on small and medium industrialists to produce higher quality goods. This is certainly the case in Buenos Aires and Córdoba, Mexico City and Monterrey, and Belo Horizonte and São Paulo. In fact, small and medium industrialists interviewed in Argentina, Brazil, Chile, and Mexico saw the twin specters of Castroism and government intervention as less immediate threats than extinction through local competition. Colombian and Venezuelan industrialists, in contrast, tended to subordinate the dangers of excessive competition to those of Castroism and potential government control.

On Inflation and Growth

The belief that inflation is an indispensable, readily available, and indefinitely applicable tool for increasing capital formation is held to varying degrees by native industrialists everywhere in Latin America. It is most pronounced among Argentine, Brazilian, and Chilean industrialists, and least pronounced among Mexicans. Mexicans anticipate less inflation than Colombians and Venezuelans, and the latter expect decidedly less than Argentines, Brazilians, and Chileans. Awareness of the real causes of inflation is universally low among industrialists, as could be expected. While more sophisticated perspectives on economic development are discovered among large industrialists, willingness to support political reforms leading to the changes in social structure necessary for sustained economic growth—as contrasted with continued reliance on the inflation-devaluation cycle—is rare among Brazilian industrialists and infrequent among big Argentine and Chilean industrialists. The conviction among big industrialists that expansionist monetary policies must be avoided is most noteworthy in Mexico, Peru, and Venezuela.

Argentine, Brazilian, and Chilean industrialists appear insufficiently concerned with the ways excessive inflation distorts patterns of investment and hinders real growth to reshape their inflation-mindedness voluntarily. Specialists on the ABC countries differ on whether expansive monetary policies have been a deterrent to industrial investment in these countries. Some specialists contend that the industrialist in the ABC countries borrows as much as he can and invests as fast as possible because he can repay in depreciated currency, or if his funds are in plant investment, their value will increase with inflation. They further argue that budgetary and balance-of-payments assistance from foreign governments and international agencies has tended to retard the internal solution of basic problems. If the attitudes of private industrialists in the ABC countries are taken into account in an anatomy of local industrial growth, the traditional assumption that inflation is a deterrent to investment requires some refinement. The differences between structuralist and monetarist schools of thought on inflation in Latin America lead to one conclusion: there is no stock explanation for the causes of inflation and its effects on growth.

.   .   .

On Labor Relations

In much literature about the region, the Latin American industrialist appears as a paternalistic, authoritarian mogul, who expects government to guarantee him a docile, obedient labor force. But in fact, entrepreneurial practices are adapted to advanced labor laws and privileges. The private industrialist may prefer lower wages to higher wages; a conciliatory labor force to obstinate strikers; merit, skill, and modernization to job security; unilateral managerial decision making to collective bargaining; and lower costs to higher costs. But he must often obtain the sanction of the government, union leaders, or both, if he expects to increase his efficiency under existing legislation on minimum wages, maximum hours, social and job security, union organization, and collective bargaining.

The key to labor policy rests in the hands of government. When industry-wide circumvention of labor legislation passes unchallenged, the fact may usually be taken as evidence that it coincides with the government's labor and development policies. When organized labor persists in exceeding the boundaries of collective bargaining or otherwise enjoys favored treatment, it is almost certainly because the government sanctions such action. Governments lead; most businessmen and trade unionists follow. Both labor and private industrialists are subject to the mixed blessings of labor movements inextricably tied to politico-governmental machinery.

The cost structure of Latin American industry is automatically determined by certain basic labor rights and welfare legislation. These became well established in Brazil and Mexico in the 1930s, in Argentina in the 1940s and early 1950s, in Chile in the late 1930s, and in Colombia in the 1950s. They have proven difficult to alter. Severance payments, indemnities, and sometimes the requirement of prior court consent make it difficult and expensive to discharge employees. In most Latin American nations, even bankruptcy does not discharge an industrialist's liabilities to his workers, since employees may exercise prior rights in enjoining the liquidation and distribution of physical assets. Labor legislation is advanced even by U.S. standards, and presently enforced social welfare laws are decidedly more comprehensive and liberal than those of Western Europe and of virtually every country in Africa and Asia.

Latin American industrialists protest the constant pressure by industrial labor to extend the scope of social welfare measures. They believe too large a share of industrial output is already put aside for social security and other welfare benefits. Such "savings" are unconvertible into new private investment. Businessmen say they cannot finance extensive welfare measures and simultaneously provide new industrial investment to the extent required for accelerating the growth of national income and employment.

A considerable number of medium and large industrialists believe that the true interests of workers are advanced faster under a company union than through national or regional trade union affiliation. They feel that a closed shop subjects an industrial plant to the vicissitudes of predatory unionists and politics. They point for substantiation to the rarely matched privileges enjoyed in the company unions of the Garza Sada–G. Sada industrial complex in Monterrey, of the Ruiz Galindo industries in Mexico City, of Eugenio Mendoza industries in Venezuela, of the Bangu textile mills and Ypiranga paint factories in Brazil, and of the subsidiaries of several foreign corporations.

Viewpoints of local industrialists diverge on presumed behavior of workers in spending pay increases. Small and medium industrialists tend to believe that higher wages tempt laborers into working fewer hours and into spending pay increases on alcohol and mistresses, and at the race tracks. Large industrialists emphasize that higher wages are spent on the purchase of bicycles, automobiles, television sets, vacations, and education for children, or are set aside to finance business.

Perhaps the most serious shortcoming in the attitude of many Latin American businessmen on collective bargaining is their apparent inability to relate labor-management relations to real national economic growth. Pay increases, immediately accompanied by expansionist monetary policies, accomplish dubious advances in real income and output. A healthy private sector, as one recommendation at the end of the chapter indicates, requires greater consideration of the concept of the national interest by both management and labor than is the case today virtually everywhere in Latin America.

On Government Intervention and State Ownership

Latin American industrialists generally believe that private business deserves much better recognition, treatment, and encouragement from government than it has been receiving in recent years. Mistrust and misunderstanding on the part of both private and public sectors keep tempers continuously on edge, obstructing the cooperation between these two parties which is so necessary to achieving the goals of the Alliance for Progress.

The outlook of industrialists ranges from antagonism toward virtually all quarters of government to constructive assistance on much of what government is attempting under Alliance for Progress auspices. The commonest opinions include the following:

Industrialists believe government should not promote any new state industries at all, or at least not before eliminating weaknesses in existing government enterprises. Industrialists assert that some state enterprises enjoy too much freedom from central government control, while others have too little. Industrialists want a voice, which they contend is now rarely solicited and more rarely respected, in determining which economic activities should fall under state ownership and which under private or mixed ownership. Industrialists also contend that government indictment of private enterprise for its unwillingness to invest oftentimes overlooks the simple inability to invest because of political hindrances and lack of capital, technology, credit, infrastructure facilities, raw material supply, and marketing media. Industrialists seek maximum price, tax, and wage incentives; maintenance of law, order, and constructive political stability; tariff protection; and, in numerous cases, government loans, grants, contracts, and technical assistance. Industrialists further submit that arguments for higher and more effective taxation ignore the low morality of high public officials, such as the huge pilfering of public treasures by Perón in Argentina, Pérez Jiménez in Venezuela, and others whose cupidity is less well known but nonetheless large.

At the heart of the entrepreneurial outlook on government is a belief that business cannot flourish under political demagoguery and irresponsible officialdom; that leadership intent on establishing political stability is needed; that subversive elements should be removed from government; that freedom as well as investment is endangered by violence, sabotage, and terrorism.

.   .   .

On Foreign Investors

In general, foreign investors are welcomed by the most progressive Latin American industrialists. The tensions which arise usually relate to the extent, nationality, purpose, and performance of foreign enterprise, and not to the intrinsic merits and evils of foreign capital *per se*. From time to time, industrialists, like other occupational groups in Latin American countries, find themselves temporarily engulfed in the tides of excessive nationalism. Of late, small industrialists in Brazil appear especially susceptible to antiforeignism of virtually every mold. The largest business chamber of small Mexican manufacturers, the CONACINTRA, also emits regular blasts at foreign investment. But few big or medium industrialists persistently attack U.S. private investment.

Industrialists sometimes work in concert with government in influencing foreign subsidiaries to admit local equity capital, in preventing foreign industrialists from entering into competitive local manufacture in the first place, or in circumscribing foreign investment by other means. Local industrialists of one region may be more inclined than those of another to support foreign investment: those in Bogotá and Cali more than those in Medellín; those in Buenos Aires more than those in Mendoza or Rosario; those in Rio de Janeiro and São Paulo more than those in Porto Alegre or Recife; those in Mexico City more than those in Morelia or Puebla. In some instances—notably in the case of certain Brazilian and Colombian provincial centers —resistance arises not only when the potential investor is a foreigner but also when he is not a home town product.

15

Indicators of the Need for
Agrarian Reform

————◄◆►————

T. Lynn Smith

Latin America's emphasis on industrialization since World War II has led to the neglect of agriculture, and food production has either lagged behind or barely kept pace with population growth. Complicating the problem of inadequate food production is the fact that much of rural Latin America is plagued by the social and economic ills which rural sociologist T. Lynn Smith of the University of Florida calls indicators of the need for agrarian reform. However, although the demand for agrarian reform has won at least token acceptance throughout Latin America, there are strong differences of opinion over the methods and objectives that ought to be adopted in order to provide land for the landless and improve the quality of rural life. Nor is there any guarantee that agrarian reform will result in increased productivity, even in the long run. In Mexico, where agricultural production has made impressive strides since 1950, there still is debate over whether it took place because of or in spite of the agrarian reform programs of the Mexican Revolution.

The social and economic ills or the indicators which reveal the need for agrarian reform mentioned in these pages are those frequently encountered in the writings of various Latin Americans. To a considerable degree they correspond with those I have concluded are most significant, but the list that is given is by no means identical with the one that I would use if I were discussing agrarian reform in general. Some . . . would probably prefer to delete some of the items and substitute others that go unmentioned, and to this there would be no particular objection except in the case of some, such as *latifundismo* and the concentration of ownership and control of the land in general, which figure in almost every Latin American discussion of the need for agrarian reform. Moreover, it should be stressed that all of the items enumerated here are highly interrelated, since all are central features of essentially the same social system. In all probability some of them are merely reflections of others in the list; nevertheless, they are thought to be adequate for purposes of the present diagnosis.

Latifundismo

In many parts of Latin America, and especially in such countries as Brazil, Colombia, and Venezuela, *latifundismo* has a special connotation which differs substantially from its meaning in other parts of the hemisphere. In these countries, only during recent years, and as the debate over agrarian reform waxed in volume and importance, has there been any tendency to designate as *latifundia* the highly developed plantations engaged in the production of sugar, coffee, rice, and so forth. Rather, the general rule has been to restrict the use of this term, presently so highly charged with opprobrium, to the extensive tracts of land that are either held in complete idleness or devoted to much less intensive uses than those for which they are eminently suited. . . . there has occasionally been a logical and eloquent plea for the imposition of a general property tax as a means of putting an end to the obvious disadvantages of these large unused or poorly used holdings, but until the recent imposition of taxes of 5 per mil by the state of São Paulo[1] in Brazil and 4 per mil in Colombia, such endeavors amounted to little more than voices crying in the wilderness. The powerful, landowning, upper-class families have seen to it that the right to levy a substantial tax on the land would not be invested in any governmental unit which they could not control. As a result land has gone untaxed, or practically untaxed, and the ownership of land has been in effect an asylum for capital. Economic pressures that would force the use of the soil have been lacking, and . . . agriculture has indeed been encircled by a barrier that could not be overcome by the man of modest means. In brief, in many parts of Latin America latifundismo per se, or the existence of millions of acres of fertile lands that are entirely unused, or utilized very poorly, in countries where the rural masses are unable to find land to cultivate and where the production of food and fiber is far below national needs, is a strong indicator of the need for agrarian reform.

---

[1] This measure was invalidated in 1963 by a constitutional change which terminated the right of Brazilian states to levy a general property tax, and, without any preparation whatsoever, gave this right to the *municipios*.

High Degree of Concentration in the Ownership and Control of the Land

Merely because huge landed estates are not permitted to vegetate in idleness, so as to qualify them as latifundia in the Brazilian or Colombian sense of the term, does not mean that there is no need for agrarian reform in the areas in which large estates dominate the scene and determine the nature of the prevailing social system. As a matter of fact, if viewed from the standpoint of the world as a whole, a high degree of concentration in the ownership and control of the land is probably the most generally recognized indicator of the need for agrarian reform (exception being made, of course, for those countries in which experience runs a poor second to ideology and the huge state farm is idealized as a solution for their chronic agricultural problems). Certainly I would place this indicator first in importance, a conclusion, incidentally, which was reached on the basis of the sociological study of two sharply contrasting social systems in the United States some years before I was privileged to visit Brazil and other parts of Latin America. In one of these social systems which dominates rural life in the Midwest and many other parts of the United States, the family-sized farm is the central element in the complex; in the other, which is all important in many parts of the South and which also prevails to some extent in California and other western states, the large plantation is the nucleus of the social system which has generated so many of our nation's perennial social, economic, and political problems.

That there is a high degree of concentration in the ownership and control of the land throughout most of Latin America is made evident by practically every census of agriculture that is taken. In Brazil, for example, a country for which the data are among the best, the 1950 materials make it apparent that not more than one in four of the families that are dependent upon agriculture for a livelihood is headed by a person who could be classified as a farm operator. Moreover, even this proportion is inflated because the considerable number of squatters is included in the category of farm operators. This means that at least 75 per cent of Brazil's agriculturists fall into the unenviable category of farm laborers. Furthermore, of the minority that legitimately may be classified as farm operators (owners, renters, managers, and even squatters) almost 20 per cent have the use of no more than 13 acres, and 75 per cent have farms of less than 125 acres in size. Collectively this three fourths of all Brazilian farm operators have the use of only 10 per cent of the land in farms, whereas the 0.5 per cent of the operators with farms of more than 6,250 acres have more than 36 per cent, and the 0.1 per cent with estates of more than

25,000 acres have control of almost 20 per cent of the land in farms. Furthermore, between 1940 and 1950 the trend was in the direction of an increased concentration of the control of the land by the few.[2] It is true, of course, that the subdivision of land by inheritance is a powerful factor in fragmenting some of the holdings, but in Brazil its effects are apparently more than offset by those of other forces, and the need for agrarian reform becomes more acute as one decade is succeeded by another. In interpreting this information the reader should keep in mind that the Brazilian material represents the situation in a country that contains more than a third of the population and much more than a third of the area of all Latin America, and that the Brazilian data probably are fairly representative of what would be the case if the information for all twenty of the countries were available.

High Proportion of Laborers in the Agricultural Population

The predominance of the large estate *ipso facto* means that a high proportion of the heads of all rural families are doomed for life to a position near the bottom of the social and economic scale. In Latin America, as elsewhere, unskilled workers inevitably have lower-class status, and of these the ones who are engaged in agriculture constitute huge segments of the lowest of the lowly. In addition, in many parts of Latin America large numbers of the agricultural laborers lead wandering, migratory lives; this residential instability makes their status and the social and economic roles they perforce must play much less enviable than they would be otherwise. Obviously, a high proportion of laborers in the agricultural population is merely a reflection of an extreme degree in the concentration of landownership and control, which was discussed above. Even so, the mere fact that three fourths of the heads of Brazilian families who live from agriculture are farm laborers, and the fact that the proportion in the remainder of Latin America is probably equally high, is a strong indicator of the need for agrarian reform. Until this proportion is substantially reduced one may confidently predict that it will be impossible either to increase the input of management in agricultural enterprises to effective levels, or to bring rural levels and standards of living up to the desired planes. Thus the need for agrarian reform shown by this indicator will continue until the vast majority of those

---

[2] For more details, see T. Lynn Smith, *Brazil: People and Institutions,* 3rd ed. (Baton Rouge: Louisiana State University Press, 1963), pp. 330–337.

who now gain a precarious livelihood through the sale of poorly executed and ineffectively applied labor, or their descendants, can either ascend the agricultural ladder and become farm operators or find remunerative employment in non-agricultural activities.

The Prevalence of Minifundia

In many parts of Latin America there is an acute need for agrarian reform even though high proportions of the agriculturists must be classified as farm operators, and even as owner-operators. This is true in extensive portions of such Andean countries as Venezuela, Colombia, and Ecuador where the mountainsides are blanketed with small, pocket-handkerchief-sized parcels of land, farms so small that they are utterly incapable of producing enough food and fiber to meet even the creature needs of those who live from agriculture. In a lesser degree a comparable phenomenon is present in many other countries. The existence of hundreds of thousands of minute, badly shaped, poorly tilled, and inefficient farm units is only slightly less disadvantageous for those who live from the soil than a high concentration of owner-ship and control of the land. In a word, *minifundia* and *minifundismo* on a substantial scale is another of the indicators of the need for agrarian reform.

The statements above are founded for the most part on rather casual observation supplemented by the information from a few local surveys. As more adequate statistical data become available, though, these statements are found to be thoroughly justified. At the present time, for example, the materials from Colombia's first census of agriculture, taken in 1960, are beginning to appear. Unfortunately, the national summary that has been published fails to present a tabulation show-ing the distribution of farms according to size. The report for the Departamento del Valle del Cauca, however, which was prepared under the direction of the man who was dean of the Faculty (or College) of Economics at the Universidad del Valle at the time of the enumeration, does give this all-important information in considera-ble detail.[3] It is quite unlikely that minifundismo in Colombia is most pronounced in the Departamento for which the data are available. Nevertheless, this enumeration indicated that of 50,171 farms in the Departamento, 25,957 (or 52 per cent) were plots of less than 5 hectares (about 13 acres) in area, and that 10,040 (or 10 per cent of all)

---

[3] *Cf.* Antonio J. Posada, organizer, *Censo Agropecuario del Valle del Cauca, 1959* (Cali: Facultad de Ciencias Económicas, Universidad del Valle, 1963), p. 11 *passim.*

of them were less than 1 hectare in size. Were the data tabulated properly for such Departamentos as Cundinamarca, Nariño, and Boyacá an even greater prevalence of minifundia would undoubtedly be revealed, and it is highly probable that if materials for all of Colombia were available the percentage of the farm operators having less than 5 hectares of land for their enterprises would exceed the 52 per cent registered for El Valle.

Brazil, of course, is not plagued by minifundia to the same degree as Colombia, Ecuador, and Venezuela. Nevertheless, as indicated by the 1950 data, one of five of her farm operators are utilizing tracts of land that contain less than 5 hectares; and it may be stated without fear of refutation that in many sections in South Brazil settled by peasants from Germany, Italy, Poland, and elsewhere in Europe, a continuous subdivision by inheritance of farms that originally were small is bringing the problem of the minifundia to an acute stage. There, as in southern Chile and in specific localities in all of the countries from Argentina to Mexico, small uneconomic farm units are indicative of a considerable need for agrarian reform.

Low Production per Worker

Although here and there one may find an exception, throughout nearly all of Latin America the production per worker engaged in agriculture is very low. This fact has been documented by so many economists and governmental officials that it seems unnecessary at this point to give any statistical demonstration of it. This low production per worker, in turn, is probably no more than a reflection of the effects of the socio-economic factors that are engendered and kept in force by a social system based on large estates, that is, by a high degree of concentration in the ownership and control of the land. Of all the factors involved, though, the following deserve specific mention: (1) the paucity of skills possessed and used by those who do the manual labor; (2) the extremely small input of management in the productive processes involved in Latin American agricultural and livestock enterprises (this deficiency is inevitable wherever the necessary capacities are not "built in" each person who participates in the tillage of the soil so that they may be applied day or night, any day or season of the year, to any particular square yard of soil, to any or all of the plants in any stage of their development, to every farm animal irrespective of where it may wander, and to every piece of farm equipment or machinery no matter to which part of the farm it may be taken); and (3) the lack of propulsions which will lead to regular work activities on the part of those who live from agriculture. All of these features are presently prominent parts of the systems of agriculture in vogue in most parts of Latin America. Indeed, in Brazil, Haiti, and the eighteen Spanish American countries taken as a whole at least one half of the agriculturists are dependent upon methods of extracting a living from the soil that are more primitive, less efficient, and more wasteful of human energy than those the Egyptians were using at the dawn of history.[4] The persistence of the complex of factors and forces which results in low productivity per worker, the inefficient combination of the factors of production, and the actual demeaning of the rural population is eloquent testimony of the need for substantial agrarian reform.

Low Average Levels and Standards of Living

In the second half of the twentieth century man's knowledge of the earth on which he lives and of the ways of cooperating with nature in order to get products from the soil is sufficient to make possible a far greater abundance of goods and services than is presently being enjoyed by the people on most parts of the earth. In Latin America the aspirations of the people and the actual amounts of goods and services enjoyed are not as abysmally low as they are in some countries. Moreover, since the close of the Second World War, and, it should be emphasized, frequently in quite unrealistic and sometimes in fantastic ways, the aspirations of the common people have risen spectacularly, whereas the rise in the actual level or plane of living has been in much more modest proportions. This has resulted in the broadening of the gap between the aspirations, or what properly is designated the standard of living, and the average amounts of goods and services consumed, or the level of living. In many places this gap has become so wide that it may reasonably be designated the "zone of exasperation." Probably this problem is not as great in the rural districts as it is in the urban centers of Latin America, but even in the agricultural and pastoral areas it is a problem that demands attention. Indeed, in most of the rural sections of Latin America the poorly directed aspirations of the masses and the prevailing low levels of living are indicative of the need for substantial modifications in the distribution of landownership and control, the systems of agriculture, the availability and functioning of educational institutions, the nature and vigor of local governmental institutions, and in various other aspects of a genuine agrarian reform.

---

[4] For a discussion of the nature of the cultural complex in action, which the present writer calls "the system of agriculture," and its role in social and economic progress, or the lack of it, see T. Lynn Smith, *The Sociology of Rural Life*, 3rd ed. (New York: Harper & Brothers, 1953), Chap. 14; and Smith, *Brazil*, Chap. 15.

Extreme Degrees of Social Stratification

Reference has been made above to the two-class system introduced into Latin America during colonial times and perpetuated there to a very considerable extent until the present time. In Latin American societies, as in others in which a system of large estates has dominated the social, economic, and political aspects of life, this has determined that there would be a small class of elite families at the apex of the social scale, and a large mass or class of impoverished, uneducated, unskilled, and only slightly productive workers at the base of it. Until late in the nineteenth century, when many thousands of peasant families were settled in southern Brazil, southern Chile, and parts of Argentina, Latin America's almost exclusively rural societies contained little or nothing in the way of middle-class farm families to help fill the broad void that existed between the upper and lower extremes of their two-class societies, that is, between the small stratum of the elite and the huge masses of servile or semi-servile workers. If evaluated in terms of the standards which prevail widely in the world during the second half of the twentieth century, any society so constituted is certain to exhibit all of the indicators of the need for agrarian reform. Even if it were the only indicator available, however, such a system of social stratification would point strongly to the necessity for substantial changes in the institutional arrangements governing man's relations to the land.

This enumeration could be continued indefinitely, for wherever there is any considerable degree of concentration of the ownership and control of the land (even if this be in the hands of the state), low productivity, huge wastes of human potentialities, and a host of other social and economic ills are certain to abound. This is particularly true in areas such as Latin America in which the absence, or practical absence, of the general property tax enables land to become an asylum for capital and the problem of latifundismo to acquire sizable dimensions. The seven items included in this section, though, should serve present purposes of indicating that there is substantial need for agrarian reform in a great many parts of Latin America. . . . To these may be added the list of indicators of the need for agrarian reform that was prepared in 1961 by the most noted writer in Brazil's lay Roman Catholic group. These are as follows:

1. A high proportion of illiterates and the consequent general lack of culture.
2. Poor sanitary conditions and high indexes of mortality.

3. Low agricultural production and overpopulation.
4. Low levels of marriage and family organization.
5. The absence of or an extremely low rate of technical progress.
6. The destruction of the soil, and, in general, the poor use of the land.
7. Defective distribution of landownership.
8. Serious smothering of the civic consciousness because of the debility of municipal [county] life, and more remotely through the general weakening of democratic life.
9. Lack of leadership.
10. A low degree of vertical social mobility and a high degree of geographical mobility.
11. Technical and legal deficiencies in the registration of titles to the land.[5]

. . .

[5] Gustavo Corção, "Conceituação da Reforma Agrária" (Mimeographed), presented to the Simpósio sôbre Reforma Agrária, organized by the Instituto Brasileiro de Ação Democrática, Rio de Janeiro, April 17–22, 1961. For a report of the proceedings of this symposium see José Arthur Rios, ed., *Recomendações sôbre Reforma Agrária* (Rio de Janeiro: Instituto Brasileiro de Ação Democrática, 1961).

16

The Dilemma of the Middle Class

————◄◗►————

Charles Wagley

Most observers of twentieth-century Latin America have commented on the increasingly large proportion of the population that can be said to comprise a middle class or middle sector. It has often been assumed that the existence of a numerically significant and politically powerful middle class will automatically produce stable and democratic government and social and economic reform, but some students of contemporary Latin America have begun to question this belief. The political, social, and economic dilemmas facing the Latin American middle classes are discussed in this selection by Charles Wagley, Professor of Anthropology at Columbia University. A perceptive and sympathetic student of Brazilian society for many years, Professor Wagley pays special attention to the part played by the Brazilian middle class in the political upheaval of 1964.

How Large Is the Middle Class?

It seems self-evident to me that the middle class is a distinctive and recently emerged sector of Latin American society. It seems evident, too, that they are numerically important in certain countries and in certain regions of some countries. But these are impressions gained by reading, visiting, and casual observation. It is very difficult to estimate their numerical strength. There have been several educated guesses as to the numerical strength of the middle class in various Latin American countries, but most often such estimates have defined the middle class in terms of both an upper and lower strata. Most writers include the wealthy industrialist and the high level administrator with the shopkeeper and the government or business office clerk. Using this broader definition (he calls it "middle sector"), J. J. Johnson [*author of Article 17*] estimates that 35 per cent of the people of

From Charles Wagley, "The Dilemma of the Latin American Middle Class," in *The Latin American Tradition* (New York: Columbia University Press, 1968), pp. 194–212. Reprinted by permission of the publisher. Footnotes deleted. Italicized bracketed notes in the text are by Helen Delpar.

Argentina, 30 per cent of Chile and Uruguay, 15–20 per cent of Brazil; and 12 per cent of Venezuela are classified as members of the middle class.

Gino Germani [*author of Article 27*] and [*political scientist*] Kalman Silvert using a broad definition of middle class also provide us with a classification of Latin American countries in regard to the strength of the middle class. They classify the various nations in four groups. Group A is made up of Argentina, Uruguay, Chile, and Costa Rica. This group has a middle strata of 20 per cent or more. This is a middle class with cultural, psychological, and political identity. Group B is made up of Mexico and Brazil with an approximate middle strata of between 15 and 20 per cent of the population. Although a middle class exists, it is highly concentrated in certain regions of each country (that is, in Mexico and other provincial capitals, and in south Brazil). Group C includes Cuba (pre-Castro), Venezuela, and Colombia. The estimated middle strata of these countries is also between 15 and 20 per cent, but they are considered to have only an emergent middle class. There is considerable disagreement as to the strength of self-identity among the middle strata in this group. And finally, there are all of the other countries with less than 15 per cent in the middle strata, with only a nascent "middle class" in some countries and a clear persistence of the traditional two-class system in others. In most of the countries with a small middle strata, a large proportion of the total population is marginal to the national economic and political life.

While neither Johnson's rough estimate of the "middle sectors" nor Germani and Silvert's more careful estimate of the "middle strata" gives any precise figures for the numerical strength of the "middle class," they do indicate the countries where the middle class is strongest —Argentina, Uruguay, Chile, Costa Rica, Mexico, Brazil, Venezuela, and Colombia. And perhaps Peru and Panama should be added to this list. In general, these are the countries with the highest indices of urbanization and the highest rate of literacy (Brazil is an exception). They are also the countries with the highest annual income per capita, although in 1961 this ranged in the countries mentioned above from $799.00 for Argentina to $361.60 for Costa Rica. It is also these same countries that are leaders in mass media—in newspaper circulation, cinemas, television and radio stations, and the publication of books and magazines. It is quite clear that the size of the middle class corresponds closely with the degree of urbanization, industrialization, ethnic and cultural homogeneity, literacy, and the demand for public services. In other words, the larger the middle class in a Latin American nation, the greater the degree of technological, economic, and social modernization. However, it is to be noted at once that its presence in significant size in a nation does not correlate necessarily with political stability. Argentina, Brazil, and Venezuela—countries with relatively large middle classes—have been plagued with political difficulties during the last ten years or more. Colombia has suffered from terrible internal violence at least partially of political origin, and Cuba has experienced a communist revolution.

The Middle Class Dilemma

This Latin American middle class finds itself in an economic, political, and social dilemma. The realities of present day Latin American society run contrary to the needs, the aspirations, and the ideology of this new social group. Although it holds many traditional values, the new middle class has modern needs and aspirations. But it is still living in a society in transition from a rural agrarian semifeudal and personalistic social system to an urban, industrial, impersonal social system.

Middle class people in Latin America are consumers. They are accustomed to adequate housing. Since they work in offices, classrooms, stores, and other public places in a white-collar capacity, they need to dress well. They want television sets, electric refrigerators, washing machines, and other accoutrements of the modern world. They would like to have an automobile if that were possible. But the realities of their economic situation are otherwise. Manufactured goods are expensive in any terms—because even if not imported, they are produced by a protected national industry. Rents, clothes, medicines, and even food are expensive for the poorly paid middle class. Between 1953 and 1960 the indices of cost of living rose from 100 to 436 in Rio de Janeiro, from 100 to 593 in Buenos Aires, from 100 to 1182 in Santiago, Chile. Furthermore, inflation is constant, sometimes rampant, in countries with a significant middle class. The middle class lives on fixed income, almost always salaries, which lag behind the rising cost of living and are adjusted slowly in face of inflation. Middle class people are often heavily in debt.

There is only one answer to the economic dilemma of the Latin American middle class, namely, to make more money. Thus Latin American middle class men—teachers, poorly paid professionals, government employees, and others—"moonlight," holding down several jobs. It is common for a government employee to work also in a private firm. Obviously he neglects his relatively secure government job. It is common for professors in universities to teach in more than one faculty and for secondary school teachers to teach their subject in several schools. Furthermore, the budget of most middle class families in Latin America can only be balanced if there are several wage-earners contributing; thus, sons and daughters work while still studying, and it is more and more common for the wife to work.

The middle classes are also frustrated by the lack of public services in the cities in which they typically live. Public services have not been able to keep pace with the extremely rapid growth of cities; in some cases, they have actually deteriorated. The middle class spends endless hours waiting for infrequent and poor public transportation. They bear the lack of water and lack of telephones with amazing patience but also with irritation. Public services, until recently, were foreign owned. Nationalists were certain that foreign transportation and utility companies were extracting tremendous loot from their countries and in many cases this was probably so. Such corporations were not allowed to increase their rates and in turn they refused to improve facilities, expecting that they would be expropriated. By now most of them have been nationalized. But compensation to these foreign companies has put a heavy weight on countries which are short in foreign exchange. And, once nationalized, the public transportation and utilities were in poor condition. Water supply systems, sewers, roads, telephone systems, public transportation, and the other public services—which the middle class needs more than any other sector of the Latin American population—call for heavy capital expenditures. If this is to be done, then taxes must be increased. Neither the Latin American elite nor the middle class is accustomed to paying heavy direct taxes, but they are now learning. Increased taxes are an added burden to a middle class which hardly lives within its income. (I might add that this is not a distinctive Latin American phenomenon.)

As it is with public facilities, so it is with education. The Latin American middle class, as we have said, places a high value on education, and they want public schools for their children. They are no longer satisfied with just the primary education to which many of the present day adults were limited, and their children crowd into secondary schools and universities. Public primary schools are crowded; public secondary schools are too few in many cities. So the middle class must take on the extra cost of private secondary schools. They are willing to make sacrifices to allow their children to attend the university. Yet even though universities are almost free, most university students, especially those from the middle class, work as they study.

The dilemma of the Latin American middle class is not only material and economic. They are faced with ideological and cultural conflicts as well. They are traditionalists but they are also liberal democrats, and they believe that equality of opportunity should be extended to the mass of people in their countries. Their children may be university students who vibrate with nationalism and with the ideal of equal opportunity for all. Yet, given the relatively under-developed economy of their nations, to provide the same conditions of life for the mass of people which the middle class itself struggles to maintain might well destroy their relatively favored position. They may not be overtly aware of this dilemma but it lies ominously in the background.

A single example of what I mean will have to suffice. As stated several times, the Latin American middle class believes strongly in the extension of free public education to the entire population. In most Latin American countries, this is an ideal far from realized. It is estimated that in 1950, 49 per cent of the population of Latin America over fifteen years of age had never attended school or had dropped out before completing one year. The educational institutions of most countries were originally established for the elite—a very small pro-portion of the total population. The educational system inherited from the past provides a poor basis for the building of a system making education available to all. Then too, the well-known population ex-plosion which in a generation or so more than doubled the number of Latin Americans (even greater in the school population), does not make the task easier. To make universal education a reality, a massive undertaking—of training teachers, building schools, and reorganizing the curricula—would be necessary. This would call for a financial outlay by the governments far beyond that now made for education. In the process, the quality of the existing schools would certainly de-teriorate. If a rich nation such as the United States has such problems in racial integration of its schools, one can only imagine the problems most Latin American nations would face in assimilating the entire mass of people into its educational institutions. Although this is the stated ideal of the Latin American middle class, it has to settle for less.

Furthermore, the Latin American middle class equivocates in its liberal democratic views. It favors universal suffrage and freely elected governments. Literacy is a qualification for voting in most of Latin America, thereby automatically disfranchising a large sector of most national populations. Although several writers have spoken of some sort of middle class alliance with the workers, the facts do not seem to support this theory. It may be true that for a time the Argentine middle class sided with Perón and the *"descamisados"* against the oligarchy, or that the Brazilian middle class supported Vargas and his Brazilian Labor Party (P.T.B.). But, at the time, the middle class felt that it was in control. They did not cogitate turning over the domi-nant political power to the workers. And the so-called "alliance" ended when the working groups took, or seemed to take, control.

The middle class has a real political dilemma. Middle class people are energetically interested in politics. They know and appreciate the power of government. In fact, a large percentage of them owe their very class position to the expansion of government bureaucracy. They believe in honesty and morality in politics and in government. They are perforce adherents of statism, for they are not convinced that capitalism and free enterprise will lead to social and economic development of their countries as it seems to have in the United States. But, with few exceptions (perhaps the Christian Democrats of Chile, Peru, and Venezuela, as examples), there are no political parties that clearly represent their interests despite the high sounding names of many Latin American parties (Social Democrat, Liberal Party, National Democratic Union, and so forth). With their dependence on the state, the Latin American middle class becomes jittery in face of rapid change and the increased power of the urban and rural masses. Faced with a crisis, the middle class acquiesces; it remains passive before a military coup that guarantees stability or it actively supports a political party or a coalition of parties aimed at stability rather than abrupt change. There is no guarantee at all that the development of a strong middle class in Latin America will lead to the strengthening of democratic institutions.

The Case of the Brazilian Middle Class

Perhaps I may illustrate the economic, social, and political dilemma of the middle class by the case of the Brazilian middle class—a group about which I have had considerable knowledge. The Brazilian middle class is not numerically the strongest in Latin America in relation to the total population of the country. But, since World War II, it has gained remarkably in numerical strength and in self-identity, especially in south Brazil—in Rio de Janeiro, São Paulo, Belo Horizonte, Porto Alegre and other rapidly growing cities. The Brazilian middle class has suffered, perhaps more intensely than their counterparts in other countries, all the ills we have described: lack of public facilities, crowded schools, and low salaries that do not keep up with rampant inflation. Furthermore, Brazil has suffered a series of political crises since 1954 when the ex-dictator and then elected President, Getulio Vargas, committed suicide. In 1961 there was the dramatic resignation of President Jânio Quadros, a man who seemed to have a basis of political support and whose political symbol "the broom that swept the house clean" was pleasing to middle class morality. Then, the elected vice-president, João Goulart, was allowed by the Army to assume the Presidency only after a constitutional amendment establishing a parliamentary form of government was passed. This was done to curb Goulart's power. A plebiscite in 1963 returned the country to a presidential form of government restoring most of the executive powers.

The year 1963 and the first months of 1964 were marked with continual crisis in Brazil. In 1963 a series of strikes upset transportation and industrial production. Inflation continued at an increased rate. The cost of living is said to have increased 80 per cent in 1963.

In the first three months of 1964, it almost seemed that Brazil was in a state of chaos. The cruzeiro dropped in value from 600 to the dollar in January to 1360 in March. A new round of strikes broke out among the dock workers, the bank employees, the transportation workers, and others. President Goulart seemed to be seeking his support from labor, the peasants, and the students. He announced a series of "basic reforms"—including a land reform bill authorizing the federal government to expropriate unused lands along highways, railroads, and waterways. He signed a bill lowering the rates on rent control. He was said to favor granting legality to the Brazilian Communist Party and there were discussions about the feasibility of recognition of Communist China. Goulart also announced that he was in favor of amending the Constitution of 1946 to grant suffrage to illiterates and to allow military personnel to run for elective office by placing themselves on inactive status. (Several noncommissioned officers had petitioned for this right.) There was a round of increases for labor but little help for the low-level white-collar worker. The middle class suffered and they were frightened.

There was a strong reaction from the middle class (and the upper class). *O Estado de São Paulo* and *O Globo,* conservative papers of wide circulation, warned of "socialist" and "communist" policies of Goulart's government. Carlos Lacerda, the Governor of Guanabara state in which Rio de Janeiro is situated and a critic of almost all federal regimes, fanned the flames by spectacular speeches over television lasting for hours. Anti-communist groups called for demonstrations in the streets to protest against the leftist trends of the Goulart government. In March of 1964 an estimated 500,000 people in São Paulo took part in a "God and Family" protest. Stories of the influence of China, Russia, and Cuba among the peasants in north Brazil were rife. It was rumored that Goulart planned to declare himself a dictator of the left. The middle class (and certain elements of the upper class) were in near panic.

The result is well known. Set off by a "sit down strike" or "mutiny" among 1425 enlisted men and noncommissioned officers which Goulart supported on March 31, 1964, the Brazilian Army took over the national government of Brazil within 24 hours. There was almost no resistance. Reportedly over 7000 people were arrested in a few days following the take-over, including important legislators and officials. On the evening of the coup, tons of paper was thrown from the windows of apartment houses and office buildings—obviously by people of the middle class. White candles of victory were lighted in middle-class apartment windows in Rio de Janeiro. And a march of protest similar to that which was carried out in São Paulo became a march of victory a day or so later. Evidently the middle class was pleased; it was relieved to have the military take over.

In the first months after the March 31 "revolution," the middle class seemed to give it its support despite the numerous actions contrary to middle class liberal democratic ideology. On April 9, 1966, the military command proclaimed the first Institutional Act (two more have followed) decreeing that "the victorious revolution dictates juridical powers without being limited in this right by the norms existing prior to its victory." On April 11, 1966, contrary to the existing Constitution, Marshal Humberto Castelo Branco was elected by the Chamber of Deputies as President of Brazil to serve until January 1966 (later extended one year). In the first two months, some four hundred people lost their political rights, among them three ex-Presidents and six state governors. These governors, fifty-five federal legislators, public officials, labor leaders, and others were included among those who lost the right to vote, to run for public office, or to hold government jobs. Despite the trappings of a Congress and Senate, a civilian ministry, and an "elected" president, this was clearly government by the military.

The new government seriously attempted to curb inflation with only moderate success. In 1965 it allowed three state elections; anti-government candidates won in the two important states of Minas Gerais and Guanabara. This indication of loss of support, particularly in states with an articulate middle class, led the government to tighten control. Political parties were abolished and a "Pro-Revolutionary" coalition was formed. (As yet there is no true opposition coalition.) It was decreed that the forthcoming election for Presidency and State Governments would be indirect by the legislature. This was followed by further *cassações* (cancellations) of political rights seemingly to guarantee the election of government candidates. A "revolutionary" General, Costa e Silva, who was Minister of War, announced his candidacy for President and he was elected virtually without opposition. It looks as if the Brazilian government will be dominated by the military for many years to come. If this should happen, then the middle class will have made a bad bargain. As a result of its basic economic, social, and political dilemma, the Brazilian middle class opted for stability over change.

Conclusions

What happened in Brazil from 1964 to the present is not a unique phenomenon in Latin America. In its essential features, it has happened again and again—in Argentina, Colombia, Ecuador, Dominican Republic, Peru, and Venezuela. After initial support of a military regime which promised stability, the middle class found itself prisoner of a quasi-authoritarian state. And in Cuba what seemed to begin as a middle class revolution against the dictator became a communist revolution which has driven most of the middle class into exile. In all of these situations, the middle class might have been the crucial element for social and political change. It was not so; rather it faltered and acquiesced in favor of the status quo.

The Latin American middle class must solve its dilemma. It must decide to promote social and economic change and to build a society in its own image, no matter what the cost. And it will be a costly and difficult task to extend education, health, food, public services, and the right to vote to the mass of people. The middle class will itself suffer in the process. But the alternative is to live in a nation policed by the military or face a left-wing authoritarian regime which would aim at its destruction. The question facing the next generation in Latin America is whether or not the middle class is willing to pay the price of a peaceful revolution.

17

Effects of Institutionalization and Professionalization of the Military

⊷◄●►▸

John J. Johnson

Unlike their nineteenth-century predecessors, army, navy, and air force officers in contemporary Latin America are likely to be individuals of middle-class origin, often the sons of provincial, military, or immigrant families, who have received professional military training and are acutely conscious of the area's relative lack of development. Thus, although the armed forces still arrogate to themselves the right to act as supreme arbiters of political life in a number of Latin American countries, the attitudes and goals of the members of their officer corps are considerably different from those of an earlier age. The ways in which these changed attitudes and goals affect the political behavior of the Latin American armed forces are discussed here by Professor John J. Johnson of the History Department of Stanford University.

. . . In terms of the relationship between the armed forces and civilians, the junta of government has been the most important by-product of institutionalization. In its civilian context the junta goes back to the colonial period, but it has been a regularly employed military device in Spanish America only since the 1920's. In their simplest forms the military juntas are boards or committees that assume power and rule by decree following the removal of a regime by force. They represent joint efforts on the part of dominant groups in the various branches of the military establishment to present a unified front against dissident elements within the services. This is what occurred in Peru in July 1962 when the Manuel Prado government was driven from power: a junta representing a substantial cross-section of the officer corps in each of the branches of the armed services took over

From John J. Johnson, *The Military and Society in Latin America* (Stanford, Cal.: Stanford University Press, 1964), pp. 113–119. © 1964 by the Board of Trustees of the Leland Stanford Junior University. Reprinted by permission of the publishers, Stanford University Press.

the leadership of the republic. The juntas are by definition transitory and several have terminated their rule in favor of civilians but rarely without first laying down the terms under which the successor government is permitted to be selected.

As far as the evolution of the armed forces is concerned, the military junta is a manifestation of the decline of individualism and the growth of an *esprit de corps* or group identification that has accompanied the greater institutionalization of the services. The Venezuelan situation perhaps best illustrates this point. Under the old tyrant Juan Vicente Gómez, the armed forces were used against civilians repeatedly, but at the command and pleasure of the dictator. Their long-range interests were incidental to the immediate interests of Gómez. But under the tyrant the armed forces did take on a national character and did evolve institutional objectives, and when Gómez died in 1935 these developments manifested themselves. Following a number of internal crises that resulted in the younger professionals supplanting the older non-professionals in key positions, the armed forces began to act in the name of the various branches and to claim the role of custodians of the national interests. The juntas of 1945, 1948, and 1958 were the results. Although the junta may now be considered a well-established political device of the armed services throughout Spanish America, it does not follow that strongmen will not appear from time to time, as in Argentina when Perón emerged supreme two years after the military took over the government in June 1943.

Professionalization has produced officers, who, when they act politically, do so for reasons and in a manner that clearly distinguishes them from their pre-World War I counterparts. First of all professionalization has almost completely destroyed the fluidity that existed when officers moved in and out of the military life at will. Then, too, as Lucian Pye has so ably established in reference to areas other than Latin America, professionalization has created an intellectual atmosphere within the armed forces that makes the leadership acutely sensitive to the advantages of modernization and technical advancement.[1] The new officer's belief in the need to modernize involves him so deeply with the welfare of the nation that he feels obliged to take a position on all major issues. This view can place him in an unusual position at several levels. Although nationalistic, he is, for example, required to obtain his weapons abroad. Also, he can be forced to look

---

[1] See his excellent contributions in Gabriel A. Almond and James S. Coleman, eds., *The Politics of the Developing Areas* (Princeton, 1960), and John J. Johnson, ed., *The Role of the Military in Underdeveloped Countries* (Princeton, 1962). Pye's thinking is apparent throughout Max F. Millikan and Donald L. M. Blackmer, editors, *The Emerging Nations; Their Growth and United States Policy* (Boston, 1961).

outside his own society for models upon which to fashion his own career, which can make him painfully aware of the extent to which his own country is economically and technologically retarded. Or his impatience to see the complete modernization of the armed forces and of the nation may tear him emotionally between those values held over from his youth and those that tend to align him with intellectuals and students and others most anxious to bring about change rapidly. For better or worse, the emotional conflict has held up the playing out of the contest between the military bureaucracies, which have traditionally represented the countryside, and the civilian bureaucracies, historically centered in the cities and inclined to look outward for guidance. This is why when the cities appear to triumph politically, as they have on many occasions since World War I, there has remained a strong residue of rural-mindedness, which erupts from time to time either at the instigation of or with the collusion of the armed forces, who have held the balance of power more or less continuously in all republics except Uruguay, Costa Rica, Chile, Colombia, Mexico, and Bolivia.

The commitment of the new generation of officers to modernization has also meant that the traditional social-economic gap between the leader and the led has been reinforced by differences in acculturation to modern life. This, plus the fact that in contemporary military establishments there is little or no comradeship between officers and men, has created a void that tends to prevent commissioned officers from being fully aware of the concerns of the non-commissioned officers and troops. Accordingly, non-commissioned officers and troops have been encouraged to look to civilians to fill the vacuum of representation between them, their superiors, and the public. This gap also tends to keep the officers divorced from that part of the populace in which democratic aspirations are nourished. Modernization and its implications, it would seem, weigh so heavily in Spanish America's future that the "pay, promotion, pension" argument—so often used at one and the same time to discredit the armed forces and to account for their participation in politics—loses much of its significance. In the final analysis, the republics will not be made or unmade on the basis of their military expenditures, although their future may well be determined by how important the armed forces consider modernization to be.

In some respects professionalization has made the modern armed forces officer less qualified than his World War I predecessor to run the governments of the republics. The officer of an earlier generation was first of all a civilian who thought as a civilian; he could, if he chose, keep his finger on the pulse of the narrowly based civilian ruling element through direct contact—although in actual practice the military tyrants in the latter stages of their dictatorships often lost all touch with the civilian elite and depended entirely on crudely repressive tactics. And the state, which was charged with little more than defending the national sovereignty and protecting private property, could be managed with only a primitive knowledge of administration. The modern officer-statesman, on the other hand, is never free for more than a brief moment to rule exclusively in the interests of a single sector of society, and government has become extravagantly complex as the state has committed itself to action in many social and economic areas.

The contemporary officer, furthermore, must spend at least twenty years in the service before he can expect to be called by his peers to lead them when they challenge politicians on their own ground. During those twenty years he lives in near-isolation from civilian concerns. Consequently, when he plunges into politics without ethical, moral, or legal support, he must not only speak for the armed services and try to keep them happy; he must also, because of the isolation that the military life imposes, depend for advice on his military friends, who live by the same kind of conventional wisdom that he does. These advisors, like the junta member himself, are usually win-the-war-and-to-hell-with-the-cost men, and as administrators they have been inefficient planners and inclined toward ruinous financial policies, as witness Perón in Argentina and Rojas Pinilla in Colombia. Carlos Ibáñez of Chile is an excellent example of a military man elected to the presidency of a politically sophisticated republic in a free election who by the time he left office had surrounded himself with a disproportionate share of military men because he felt he understood them and they understood him.

During his first twenty years as a soldier, the military ethic teaches the modern officer that man is weak and irrational and must be subordinated to the group, a position which at times has induced officers to disdain the civilians whom they propose to rule. Furthermore, the officer is, for nearly all of his professional career, himself a subordinate, taking orders rather than giving them, carrying out someone else's ideas rather than his own, and fitting himself into the well-defined hierarchical organization of the military. Subordination, and the narrow range of alternatives that subordination in the military permits, make the officer decisive and build up in him a faith in his ability to demand decisive action from others. The professional soldier's ordered and disciplined life has unquestionably made it difficult for him to tolerate the unsettling effects of social change, the "wasted effort" and divisiveness that accompany the workings of the democratic process. Perón, for example, in addressing a class of Argentine cadets before the War's end, accounted for France's military collapse on the grounds of internal disorder resulting from its political system. Above all, it has been the officer-politician's propensity to reject democratic institutions, polemics, and personal rivalry, and to apply military regimentation and modes of thought to all types of civilian situations that has ordinarily kept him in conflict with important elements within the civilian population. In this climate of opposition, he has not been able for extended periods of time to make effective use of his best qualities—self-confidence, experience in taking orders before giving them, the ability to accept rapid modernization, and the disposition to think in national terms.

Finally, the modern officer-politician runs into difficulties never experienced by his predecessor when he insists, as he ordinarily does, on imposing not only his person but a whole system upon the nation. Officers of an earlier generation, assuming control when strains developed, simply "declared for the general will" and were content to exercise personal political power. Despite their apparent ruthlessness, they were haphazard in enforcing their will upon the public, and they invariably proclaimed representative democracy to be their ultimate objective. But the modern officer often enters politics because of ideological differences with the civilian elements in power. When he achieves power as a representative of his branch of the service he feels compelled not only to rule but to define the content of the general will, as did Perón under what he called *justicialismo*. The modern officer may attempt to brainwash his subjects through mass media of communications. He may use the schools and government-controlled labor organizations for the propagation of the ideological position he seeks to impose. He may employ economic sanctions, one of the more easily applied political weapons in a "planned" society. He may lump representative democracy with imperialistic capitalism and reject both as undesirable.

The officer-statesman's confidence in his ability to formulate and implant ideological doctrines arises from two basic causes: contact with officers from other countries, and a conscious effort on the part of the armed forces in the most advanced countries to make officers aware of contemporary developments. Thus, the rise of a totalitarian attitude in the Argentine Army in the 1930's and 1940's can be accounted for in large part by its close connections with the armies of Nazi Germany and Fascist Italy, which at that time must have seemed almost invincible. Today, middle- and senior-grade officers in all the leading countries of Latin America are expected to have instruction in both national and world affairs; as a result, they become convinced that they are qualified to play a leading role in the economics, international relations, and government of their countries. It is still too early to determine how successful these training programs will be. As yet there has not appeared an officer who has publicly displayed a greater grasp of national and world problems than have civilians. But to the consternation of the anti-military elements of the area, the armed forces have won some highly placed individuals over to the military point of view by using them as instructors and extending to them some of the privileges (free air travel, for example) that the armed forces enjoy.

18

U. S. Military Assistance Policy Toward Latin America

◄—◆—►

Charles A. Meyer

Since World War II the United States has provided different kinds of military aid to the armed forces of Latin America. Originally intended to strengthen hemispheric defenses against external aggression, military assistance programs began after 1960 to place increasing emphasis on aiding Latin American governments to combat indigenous threats to internal security. Over the years many observers in the United States have expressed concern that these programs may have encouraged military intervention in politics or contributed to the longevity of repressive regimes. The policy of the Nixon administration on military aid to Latin America is explained in a statement to the Senate Subcommittee on Western Hemisphere Affairs by Charles A. Meyer (1918–), who was named Assistant Secretary of State for Inter-American Affairs in 1969. A vice president of Sears, Roebuck & Company at the time of his appointment, Meyer spent many years in Latin America as an executive of that firm.

I welcome this occasion to appear today before this subcommittee, since it affords me an excellent opportunity to exchange viewpoints with you on our military assistance policy toward the countries of Latin America.

As I believe you know, our military presence in Latin America is sharply diminishing. Total U.S. military personnel assigned to our military groups, amounting to almost 800 in 1967, is in the process of being reduced to 505—more than 35 percent—by July of 1970. And this, gentlemen, is in an area almost 2½ times the size of the United States. Moreover, the question of personnel strength and their roles will continue to be subject to frequent review. The amount of money expended in our grant military assistance program to Latin America

From *The Department of State Bulletin*, 61 (August 4, 1969), 100–102. Italicized bracketed note in the text is by Helen Delpar.

has already been reduced by almost 75 percent from the FY [*fiscal year*] 1966 level of $80.7 million to the FY 1970 request of $21.4 million.

As you also know, all aspects of our policy toward Latin America have been undergoing intensive review and appraisal for the past several months. Along with the studies being carried out within the executive branch, I am certain that these hearings will provide a very useful part of our policy review.

Our military assistance program includes three components: furnishing technical advisers, supplying some grant materiel, and sponsoring formal training.

Although our military assistance program does not play a large role in terms of money expended or personnel involvement, it nevertheless is a significant element in our general overall Latin American policy. It is not, as perhaps some would contend, a program primarily based on such an outdated rationale as "hemispheric defense." Neither is it a program divorced or isolated from or inconsistent with our overall concern: social and economic reform leading to a better and more rewarding life for our Latin American neighbors.

On the contrary, one primary purpose of our military assistance program is to help our Latin American neighbors attain socioeconomic development by systematic evolution rather than in the volatile atmosphere of destructive revolution. Therefore, this program is a concomitant to the broader reform programs in such areas as education, land reform, and the like, which are the top-priority objectives of our participation in the Alliance for Progress. The Departments of State and Defense both continuously work together to ensure that this relationship prevails, as it should.

Some of the earlier witnesses who appeared before this subcommittee have correctly made the long-accepted and recognized point that the acceleration of the movement in Latin America toward the social and economic reform goals of the Alliance for Progress will naturally and inevitably be accompanied by instability. It can, moreover, be argued that social tensions and conflicts are necessary ingredients in promoting the accelerated structural changes the Alliance seeks. At the same time, there can be little doubt that the painful and dynamic process of change is exploited by elements which have no real interest in the kind of change sought under the Alliance and, indeed, seek to frustrate it. Consequently, there is legitimate and responsible concern that instability not attain such a level as to destroy the reform process itself.

There is, then, a very close relationship between the prospects for achieving social and economic reform and development goals and a necessary level of internal security and stability. This relationship between modernization and stability is complex even in a fully democratic, pluralistic, highly developed society such as ours. If constructive reform is to proceed, however, the acceptable forms of legitimate, healthy, necessary dissent preclude terrorism and armed insurgency.

Inasmuch as our military assistance program was shifted in the early sixties, in recognition of changed circumstances, toward strengthening the Latin American national capabilities to counter Communist sponsored or supported insurgency movements, how do we assess the threat today and for the near future? We believe that there is very little likelihood of a major external threat to the area in the foreseeable future. Communist insurgencies are currently at a relatively low ebb in Latin America. At the present time, active insurgencies of a sporadic nature continue to exist only in Venezuela, Colombia, and Guatemala.

The defeat of the Che Guevara-led guerrillas in 1967 by elements of the Bolivian Army, largely equipped and trained in counterguerrilla warfare by the United States, seems to have made the Cuban regime more cautious about initiating new areas of insurgency in the hemisphere. In view of the improved counterinsurgency capabilities of the Latin American military forces achieved by our joint efforts and programs, and the declining appeal of the Cuban-style revolution to the Latin Americans, a significant increase in insurgency movements is not likely at this time. We must recognize, however, that despite the relatively lower emphasis Havana seems to be giving for tactical reasons to overt support of insurgencies in their various forms, we have no evidence of any fundamental change in their interest in the export of revolution.

Inasmuch as the threat of an external attack is unlikely and the danger of formidable insurgencies is today reduced, legitimate questions arise as to the desirability or need to continue with a military assistance program to Latin America.

Although today insurgent forces are not a direct threat to the governments in any of the Latin American countries, they do continue to represent, in varying degrees, a nucleus which can be further supported from outside in the event of deteriorating economic or social conditions. This factor, coupled with the continuance of inadequate and inequitable economic and social structures which are vulnerable to subversion, necessitates the maintenance of the counterinsurgency capabilities of Latin American forces in order that an internal atmosphere conducive to social and economic progress can prevail. Our training of small, mobile, rapid-reaction forces and our grant materiel program geared to maintaining equipment for the support of such forces play fundamental roles in this respect.

Whereas formal training is provided to 17 countries, our grant materiel assistance has now been limited to 11 countries which remain relatively vulnerable to subversive threats and which, at the same time, are less able to cope with internal security problems solely with their own limited resources. Such materiel assistance will, of course, be phased out when these countries are able to attain and maintain on their own an effective counterinsurgency capability or the insurgent threat further declines.

Now let us look at a different and important relationship; namely, that relationship which has existed since or before World War II between the U.S. military services and the matching services of the larger Latin American countries. In these countries we have maintained military groups which were originally designated as military service missions in concert with the request or continued invitation of the host governments (often under contractual terms). These military groups have undergone reductions of personnel, to which I referred at the outset, and are subject to current and continuous reexamination both as to functions and numbers. Because, however, this relationship is longstanding, because it is a relationship with the larger nations, because three of these nations are governed by leaders from their military, and because the relative size and sophistication of these nations produce requests for up-to-date major military equipment, we, the United States, ask ourselves whether our military presence is responsible (1) for encouraging military governments, (2) for providing repressive influences against the dissent inherent in today's worldwide struggle for self-fulfillment, (3) for encouraging and then financing the acquisition of armaments which are either an unnecessary diversion of national resources or are the beginning of an "arms race."

I am not a military man. Like many in this room, I have served in one war and have seen the postwar revulsion to things military. Today, the Nixon administration is dedicated to a just and honorable termination of a controversial military action. This action has caused or has given focus to dissent within our own country, dissent which is clearly discernible around the world. But recognizing this as a common current does not convince me that our politicomilitary relationships in Latin America are responsible *per se* for its internal political struggles. Nor do I believe that our inter-American relationships will be improved by any attitude on our part which, in effect, says to the sovereign states of Latin America: "You don't need anything more advanced in military equipment than the 20-year-old items you have; and furthermore, if you elect to buy anything more advanced than what you already have from anybody, we will consider it an irresponsible act and penalize you accordingly."

In all fairness, it must be said that the record of arms expenditures by Latin America has to date been the lowest of any world area, with the sole exception of sub-Sahara Africa. Only about 2 percent of their GNP and less than 13 percent of their total central governments' expenditures have been expended for total defense costs. Moreover, only approximately 10 percent of their annual defense expenditures has been devoted to new military equipment. Naturally, we would hope that such restraint on their part would continue.

However, the time has now arrived when these nations consider that they cannot further delay their military modernization programs. They would much prefer to purchase U.S.-manufactured equipment. In this regard our policy objectives have been entirely consistent with the purposes of legislative restrictions to discourage Latin American governments from diverting their limited economic resources to unnecessary military items at the expense of development programs. However, these legislative restrictions, intended to inhibit their purchase of "sophisticated weapons systems," are, I am afraid, sowing the seeds of political estrangement with the major countries of that area.

Latin Americans have become puzzled and even suspicious of our motives. Strong nationalist resentment has arisen over what is seen as United States efforts to infringe on the sovereign rights of a country to determine its own military requirements; it is especially hard to understand in those countries which cherish the sense of close alliance with us and have showed the value they place on this association.

The net result has been negative in terms of broader U.S. political interests. There has been an increasing disposition on their part to turn to European suppliers who are able to respond promptly with firm offers of much more sophisticated as well as correspondingly more expensive equipment for early delivery on attractive credit terms. Unfortunately the long-term consequence of our paternalistic, even patronizing, restrictions will be the acquisition of more expensive items, higher maintenance costs, and greater diversion of financial resources from civilian purposes. The end result could be a real arms race, which fortunately, thus far, has been avoided in Latin America.

In conclusion, let me assure you that we believe strongly that all of our policies and activities in Latin America should be reexamined periodically to evaluate their net utility and their consistency with changing conditions. Our politicomilitary policies and activities will be no exception to this scrutiny. We are mindful that the decade of the seventies may require different levels of effort in each neighboring nation, be those efforts social, economic, or politicomilitary. And we submit with conviction that balanced attention to Latin American needs in the totality of their national personalities is a desirable objective.

❊§ 19 §❊

Development for Peace

Monsignor Marcos McGrath

To what extent should the Catholic Church actively work for social change in Latin America? Can the use of violence in the pursuit of social justice ever be justified? Both of these questions, which have been the subject of heated debate among members of the clergy in Latin America in recent years, are explored in this reading by Monsignor Marcos G. McGrath, C.S.C., Archbishop of Panama. Monsignor McGrath, who was born in the city of Panama in 1924, is also first vice president of the Latin American Bishops Council.

Recently, in the United States, I gave two conferences on the Church in Latin America. In the question periods, the very timely subject of "violence" came to the fore. I observed that the Church's position, as reinforced by *Populorum Progressio* [*The Development of Peoples, 1967 encyclical by Pope Paul VI*], holds violence to be a last resort; that one cannot exclude its being justified in particular circumstances, but that one cannot generalize about its being justified in all of Latin America; and finally, that there is a lack of clear orientation in this whole area that calls for a better developed theology or ethic to guide our people.

I was reported rather diversely on these points—in several countries. One headline spoke of a Latin American bishop approving violence, though the text specified that I had given only an analysis of the question. Another article quoted me as saying that the choice of violence in Latin America is no longer an ethical question, but is rather a tactical one. What I had said was that some few Christians hold this position for their particular situation. In a later article, I was rather rudely knocked about as a comfortable bishop, dressed in silk and eating the finest of foods, who would deny the oppressed their sole remaining recourse, namely, violence. An attempt to clarify one-sided views only

Monsignor Marcos McGrath, "Development for Peace," *America* 118 (April 27, 1968), 562–567. © 1968. America Press, New York. Reprinted by permission of the publisher. Italicized bracketed note in the text is by Helen Delpar.

seemed to give the impression of falling heavily on the other side. On the whole, it has been an unusual journalistic experience. It would be only that if the matter were not so vital.

Can one speak forcefully against the social injustices prevalent in many of our countries and on the international level, between the rich and the poor nations, without becoming an advocate of organized violence? Can one oppose general recommendations of violence for all our varied Latin American situations, without becoming a defender of the status quo? I sincerely hope so.

Perhaps the key to the dilemma is in the very concept of development. In many countries we have a situation where a few enjoy the benefits of a capitalist structure in which they alone fully share, as producers and consumers—as against a more or less large number of their fellow citizens who live marginally to this structure, producing and consuming little, not only enjoying few of the benefits of civilization, culture and religion, but often suffering the terribly contrasting situation of a daily increasing want and misery. A national per capita income of $600 a year (a high figure for Latin America) means very little when the bulk of the population may be earning less than $50 a year.

There are those who would keep this status quo. Sometimes it is because they are simply ignorant of the contrasts. I have heard rich persons in some Latin American nations teeming with city slums and burdened by primitive conditions on the land blandly remark that there are no really poor persons in their country. Obviously there is a blindness and an insensitivity there for which we, as a Church, are heavily responsible.

But the status quo is perpetuated, worsened and embittered in many cases by other factors. There is in some countries a concept of politics and political parties that views the whole political process as the manipulation of government power in favor of the economically strong—a manipulation disguised and corrupted and maintained by the distribution of government favors and jobs, often dishonestly, often to the least deserving or least competent. Even granting that a margin of inevitable corruption is typical of all human affairs, one must sorrowfully shake one's head at this situation. One is reminded of John F. Kennedy's statement to the effect that honesty in government is the prime condition of honest effort among the people in a democracy.

The system itself, with its built-in class traditions, tends to maintain the status quo—often by unjust measures (relating to the salaries, working conditions, land tenure, etc.). Sometimes these are backed up with personal violence, physical or moral, exercised publicly or privately against "social reformers" of any kind.

Certainly these abuses must be denounced. In their extreme and prolonged form they are what can provoke violent revolution; they could constitute the "manifest, long-standing tyranny" of which Pope Paul speaks in this connection.

This kind of situation in Latin America is further complicated by international economic injustices, so strongly pointed out by *Populorum Progressio,* which drain and impoverish and humiliate our nations far more rapidly than the relatively small amount of foreign aid can undo them. International economic interests favor the small capitalist sectors of our society but do little about the worsening situation of the masses.

Even many government leaders or international agencies or private individuals who wish to work for the development of our countries may be reinforcing and augmenting the contrast between "haves" and "have-nots" if their concept of development is too exclusively from the top down: through government, through new factories, public works, etc. They forget the "human factor," the man at the bottom: his formation, his association into community groups, his leadership, his active participation in development.

An example may help. One small Latin American country recently published statistics on a marked increase in food production. This was excellent for its export-import balance. But on closer inspection it was clear that the government had facilitated credit and technical assistance to the small group of large landholders who, because of their know-how, quickly produced more. This helped the balance of trade, but it deepened the contrast between these few farmers, who became richer in the process, and the bulk of the peasants, who meanwhile, unassisted, sank deeper into their poverty and discontent. A government may well argue that with its limited means it can do no more; that it cannot possibly help every isolated poor farmer, most of whom actually resist the help. But ways must be found, and are being found, by governments to help farmers, with the fullest possible action of private groups and of the farmers themselves, in their own independent organizations. Such organizations, started and promoted by leader-training centers, are the necessary bases of democracy and development in the rural areas.

Similar examples abound—in urban, suburban and rural sectors. True human and social development must concentrate not on "under-development," but on the *man* and his family and his community, who must be assisted in developing themselves. Aid from above may otherwise develop the developed and forget the rest.

For many these are common verities; but they are seldom respected in practice.

It is stated in the Constitution on the Church in the Modern World (§12): "According to the almost unanimous opinion of believers and unbelievers alike, all things on earth should be related to man as their center and crown." This is the fundamental issue. Do we believe in the dignity and possibilities of each man, however poor and ignorant, however immersed in the vices his situation may engender? Many, frankly and fundamentally, do not; or simply ignore the whole question. They therefore accept the status quo as normal. Others, who work for development within the given structure, often forget that each man's dignity requires the development of his possibilities, and his active participation in his own development. They seem to forget also that without this effort the economic development of their countries will always be limited, since a large number will remain marginal to it, both as producers and consumers; and the political development will always be insecure because this large mass will remain the dupes of politicians of Left and Right.

In the face of such obstacles, intelligent, active Christian promoters of social reform may well despair. They are burning with a desire to help the hungering masses, and they find no effective way. Eventually some are tempted to choose violence. They would break with everything, take to the hills and overthrow the existing regime. Such men often seem to manifest just as little real sense of what development means as those they would overthrow. They are surprised when the peasants do not join them or support them. But what did they expect? The great problem of the peasant or the Indian is precisely his passivity, his lack of training—and his suspicion of all the top-level, cultured leaders and redeemers, including these revolutionaries, who promise him so much. He would rather hold on tenaciously to the little he has.

That much can be said without any reference to Christian principles. The failure of the guerrilla movements in Latin America is proof of the fact. True, counter-guerrilla military strength is part of the explanation of this failure; but, more fundamentally, the masses to be redeemed are not eager or ready to share in this kind of redemption.

Let me interject here the warning, always apropos in any discussion of Latin America, that we have to guard against generalizations. The conditions I have described as existing in "some" or "many" of our nations do not exist in all of them; nor do they exist in any two of them in exactly the same way. We will have to remind ourselves of this point later on.

But now we can turn directly to the question of violence—to view it in an ethical light. A genuinely "theological" consideration of it would take us more deeply into Scripture and theology than this modest article can pretend to do.

In many countries, today, violence is a pressing subject—whether more so or less than in the past is for historians to tell us. Violence

takes various social forms: guerrilla tactics, race riots, terrorism, underground resistance and just plain war, with its widening impact upon
civilian populations. We are not concerned here with the mounting incidence of violence in petty and major individual crimes in many
countries, or with the growing mentality of violence they reveal. It is
not, of course, a subject to be studied only in a Latin American context. In Latin America, however, the particular form it takes is bound
up with the social "revolution" there. Many hold that without violence
this revolution cannot succeed.

The term "revolution," in 20th century usage, especially in the
writings of most Marxists, often carries with it the connotation of class
warfare and violence. Yet the term is used broadly throughout Latin
America with many different meanings. In one country it may refer
simply to a military *coup d'état* that changes the leaders of a society,
with or without bloodshed, but rather tends to confirm the existing
socio-economic structures. In others the term "revolutionary" is used
to describe constitutionally established and ruling political parties that
work for social progress but reject and suppress all forms of violence.
In some countries "revolution" means dictatorship obtained and maintained with violence; in others, it means socio-economic change and
progress within constitutionally guaranteed liberties. If ever a term
was equivocal in Latin America, this is it.

Yet we cannot get away from it. When one outstanding Catholic
politician in Latin America was questioned by an eminent European
prelate about whether or not we, as Christians, have to talk about
"revolution" in Latin America, he replied: "Whether we talk about
it or not, it will take place with or without us—or against us."

It is in this sense that John F. Kennedy once said that those who
obstruct peaceful revolution provoke violent revolution. President
Lyndon Johnson and other world statesmen have spoken of revolutions to uproot misery in all its forms. Some years ago, Hubert Hum-
phrey, as Senator, more explicitly contrasted the terms "evolution"
and "revolution" in connection with Latin America. He found that
"evolution" was too weak a term for what we must desire, because it
would imply simply letting things take their own course; whereas we
must provoke, plan and promote the changes required for a better
world in this continent. In this sense, "revolution" would be the more
fitting term.

If we take "revolution," then, in the broad sense of "bold transformations, innovations that go deep," of "urgent reforms [that] should
be undertaken without delay," then "it is for each one to take his
share in them with generosity, particularly those whose education,
position and opportunities afford them wide scope for action" (*Populorum Progressio,* §32). We could multiply texts from the Vatican

Council's Constitution on the Church in the Modern World, from the encyclicals *Mater et Magistra, Pacem in Terris* and *Populorum Progressio,* all of which are quite explicit on this point. Many statements, individual and collective, of Latin American bishops also stress the urgency of these changes for Latin America or for their individual nations. Yet none of these statements favors violence.

If we take "revolution" in this sense, then as Christians we must be for it wherever these changes are needed, as is the case in most Latin American countries. Yet, understandably, to avoid the ambiguities the term suggests in many minds, we prefer to avoid it in most of our Church documents, and to speak about "development" or "social change."

There have been many of late who have spoken about the need to develop a "theology of revolution." This, too, can be ambiguous. In one sense we may say that this theology is already well under way. Theology does not spell out technical solutions, but rather points out value goals consonant with the dignity of the human persons in society. These goals are more and more being pointed to and stressed by the Church.

But if this "theology" refers to the *means* by which this "revolution" or "social change" may be brought about, then we find ourselves suddenly in the area of violence as a possible solution. Certain Catholic publications of late have spoken of revolution as necessarily and in principle involving violence. I think this idea is unfortunate. It permits all the appeals for social change in Latin America, even by bishops, to be invoked rather indiscriminately in favor of violence—which is in fact what is happening in the minds of some, and in their political platforms. And it leads to a position that would oppose any so-called half-way measures, and converts the concept of social change or revolution into a political and military goal: the obtaining of total power. It is obvious that this sort of thinking tends to paralyze much that is being done in social reform today and play into the hands of those who would take power to impose not only a whole new socioeconomic and political system, but also their own ideologies, on a people.

So it is best here to set aside the terms "revolution" and "theology of revolution" and ask ourselves simply: When is violence justified as a means to the goal of required social change?

Catholics are often charged with following the maxim "The end justifies the means." Nothing is farther away from Catholic theology. No means may be employed to attain any end unless the action performed is good in itself. If it simultaneously causes an evil effect, this effect can only be permitted if the good it causes is proportionately greater than the evil. Such is the case with self-defense, which may lead to the killing of an unjust aggressor to save one's own life. Such was the classic moral example in the case of a just war to defend a nation or a people against unjust aggression. Such is the case in any defense of personal or group rights that might involve violence or be the occasion of harm to other persons. In every case the good effect must be clearly greater than the evil; and only the good effect should be directly intended and personally desired. These, I think, are familiar considerations.

Violence in all forms is abhorrent to the spirit of the gospel. The example of our Lord and His counsels rather incline us to suffer evil from others than to resist it with harm to them. The "pacifist" movement, which would reject all wars and, logically, all other forms of social or individual violence, is one expression of this spirit, and it is generally at least tolerated in nations of Christian tradition. The examples of Martin Luther King and the Hindu Gandhi, both victims of violence, are eloquent testimony in favor of "peaceful resistance" to injustice.

But, for most convinced Christians, some occasions justify war or self-defense in other forms, and the *proportionate* means to that defense, and those who fight for themselves or their nations in these circumstances are duly honored. It is, of course, precisely the *disproportion* of modern means of total warfare that makes it very difficult, if not impossible, today to morally justify any all-out war.

The matter is less clear when we speak about violence against established authority within a given society as a means to obtain social rights or social justice. This is the problem that is being posed by many in Latin America today. We cannot ignore the fact, nor should we. Many Christians are involved in the discussion of the problem. In fact, not a few Christians in Latin America have already decided in favor of the violent overthrow of their country's government. The fact that they do not act on their conviction is due to tactical considerations. They simply consider that the time is not ripe. They could not win the battle now.

Their fundamental argument, as I have heard it expressed, is that a situation of violence already exists. Where the few are established in power, and this power is systematically used to augment their own interests and block efforts at improving the situation of the majority who are in need, sometimes in dire need, then, these Christians say, violence is already present. To strike out against this violence requires no further ethical argument. It is merely self-defense. The only question is when and how to strike out. Even a just war, they say, should not be entered into if there is no chance of winning. Nor should violence against established authority be undertaken without sufficiently broad popular support and the other requirements for a real chance of eventual success.

What can be said about this argument? Obviously its proponents are condemning existent "institutional violence"—a system, national and international, that wreaks personal injustice or "violence" upon many. By the same token, they advocate "counter-violence"—against the system, or against the persons enforcing the system. This distinction is important in that it may help to expose some of the political analysis necessary in approaching the whole problem. "Counter-violence" is mostly directed at the persons—military, etc.—protecting a system. But it is the system that must be changed. A good law of agrarian or monetary reform, or treaties for international price control, do more to this end than the burning of farms or the shooting of bankers. But how may these laws be passed and applied if those in power resist? This is certainly a political process involving the formation of a conscience, of leaders, of movements, of parties, of Latin American common markets —the whole process of democratic pressure groups. True, it takes time. Yet it is beginning in many areas.

The next question is what violence will achieve. The socio-economic development of our peoples, as well as their cultural and spiritual development—are these guaranteed by "throwing the government scoundrels out"? What or who will be put in their place? What will they do? Will liberty be lost in the process? May not a worse oppression follow, for all, and especially for the very masses we wish to help? Revolutions of any kind, if they are deliberately provoked, must have clear goals and possess the means with which to reach them. I remember once, after a riot somewhere in Latin America, talking with a Catholic friend who had been throwing stones at the police. I asked him: "Were you trying to overthrow the government?" "Of course," he said. "What did you plan after that?" I asked him. "I had no idea," he said. "We would think about that later."

There is a short circuit in this kind of thinking, a romanticism that refuses to face the facts. Perhaps it refuses to face the basic fact that we have a long, slow, uphill struggle to develop our masses through basic education and social organization before they can become the productive, responsible persons of a working democracy that we want them to be. Perhaps the sort of thinking that would work the miracle of development by having a few revolutionaries simply "throw the scoundrels out" is only a new kind of paternalism. However great scoundrels the government leaders may be, this "miracle" would not be development, it would be pure magic.

So there must be a program. The next question is whether the Christians involved (since we are speaking about Christians) can continue to maintain their values in whatever action they initiate. Generally they are amateurs at the game. They have had to make a conscience judgment about resorting to violence in the first place. They have to be scrupulous about the means, so that these should not be disproportionate. Terrorism, for example, with its killing of innocent persons, raises many and very serious moral doubts. But these Christians soon find themselves associated, at least in practical matters, with professional revolutionaries or opportunists lacking any scruples as to the use of violence in any of its forms. Who will find it easiest to take over leadership of the whole process in the end? There is more than one example to prove that it is usually not the amateurs.

There is, too, another consideration: what long-sustained violence (especially if accompanied by terrorism) does in crushing the basic human and Christian values of life and respect for other human beings. Christians from Vietnam have told us that the greatest tragedy in their land is the utter loss among their people of confidence in one another. Today's friend is tonight's assassin. Death occurs anywhere and at any time—in the most violent forms. No one is excepted. No one is respected. How long will it take to rebuild the inner humanity of a people thus destroyed?

Finally, there is the basic moral judgment that violence in a particular situation is justified because, as the saying goes, violence already exists. This is a judgment that may be too easily made. First of all, I think, we must reject it wherever it is presented in generalizations that would cover all the Latin American countries. I cannot say that it does not exist in this sense anywhere in Latin America, but I can vehemently reject any generalization about the "Latin American revolution." When we talk about revolution in these terms, we must speak about specific nations and even specific areas.

We cannot exclude the possibility of some specific situation in which violence against established authority may be morally justified. History provides many such situations that were approved by the Christian conscience of the people at the time, or at least afterwards. I think it is safe to say that most Christians agreed in conscience with the armed opposition to the Batista regime, at least in its final stages. So did most of the governments of this hemisphere, and some clearly assisted in its overthrow. What happened there, afterwards, is difficult to judge. But at least it is a warning that we must keep in mind. Each situation must be judged on its own merits. Every person must make his own conscience judgment.

Secondly, the violence that is said to "exist already" may have been there for a long time. Have we just come to see it? Or may we be ridden by a guilt complex that we, as Christians, have done too little about it up till now and think by one stroke to change the whole picture or at least give testimony against it and thus relieve our guilt? May we not be forgetting that within our own country there are at least some forces of reform at work, some people just as socially Christian as ourselves whose lives are dedicated to this cause—without violence? May we not forget that those who are blind to the cause are so because we have not sufficiently preached the human and social dimensions of the gospel? May we not forget that no one particular situation in Latin America stands alone; that if our situation is perhaps intolerable, there is a bright awakening in the whole Church and in the hearts and minds and actions of many thousands of Christian leaders, and other leaders of good will, to work at this terribly difficult and complex task? May we not forget how tremendously difficult it is to solve some of the great social problems of the day—such as overpopulation and impending famine—under any system? Impatience may sometimes be holy; but patient determination may be more holy and more valiant.

I personally find more heroism in those who energetically and patiently labor at the groundwork of development (co-operatives, labor unions, community development, and the like) or in social and political action for development on higher levels, than in those others who too easily or too impatiently or too ingenuously take to violence, or simply advise others to do so. Even from a tactical point of view, those who take to violence are often doomed to failure; for their "testimony," although it may excite some admiration, often sets back the process of development itself.

Those who opt against the given structures in a total and immediate fashion—rejecting "half-way" measures, working for the "violent" overthrow of the powers that be—may well be chasing after the mythical pot at the end of the rainbow. Even if they can morally justify their violence and do take over the government, they still have before them the whole problem of the development of the masses. Will solutions then be forcibly imposed from above? With what set of values? With what concept of man and society? Neither desperation nor romanticism nor the recognized effects of demagogic slogans should prevail over a realistic dedication to man—the poor man of Latin America, who is our brother, in whom we believe, and whom we wish to assist to his full responsible manhood in a more just national and international society.

Others will speak and write more effectively and more technically about all these problems. As a theologian and pastor, I only wish to invite the reader to a fuller consideration of what the choice of violence means within the full context of the "Progress of our People."

Obviously, I am not a "Latin American bishop who approves violence." Nor can I or anyone else exclude it always and everywhere.

Each Christian must form his own conscience, but with an accurate knowledge of the situation he is in and a clear grasp of the principles and the dangers involved. He should look well, very well, before leaping. There must be real justification—as to the end, as to the means, as to a program and as to the likelihood of success, not only of the overthrow of a regime but of the program to follow. Let him remember that our greatest commandment is to love our neighbor. Even if violence may be chosen, we may not hate.

The greatest violence of all, that which "bears away the kingdom of heaven," is that of love. My experience is that wherever even a few Christians, fortified by the gospel and the clear urgings of modern Church documents, work with all their might, out of love, for the integral development of the poor, and above all if they are in contact and co-operation with the best forces working for it (beyond their frontiers if there are few at home), hope does not die in their hearts and hope rises in the hearts of others. The very talk of violence by some sincere Christians in Latin America must make us all realize that what we have done so far for the poor is very little. We must do much more, and in so doing dispel the specter of violence that haunts the minds of some and threatens the lives of many.

BIBLIOGRAPHY

An excellent introduction to the complex topic of nationalism is Samuel L. Baily (ed.), *Nationalism in Latin America* (New York: Knopf, 1971). Many other volumes deal with nationalism in Latin America in general and in individual countries. Among them are Arthur P. Whitaker, *Nationalism in Latin America: Past and Present* (Gainesville: University of Florida Press, 1962); Arthur P. Whitaker and David C. Jordan, *Nationalism in Contemporary Latin America* (New York: Free Press, 1966); Gerhard Masur, *Nationalism in Latin America* (New York: Macmillan, 1966); Samuel L. Baily, *Labor, Nationalism and Politics in Argentina* (New Brunswick, N.J.: Rutgers University Press, 1967); Frederick C. Turner, *The Dynamic of Mexican Nationalism* (Chapel Hill: University of North Carolina Press, 1968); and E. Bradford Burns, *Nationalism in Brazil: A Historical Survey* (New York: Praeger, 1968). Economic nationalism is illustrated by several of the selections in Marvin D. Bernstein (ed.), *Foreign Investment in Latin America: Cases and Attitudes* (New York: Knopf, 1966). On the implications of efforts to integrate the Indian into the European culture of Spanish America, see Frank Tannenbaum, "Agrarismo, Indianismo, y Nacionalismo," *Hispanic American Historical Review*, 23 (1943), 394–423. Divergent assessments of APRA are given in Harry Kantor, *The Ideology and Program of the Peruvian Aprista Movement* (New York: Octagon, 1966); Fredrick B. Pike, "The Old and the New APRA in Peru: Myth and Reality," *Inter-American Economic*

Affairs, 18 (Autumn, 1964), 3–45; and Richard Lee Clinton, "APRA: An Appraisal," *Journal of Inter-American Studies and World Affairs,* 12 (1970), 280–297.

A sound introduction to the subject of Latin American economic development and industrialization is offered by two anthologies: Albert O. Hirschman (ed.), *Latin American Issues: Essays and Comments* (New York: Twentieth Century Fund, 1961) and Charles T. Nisbet (ed.), *Latin America: Problems in Economic Development* (New York: Free Press, 1969), both of which contain selections examining the views of Raúl Prebisch. The following books are also important: William P. Glade, *The Latin American Economies: A Study of Their Institutional Evolution* (New York: Van Nostrand-Reinhold, 1969); Roberto de Oliveira Campos, *Reflections on Latin American Development* (Austin: University of Texas Press, 1967); Warren Dean, *The Industrialization of São Paulo, 1880–1945* (Austin: University of Texas Press, 1969); Aldo Ferrer, *The Argentine Economy* (Berkeley: University of California Press, 1967); Sanford Mosk, *Industrial Revolution in Mexico* (Berkeley: University of California Press, 1950); Manuel Germán Parra, *La Industrialización de México* (Mexico: Imp. Universitaria, 1954); and Raymond Vernon, *The Dilemma of Mexico's Development: The Roles of the Private and Public Sectors* (Cambridge, Mass.: Harvard University Press, 1963). The conditions and values that have served to encourage or inhibit economic growth in Latin America and the emergence of a native entrepreneurial class may be further explored in "Economic Development and the Business Classes," in Seymour Martin Lipset and Aldo Solari (eds.), *Elites in Latin America* (New York: Oxford University Press, 1967); Everett E. Hagen, *On the Theory of Social Change: How Economic Growth Begins* (Homewood, Ill.: Dorsey Press, 1962), especially Chapter 15; and Tomás Roberto Fillol, *Social Factors in Economic Development: The Argentine Case* (Cambridge, Mass.: M.I.T., 1961).

A lengthy list of works on agrarian reform appears in T. Lynn Smith (ed.), *Agrarian Reform in Latin America* (New York: Knopf, 1965), together with the excellent introduction by the editor, from which Reading 15 was taken. Another good, although somewhat outdated, general discussion is Thomas F. Carroll, "The Land Reform Issue in Latin America," in Hirschman, *Latin American Issues,* mentioned above. The results of agrarian reform in two countries that have experienced social revolution in the twentieth century can be seen in Nathan L. Whetten, *Rural Mexico* (Chicago: University of Chicago Press, 1948); Eduardo L. Venezian and William K. Gamble, *The Agricultural Development of Mexico. Its Structure and Growth Since 1950* (New York: Praeger, 1969); Dwight B. Heath, Charles J. Erasmus, and Hans C. Buechler, *Land Reform and Social Revolution in Bolivia* (New York: Praeger, 1969); and William J. McEwen (ed.), *Changing Rural Bolivia* (New York, 1969).

John J. Johnson, *Political Change in Latin America: The Emergence of the Middle Sectors* (Stanford, Cal.: Stanford University Press, 1958) has been extremely influential in focusing attention on the increasing political role of what are usually called the middle classes. However, Milton I. Vanger, "Politics and Class in Twentieth-Century Latin America," *Hispanic American*

Historical Review, 49 (1969), 80–93 questions the value of class analysis in interpreting the recent political history of Latin America. Also of interest is Fredrick B. Pike, "Aspects of Class Relations in Chile, 1850–1960," *Hispanic American Historical Review,* 43 (1963), 14–33.

Changes in the military establishments of Latin America can be traced in John J. Johnson, *The Military and Society in Latin America* (Stanford, Cal.: Stanford University Press, 1964) and Edwin Lieuwen, *Arms and Politics in Latin America* (New York: Praeger, 1960) and *Generals Vs. Presidents: Neomilitarism in Latin America* (New York: Praeger, 1964). Lyle N. McAlister, "Civil-military Relations in Latin America," *Journal of Inter-American Studies,* 3 (1961), 341–350 attempts to identify and describe the various types of civil-military relations in Latin America. The following works examine different aspects of the armed forces in individual countries: John D. Wirth, "*Tenentismo* in the Brazilian Revolution of 1930," *Hispanic American Historical Review,* 44 (1964), 161–179; Howard J. Wiarda, "The Politics of Civil-Military Relations in the Dominican Republic," *Journal of Inter-American Studies,* 7 (1965), 465–484; Herbert S. Klein, "David Toro and the Establishment of 'Military Socialism' in Bolivia," *Hispanic American Historical Review,* 45 (1965), 25–52 and "Germán Busch and the Era of 'Military Socialism' in Bolivia," *ibid.,* 47 (1967), 166–184; Frederick M. Nunn, "Military Rule in Chile: The Revolutions of September 5, 1924 and January 23, 1925," *Hispanic American Historical Review,* 47 (1967) 1–21; Stephen L. Rozman, "The Evolution of the Political Role of the Peruvian Military," *Journal of Inter-American Studies and World Affairs,* 12 (1970), 539–564; Edwin Lieuwen, *Mexican Militarism: The Rise and Fall of the Revolutionary Army, 1910–1940* (Albuquerque: University of New Mexico Press, 1968); and Robert A. Potash, *The Army and Politics in Argentina, 1928–1945* (Stanford, Cal.: Stanford University Press, 1969). On U.S. military assistance to Latin America see Michael J. Francis, "Military Aid to Latin America in the U.S. Congress," *Journal of Inter-American Studies,* 6 (1964), 389–404 and W. F. Barber and C. Neale Ronning, *Internal Security and Military Power: Counterinsurgency and Civic Action in Latin America* (Columbus: Ohio State University Press, 1966).

The challenges faced by the Roman Catholic Church in contemporary Latin America are discussed in the following books: John J. Considine (ed.), *The Church in the New Latin America* (Notre Dame, Ind.: Fides Publishers, 1964); William V. D'Antonio and Fredrick B. Pike (eds.), *Religion, Revolution and Reform: New Forces for Change in Latin America* (New York and Washington: Praeger 1964); and François Houtart and Emile Pin, *The Church and the Latin American Revolution* (New York: Sheed and Ward, 1965). Germán Guzmán, *Camilo Torres* (New York: Sheed and Ward, 1969) is a sympathetic account of the life and work of the radical Colombian priest killed in 1966.

❧ THREE ❧

THREE FACETS OF CHANGE

Although all of the Latin American republics have experienced change during the twentieth century, discussion of the sources, extent, and consequences of the change is more likely to produce disagreement than consensus. Such differences of opinion are, of course, the result of the complexity of the task confronting those who attempt to identify the patterns of change and the forces, institutions, and individuals responsible for its occurrence.

The fact that both Mexico and Cuba have experienced radical change as the result of violent revolution perhaps facilitates to some extent the analysis of developments within these countries. The initial phases of both the Mexican and Cuban revolutions were characterized primarily by demands for political reform and the restoration of constitutional government, but in both countries the triumph of the revolutionaries brought far-reaching social and economic changes which drastically altered the structure of society. In Mexico, reform occurred sporadically over a period of three decades, reaching its apogee during the administration of Lázaro Cárdenas from 1934 to 1940. Cuban society, on the other hand, was transformed within three years of Fidel Castro's assumption of power and, it has been argued, without significant pressure from the supposed beneficiaries of the Revolution. The Cuban Revolution also differed from that of Mexico in that its leaders formally embraced Marxist-Leninist ideology, though the Communist Party played a role different from that foreseen by Lenin. The key events of the Cárdenas administration are described in the readings in the first section of Part Three, while the selections in the third section discuss various aspects of the Cuban Revolution.

It is more difficult to determine the extent to which the Perón era in Argentina—the subject of the second section in Part Three—can be labeled as revolutionary in the sense of having effected or even attempted the destruction of the established order. Even if Peronism is regarded as being essentially nonrevolutionary, however, the emphasis of the regime on industrialization and economic independence—both of which were imperfectly achieved, at best—justifies its being classified as an agent of change in the twentieth century. Perhaps even more important in this respect is the fact that during the Perón era the Argentine worker not only made real economic gains through wage increases and improved social security benefits, but he also acquired a new sense of self-awareness and importance. As an Argentine labor leader explained to an American political scientist in 1963: "Look, before 1945 we had nothing and we were nobody. Since 1955 we haven't had anything either, but we know we're somebody. And because of him." [1]

---

[1] James W. Rowe, "Argentina's Durable Peronists: A Twentieth Anniversary Note" (Part I), *American Universities Field Staff Report* (April 1966), pp. 22–23.

[A] Mexico Under Cárdenas

❧ 20 ❧

The Ideology of the
Mexican Revolution

———◄►◆►———

Moisés González Navarro

*The six years (1934–1940) during which Lázaro Cárdenas (1895–1970)
occupied the Mexican presidency constituted the culmination of the
revolutionary process that had begun in Mexico in 1910, for Cárdenas
surpassed any of his predecessors in his efforts to make the primary
objectives of the Revolution, particularly agrarian reform and economic independence, a reality. The ideological course of the Revolution is traced in this selection by Mexican historian Moisés González
Navarro, who maintains that the inauguration of Cárdenas brought to
power a new generation, which used Marxism to revivify the faltering
Revolution.*

If by ideology is meant the combination of doctrinal foundations of
any system—political, economic, and so forth—and by revolution the
violent change of the social structure, then the study of the ideology of
the Mexican Revolution should be limited to its destructive phase

From Stanley R. Ross (ed. and tr.), *Is the Mexican Revolution Dead?* (New
York: Knopf, 1966), pp. 177–187. Copyright © 1966 by Stanley R. Ross. Re-
printed by permission of Alfred A. Knopf, Inc. Deletions in the text are by
Stanley R. Ross. Italicized bracketed notes in the text are by Helen Delpar.

and the period immediately following. Nevertheless, from convenience, inertia, or whatever reason, it is pretended that the Mexican Revolution is something like a permanent revolution and therefore has not ended, and that one can speak of the armed conflict initiated fifty years ago and of the present more or less peaceful epoch as a single social phenomenon. We provisionally accept the unity of the Mexican Revolution from 1910 to present.

First, it is appropriate to indicate the dominant features of the society which the Revolution sought to destroy or, at least, to replace. The Porfiriato was fundamentally characterized by the predominance of a system of large estates coupled with an incipient industrialism which was beginning to displace the handicraft economy dependent on the international trusts.

Positivism, the dominant philosophy of modern Mexico, was beginning to be attacked by the Athenaeum of Youth. [*Mexican educator and man of letters*] Justo Sierra himself, having overcome his Spencerian positivism of thirty years earlier, in his speech inaugurating the National University referred to philosophy as that beggar figure which for years has loitered on the periphery of official education and than which there is "nothing more respectable or more beautiful." It does not appear that the Athenaeum of Youth directly influenced the formulation of the revolutionary ideology, although some of its members participated in the Revolution—principally on the side of Francisco Villa. Nevertheless, it is possible that by breaking with the official philosophy the Athenaeum of Youth contributed to a broadening of the spiritual horizon of the intellectuals who fought in the Revolution, although there can be discerned traces of positivism in certain revolutionary politicians and especially in the *Carrancistas* [*followers of Venustiano Carranza*].

Some consider the journalists who opposed Díaz's regime as the ideological precursors of the Revolution, but besides being a very heterogeneous group—including classical liberals like Iglesias Calderón, Catholics preoccupied with social problems like Trinidad Sánchez Santos, and the Flores Magón group—only the last named could be considered as precursors since the others were reformers.

During the final years of the Porfiriato, writers like Calero, Emilo Vázquez, Querido Moheno, and Madero prepared the ground for political change. They were the theorists of political reform, exponents of the interests of a landed bourgeoisie and an intellectual middle class which seemed to view the Revolution solely in terms of the slogan popularized by Madero: "Effective Suffrage. No Re-election."

Obviously there existed a much more serious ill than the need for political change. The defenders of the old regime surmised that although Madero's slogan was relatively moderate, the movement he headed was capable of unleashing a social cataclysm. Therefore there is nothing strange about the vile language with which the newspaper *El Debate* . . . defined the contending elements: "Before Madero is the mass, the stupid multitude, half-naked and pestilent, which cheers the sandal and the peasant cloak and lacks only a hurrah for the louse!" Those who saw in this conflict a more profound ill were not mistaken. Francisco Bulnes said it in December 1911: "The profound and true causes of the revolution for the popular elements were neither 'no re-election' nor 'effective suffrage,' because what they really needed were 'no misery and effective—cheap and abundant—nourishment.' "

A month earlier Emiliano Zapata had issued the Plan of Ayala in which he proclaimed his opposition to the oblique form in which Madero sought to resolve the agrarian problem. According to the account of one of Zapata's biographers, this plan was the direct result of the work of the peasant leader in collaboration with Professor Otilio E. Montaño. In passing, it is appropriate to mention the important role which elementary teachers played in the formulation of the revolutionary ideology, since a goodly number of them served as advisors to the military leaders and some of them even came to occupy important governmental posts. Perhaps this helps to explain why the formulation of the revolutionary ideology was weakened by that "watered" culture . . . of which the elementary teachers are the best exponents.

The hunger for land was a general aspiration, but its nebulous initial formulation at certain times and places gives the impression that the agrarian revolution began as a simple *jacquerie* [*peasant revolt*]. That even the Porfirian authorities recognized the existence of the agrarian problem can be observed in Porfirio Díaz's presidential message of April 1, 1911, and in the proposal presented by the Secretary of Development to the Chamber of Deputies on May 13, 1911 to use national lands for the creation of small landholdings. There were many other proposals made by individual reformers associated with the old regime and by members of the 26th Legislature in 1912 which sought to resolve this problem by indirect means such as making agricultural credit available, aiding the farmers through irrigation projects, and establishing a tax policy favorable to the small farmer. Aside from their superficiality, these measures failed in the atmosphere of political instability after the fall of Díaz, during the transitional (and, in reality, restorative) regime of León de la Barra and the vacillating policy of Madero.

The agrarian projects of the 26th Legislature reached a radical climax on December 3, 1912, with Luis Cabrera's proposal for the restitution and granting of lands to the *ejidos*. It was Cabrera's view that Andrés Molina Enríquez's book *Los grandes problemas nacionales*

(*The Great National Problems*) was judged disdainfully by those who had no interest in solving the agrarian problem and carried no weight with them because it did not cite French, English, or German authors and was limited to an analysis of the national reality. Almost twenty years later Cabrera explained that this book by Molina Enríquez was the most important precursory social document of the Revolution and that even in 1931 he considered it "the best catalogue of our national problems" because in it the division of the haciendas, the promotion of small landholdings, and the protection of communal property were studied in depth. However, he added that neither Madero nor the democratic revolutionaries had read the book. Cabrera had talked long and frequently with Molina Enríquez about the agrarian question. From him Cabrera drew his agrarian ideas, but applied them in accordance with his personal experience—experience which prompted him to regard as the fundamental problem the reconstitution of the ejidos by effective and radical means, rather than by juridical evolution as recommended by Molina Enríquez. Carranza, due to pressure from some of his military chiefs and the necessity of snatching the agrarian banner from Zapata, or because he was convinced of the need for solving the ejido problem arising from actual experience in the center of the country, promulgated the Law of January 6, 1915, the work of Luis Cabrera. According to Molina Enríquez, the nine introductory clauses justifying this law summarized ideas which he had expressed in his book . . . : to give land to those who, due to their stage of development or lack of economic resources, were not able to adapt to the individualistic system of property established by the Spanish conquest.

In summary, the Revolution in its agrarian aspect has some characteristics of jacquerie, received its greatest impulse from Zapatista tenacity, and had its best formulation in the ideological work of Molina Enríquez, in the legislative work of Luis Cabrera . . . , and in the drafting of Constitutional Article 27 in which Pastor Rouaix played a decisive role.

The Revolution was until 1917 fundamentally agrarian. However, it also had sought to solve the problems of the workers despite the fact that the number of industrial workers was not great. Nevertheless, during the Porfirian regime labor had become better organized, with the miners, railroaders, and textile workers constituting important union groupings.

With the organization of the Casa del Obrero Mundial (House of the World Worker), anarchosyndicalism—of Catalán origin—achieved some importance which increased when the "Red Battalions" participated in the armed conflict in support of Carranza. Except for this contribution, well defined but lacking legislative consequence, the revolutionary ideology in this field as well appeared and developed spontaneously.

There was a positive coincidence in the timing of the proposals for the protection of the workers which emanated from diverse and even opposing political groups. Huertist deputies . . . , renovator deputies . . . , Juan Sarabia and Heriberto Jara among the independent legislators, various revolutionary governors, and the Sovereign Revolutionary Convention . . . presented between 1912 and 1915 various legislative proposals dealing with working women and child labor, industrial accidents, Sunday and holiday rest, payment in real money, suppression of company stores, legal recognition of unions, the right to strike (this last particularly proposed by the conventionists), and so on. This does not imply that the conservatives would have accepted the Revolution itself, for this presupposed not only recognition of those social guarantees, but also destruction of the power of the old regime.

During the reign of Díaz various Catholic congresses were held, due principally to the efforts of Trinidad Sánchez Santos and Bishop José Mora y del Río. During the initial years of the Revolution they continued their work, including the enactment of some legislation, particularly in Jalisco. In regard to employer-employee relations they reached the point of anticipating, in some respects, the Constitution of 1917. But in regard to the agrarian problem they proceeded more cautiously, almost always proposing indirect means for its solution. Because of the accusation, directed against some segments of the clergy but generalized to include all wearers of the cloth, of having supported Huerta's regime, there resulted the paradox, especially in the 1920's, of the revolutionaries attacking the clergy with the Church's own social doctrine, accusing them of opposing the social work of the Revolution in contradiction to Christian thought.

The revolutionary ideology arose spontaneously and was elaborated in the heat of conflict. Madero and Carranza, for whom the Revolution was principally political, found themselves obliged by more radical elements to adopt agrarian and labor measures. Until then, the Revolution had had a democratic character with regard to its political and agrarian (predominantly small landholding and only secondarily communal) aspects. It had also been nationalistic, laical, and anticlerical (although this last characteristic was almost unknown in Zapatism). Professors and [*Mexican agricultural workers in the United States, the*] *braceros* (frequently influenced by Protestantism) contributed to the formulation and spread of the revolutionary ideology. That ideology, down to the Constitution of 1917, even in its most radical aspects was the work of a rising urban middle class which sought to protect the great peasant masses and the growing worker groups while respecting and augmenting the capitalist structure.

Luis Cabrera called this initial stage of the Revolution "the revolution of then" in contrast to the Cárdenist "revolution of now" which he considered as communist. This conflict presented an obvious struggle of generations which General Cárdenas noted in his message of November 30, 1938, when he accused certain veterans of the Revolution of trying to confine it within rigid limits, thereby preventing it "from being perfected by its own dynamic virtue." He went on to charge that they were ignoring the fact that the Mexican Revolution was an "indivisible combination of popular aspirations which does not stagnate, but rather flourishes as an organic movement of renovation." Those veterans were seeking to block the revolutionary youth, who because of their age had not been able to participate in the warring phase, from developing a new dynamic of the Revolution.

In effect, the generation which had made the Revolution during its initial phase had almost disappeared or was well advanced in years: Ricardo Flores Magón and Madero were born in 1873; Antonio Díaz Soto y Gama and Pastor Rouaix in 1874; Luis Cabrera, Federico González Garza, and Pablo González in 1876; Francisco Villa, Plutarco Elías Calles, and Aquiles Serdán in 1877, and so on. On the other hand, the generation which collaborated with General Cárdenas was born during the final decade of the last century: Vicente Lombardo Toledano in 1894; Eduardo Suárez and Cárdenas himself in 1895; Manuel Ávila Camacho in 1897; and Luis I. Rodríguez in 1905, bringing the group into the present century.

However, the conflict was not only a matter of generations, but also involved divergent concepts of the revolutionary ideology which, of course, corresponded to the interests of different groups. When the Revolution underscored its agrarian character in the Constitution of 1917, those who had participated in the interest of political change, like F. Vázquez Gómez, considered the new fundamental law Bolshevik while Roque Estrada predicted agricultural ruination as a result of the ejidal program. On more than one occasion Molina Enríquez insisted to Obregón that the object of the Revolution had been to divide the large estates in order to expand the small individual property with a resultant increase in agricultural production, and to give ejidal lands to the communities in order to free the peons from the servitude of the haciendas and convert them into free day laborers. For his part, Pastor Rouaix was convinced that the purpose of the Revolution was to create a vigorous middle class whose existence and development could already be discerned.

The "constructive era" of the Revolution, initiated with the Plan of Agua Prieta [*1920*] with the object of providing guarantees both to nationals and foreigners and most particularly of protecting industry, commerce, and every variety of economic activity, was continued faithfully during the decade and a half which separated this plan from the Cárdenas period. If that tendency had been continued, the Revolution would have begun its Thermidor with Cárdenas.

Cárdenas' six-year term has the distinction of having made the Revolution more radical, employing an ideology—Marxism—which differed from that of the initial phase of the movement. Marxism had had a gilded era during the years from 1917 to 1925, and then under Cárdenas the gospel of Marx, mixed with certain traditional nationalist aspects, received a kind of extraofficial sanction.

Immediately strengthened was the agrarian concept which viewed the ejido as preferable to the small property and as an end in itself, rather than as mere salary supplement for the day laborer. This does not mean that Cárdenas endeavored to establish a Marxist regime— although education was given a Marxist orientation complete with demagogic excesses—inasmuch as the capitalist structure of the country was maintained, although limited, to be sure, by a firm and fundamental application of Constitutional Articles 27 and 123, which frequently were justified with Marxist terminology. Perhaps it is justifiable to distinguish those doctrines which helped to destroy the old regime from those which, in re-elaborated form, created the new. Perhaps in the same way that Proudhon, Kropotkin, Henry George, and others were used to attack the past (without all their ideas being utilized), Marx was utilized to rejuvenate—to bring up to date—the Mexican Revolution. . . .

It has been said that it is significant that the two most eminent North American investigators of the Mexican economy, Simpson and Mosk, writing fifteen years apart, should have seen fit to emphasize respectively the ejido and the industrial revolution. For those who see the Revolution as an integrated process, the emphasis on industrialization is merely the new concrete task for the Revolution. They argue that this new task was made possible by the expansion of the national market resulting from Cárdenas' land reform. Rejecting the facile characterization of Cardenism as more or less a peasant philosophy, they explain that the Cárdenas regime stimulated industrialization by the creation of the *Nacional Financiera,* the establishment of the National Polytechnic Institute, and the expropriation of foreign petroleum holdings which facilitated the task of subsequent regimes. Cardenism apparently has the double significance of having made the Revolution more radical and, simultaneously, of having accelerated the growth of its antithesis. During the last two decades the Revolution emphasized one of its objectives at the expense of the other: the strengthening of a national bourgeoisie over a proletariat which should collaborate in this undertaking well protected by the social guarantees established in the Constitution of 1917.

The present era of the Revolution appears to be its true Thermidor. Certainly the goal of Madero is far from being attained. We have passed from democratic Jacobinism—perhaps a bit ingenuous, but nonetheless sincere—to an enlightened despotism reminiscent of the ideal of the Porfirian *científicos*. It could be assumed that the preference which in recent years has been accorded to the small property, favored by irrigation projects and only infrequently acquired by illicit means, would have satisfied the agrarian thinking of men like Molina Enríquez, Cabrera, and Pastor Rouaix. The emphasis on the necessity of social peace clearly reveals the pre-eminence of bourgeois over proletarian interests. Revolutionary thinking is increasingly an urban and academic product, in contrast to the initial years when it was agrarian and spontaneous.

According to Mannheim, utopia is the complex of ideas which tends to change the existing order while ideology is the complex of ideas which spurs activity to maintain it. In this sense, the revolutionary "utopia" has been converted into a true "ideology": revolutionary rallying cries are now repeated almost like mere slogans.

⤳ 21 ⤵

The Cárdenas-Calles Break

Albert L. Michaels

A veteran of the Revolution who had attained the rank of division general and had served as governor of his native state of Michoacán, Cárdenas was picked for the presidency in 1933 by ex-President Plutarco Elías Calles, who had been Mexico's strong man since the assassination of Alvaro Obregón in 1928. Although his election was a certainty, Cárdenas embarked upon a then unprecedented "whistle-stop" campaign tour that took him into the most isolated corners of the republic; one of his first acts upon taking office in December 1934 was to move out of the sumptuous Chapultepec palace into more modest quarters. Calles named Cárdenas' first cabinet, and it was expected that Cárdenas would be a puppet president, but the new chief executive soon showed his determination to assert his independence from Calles. The reasons underlying the conflict that ensued are discussed in this reading by Professor Albert L. Michaels of the History Department of the State University of New York at Buffalo.

Lázaro Cárdenas and Plutarco Elías Calles had much in common. They had fought side by side in the Revolution and in the civil war against Pancho Villa. As Calles rose to power, Cárdenas faithfully backed him against all opposition. As a reward for this loyalty, Calles oversaw Cárdenas' appointment to several important national posts in the late 1920s and the early 1930s. The two men were good friends, yet it was inevitable that they part as enemies.

In 1934 Lázaro Cárdenas was young and vigorous and he wanted to govern in fact as well as name. Furthermore, he and his supporters wanted power for themselves. They knew Calles would have to go before they could have real power. As Frank Tannenbaum has noted:

From James W. Wilkie and Albert Michaels (eds.), *Revolution in Mexico: Years of Upheaval, 1910–1940* (New York: Knopf, 1969), pp. 219–221. Copyright © 1969 by James W. Wilkie and Albert Michaels. Reprinted by permission of Alfred A. Knopf, Inc. Italicized bracketed notes in the text are by Helen Delpar.

"Traditionally speaking, the President of Mexico must be able to do everything or he will be unable to do anything he wants."

By 1933 Mexico was tired of *Callismo* [*rule by Calles*]. The Catholics had been placed in a tight position and were desperate. The *campesinos* feared they would never own the land that had been promised them. The workers were chafing under the dictatorship of [*labor leader Luis*] Morones and his moratorium on strikes. The younger politicians wanted the positions of authority so long held by Calles' friends. Furthermore, Calles' ideas were out of date; his capitalism and individualism, which were a heritage from the prevalent liberalism of the nineteenth century, had been temporarily discredited all over the world. Even across the northern frontier President Roosevelt was experimenting with social reform. It was only natural for the Mexican to want a "New Deal" of his own. In the Six-Year Plan [*of 1934*] Calles attempted to meet the demands of the new generation, but this effort came too late. The radicals no longer trusted him; a vacuum had been created that sooner or later would have to be filled.

General Cárdenas came from the poor, overpopulated state of Michoacán. He grew up in a region with a tradition of Indian collectivism and a centuries-old struggle of the poor for a right to live. This background made him particularly open to Marxist theories based on collectivism and the struggle of poor against rich. He had gone into the country and had seen that the poor needed immediate help. It was, therefore, not surprising that he expressed a popular nationalism based on class warfare with immediate benefits to the oppressed classes. General Calles came from the richer, sparsely populated state of Sonora with its tradition of mining and small ranching. In Sonora, the enemy had been the man across the border in the United States rather than a countryman of a different class. The Northerner was proud of his white blood and skeptical of the Indian's ability to become the equal of the Spanish-descended white. Cárdenas, on the other hand, loved the Indian and named his son Cuauhtémoc after the Aztec hero. As Cárdenas readily accepted collectivism and class warfare, Calles opted for a nationalism of individualism and class harmony. He believed in a measured economic development benefiting all classes equally. He thought that by giving free rein to the man of ambition and initiative, individuals could develop the economy as the Spaniard had developed the North. Once economic development was underway, the rewards would trickle down to all classes. Both of these ideas of collectivism and individualism were enshrined in the Constitution of 1917. Calles extracted the latter ideal and attempted to mold Mexico in its image; Cárdenas extracted the former and tried to build a collectivistic Mexico. Both men had the same aim, the development of Mexico for the Mexicans, but they were trying to use different ideological tools to achieve this object. Calles and Cárdenas represented different nationalisms; they were bound to clash, and it was this clash, as much as political rivalry, that led to the split of June 1935, followed by Calles' self-exile.

When Calles returned to Mexico after six months in order to re-establish his position, he found himself in difficulties which finally resulted in his deportation by the Cárdenas government on April 10, 1936.

22

Formation of the PRM

————◄◆►————

Robert E. Scott

After Cárdenas had established his political authority over Mexico, he proceeded to a drastic reorganization of the official Partido Nacional Revolucionario *(PNR), which had been founded in 1929 at the instigation of Calles. The result was the* Partido de la Revolución Mexicana *(PRM), which was organized on the basis of four functional sectors: agrarian, labor, popular, and military. The events that led to the formation of the PRM are recounted here by Robert E. Scott, Professor of Political Science at the University of Illinois.*

During the first years of his term, President Cárdenas' left-liberal policies were in strong contrast to the growing evidences of conservatism (or, perhaps, of self-aggrandizement) displayed by General Calles. Before he could hope to assert his own attitudes fully, however, the president had to reorganize the political power structure in his own favor. For two years, therefore, Cárdenas realigned the principal functional power groups participating in national politics and particularly in the PNR.[1] Where previously its permanent membership had been composed primarily of government employees and office-holders, the party now sought workers and peasants on the basis of alliance with their trade unions and the inclusion of members of *ejido* communities. By 1936, the revolutionary party could boast of a membership of almost a million members.

In rebuilding the power structure of the PNR, Cárdenas was careful not to arouse the enmity of existing interests. He appeased the bureaucrats by supporting legislation establishing the theory of a permanent civil service and recognizing the right of government employees to strike, as well as by granting them economic benefits. He

---

From Robert E. Scott, *Mexican Government in Transition,* rev. ed. (Urbana: University of Illinois Press, 1964), pp. 127–134. © 1959 and 1964 by the Board of Trustees of the University of Illinois. Reprinted by permission of the publisher. Italicized bracketed note in the text is by Helen Delpar.

[1] Organized in 1929, the PNR, or *Partido Nacional Revolucionario,* was the official political agency of the Mexican Revolution. [H. D.]

attempted to impose as many national and state officers who were personally loyal to him as possible, but he carefully avoided open conflict with General Calles' adherents, at least until he could organize the mass bases of his strength. In doing this, the president had all of the advantage on his side, for General Calles had long since lost sight of the interests and needs of labor and agrarians, as well as direct contact with lower-rank politicians. As chief executive, on the other hand, Cárdenas had all of the legal and extralegal resources of government to win their support, and both groups were ripe for organization.

No new, dynamic labor organization had risen during the years of the puppet presidents to replace Luis Morones' Regional Federation of Labor (CROM) after it had lost official support, together with most of its national political importance, first during the election campaign of 1928 and later with the formation of the PNR. Similarly, the integration of the politically active part of the old *agrarista* party [*Partido Nacional Agrarista—the National Agrarian Party*] into the PNR had left the rank-and-file agricultural worker with few independent farm organizations and less leadership. President Cárdenas had merely to offer a minimum of government support to a clever organizer and these potentially important sources of political power would speedily rally to his standard. He found the man for his purpose in an ambitious young leftist intellectual, Vicente Lombardo Toledano.

Lombardo Toledano had been one of Morones' more able aides in the CROM, but when the CROM fell from favor he left it in order to organize his own group, the General Confederation of Mexican Workers and Farmers (CGOCM). Under his able leadership, conveniently coupled with the friendly influence of the 1931 federal Labor Code, the CGOCM grew until it could act as the nucleus for a new and more inclusive labor and farm organization. This new agency came into being in 1935 as the Mexican Federation of Laborers (CTM). From the very first the CTM flourished, for widespread knowledge and evidence that it enjoyed presidential favor attracted previously independent unions and encouraged individuals to join the new unions its organizers set up. Its membership, which included both industrial and agricultural workers, soon became the single largest organized group in Mexico.

Despite the friendly assistance Cárdenas had offered Lombardo Toledano, the president had no intention of putting a monopoly over the massive political power represented by a combination of labor and agriculture into the hands of a possible rival. Nor did he want these newly awakened interests to overbalance the other factors of the revolutionary power structure. Consequently, Cárdenas set the official party organization to work establishing separate Peasant Leagues in each state, "with the help of the federal personnel of the executive dependencies . . . , principally the Agrarian Affairs Department and the Secretariat of Public Education," as one PNR publication puts it. These state Leagues were then united in a National Farmers' Federation (CNC), to which some of the previously organized CTM agricultural groups were then attached.

Quite naturally, the leaders of the CTM objected to depletion of the group's membership by taking from the parent organization the farmers it had organized. Only the strength of the president's personality convinced Lombardo Toledano that he should give up the farm groups he had formed, and then he did so with the understanding that the component members of the newly independent CNC Peasant Leagues should have the right to consult with the CTM on matters of mutual interest.

By the beginning of 1936, as a result of these organizing activities, the major organized interest groups, with the exception of the army, were led by individuals personally loyal to President Cárdenas. The old Mexican game of playing one political force against another in order to balance out possible rivals finally had worked against General Calles; he had not kept up with the growth of the new political forces. Only the military remained to be won over or kept neutral, and if the generals had personalistic ties to the older general they also liked the younger general. President Cárdenas held most of the trumps in his hand.

The climax came when General Calles made his first overt attack on the administration's liberal policy of permitting industrial strikes, together with a thinly veiled threat against the president himself. A so-called Proletarian Defense Committee rallied to the side of President Cárdenas immediately. This show of organized strength, backed by the bureaucrats, together with the obvious intention of the army to remain neutral, was sufficient to decide the great mass of politicians. In April, 1936, General Calles was forced to leave Mexico, demonstrating graphically to anyone who might need further convincing that President Cárdenas was master of the political situation.

Once his undisputed leadership had been established, the president cast about for means of formalizing relationships among the various organizations and interests, both in and outside of the PNR, which had supported his administration. For a time he seemed to favor formation of a Popular Front similar to those in France and Spain at the time. Early in 1937, the CTM sent out feelers on the matter to the PNR, to the farmers' organizations, and to the Communist party, although the Labor Code at that time specifically forbade political action by unions.

Nothing ever came of the plan, however, for various reasons. The army completely rejected any coalition including the Communists.

Moreover, the chance of any coalition of leftists succeeding had diminished markedly about this time, for the arrival of Leon Trotsky in Mexico had split them wide open. The Communists would never enter a government accepting the presence of the exiled Russian, but he could not be expelled without alienating other important leftist leaders. On this issue, Vicente Lombardo Toledano, following the Communist party line, came into almost open conflict with General Francisco Múgica, who accepted Trotsky. This disagreement may have cost either Múgica or Lombardo Toledano the nomination at the next presidential election, for they had been the two most likely heirs apparent. Certainly it weakened the position of the leftists, resulting in the nomination of Manuel Ávila Camacho, a middle-of-the-roader. Diego Rivera, too, accepted Trotsky, suffering a long excommunication from the Communist party as a result. A few years later he recanted his heresy, but it was only a short while before his death in 1957 that he managed to win readmittance to the party.

Most important, the concept of a Popular Front simply did not fit the needs of Mexican political conditions. It had developed as a political device in countries where an institutionalized multiparty system already existed. Rather than a device of this sort, which would turn interest groups into competitive hard-core class parties, during this period Mexico required some sort of political mechanism that could channel the activities of the developing specialized interests into a constructive and integrated political system. As a consequence, President Cárdenas gave the projected Popular Front the *coup de grace* when, in December, 1937, he called for dissolution of the PNR and formation of a new revolutionary party.

The PRM—Corporate Centralism

The new Party of the Mexican Revolution took as its organizational basis a corporate structure embracing the diverse interests which supported President Cárdenas' version of the Revolution. Although no attempt was made to change the conventional system of geographically designated electoral districts established by the Constitution of 1917, the PRM abandoned the classical concept of nominations on the basis of popular primaries.

The party's corporate structure divided organized political activity into four functionally based "sectors"—agricultural, labor, popular, and military. Where once candidates had been selected by the entire party membership, voting in national, state, or local primaries, the revolutionary party's candidates now were to be apportioned among the several sectors. Before each state or national election, the sector organizations, meeting jointly, determined how many and which candidacies, except the presidential one, were to be allotted to each sector.

The sector organization or, in actual practice, the sector's leadership, then named individual candidates for the offices allotted to it. The individuals so nominated then were supported in the campaign and at the polls by the combined efforts of all four sectors. The only exception to this practice was that the military sector did not nominate or participate in local and state-level elections. Not unexpectedly, considering that members of the same party manned the electoral machinery and counted the votes, the candidates so nominated enjoyed amazingly uniform success at the polls.

Presidential nominations also reflected a corporative tendency. Selection of the revolutionary party's candidate at the national nominating convention required the support of a majority of the sectors, at first three of the four and later, when the military sector had been dissolved, two of the three sectors.

Taking their cue from President Cárdenas' speech calling for formation of the new party, official apologists stressed two points. The PRM was a genuine national organization, in that both popular participation and the sources of financial support had been broadened considerably. Second, they pointed out, at long last the military had been brought openly into politics, obviating the need for its constant illegal intervention in political affairs.

As to the validity of these points, it certainly is true that the PRM represented a broader scope of interests than had its predecessor, and that temporarily at least the military did participate formally in politics. Moreover, the new sector organization represented rather faithfully the structure of power that Cárdenas already had developed in the old PNR during the last few years of its existence. Most of the interest groups and functional organizations in existence at this time which could or would work with the new, more active revolutionary leadership were included in one of the four sectors.

The basic unit in three of the four sectors was the local organization —the Peasant League, the labor union (or confederation of local unions), or the political association. These in turn were grouped in a statewide federation of other similar functional units, according to sector. The state federation then represented the organizations in the state affiliated with the sector in a nationwide sector organization. The only sector not so organized was the military, which employed the regular army subdivisions as its units.

The *Confederación Nacional Campesina,* with its paper membership of two million (every *ejido* farmer was enrolled automatically), became the farmers' sector of the new party. Although its effective membership undoubtedly was a good deal smaller than was claimed, the CNC broadened the base of members in the party and strengthened its dominant role in Mexican politics, for the isolated and politically naïve farmers were easily manipulated by their leaders. The announced aims of the farm sector were to hasten land distribution, to combat local officials who obstructed land reform or other activities beneficial to the farmer, to carry grievances to the national capital, and in general to aid peasants in solving their problems. In practice, a fair start was made in achieving these goals, for the CNC was at that time the only agency formally representing agriculture in the official party, so that its leaders had an enormous influence over the president in all phases of policy-making for the farmer. This was especially true while Cárdenas was president, for he identified Mexican progress and fulfillment of the revolutionary goals with agricultural development to a greater extent than have any of his successors.

The Labor sector also had a mass membership but, unlike the farmers, even in 1937 no single agency represented the organized workers. The Mexican Federation of Labor (CTM), at that time still led by Vicente Lombardo Toledano, dominated the sector and took the lion's share of patronage, but other labor organizations participated in its activities. Among these were two federations, the *Confederación General de Trabajadores* (CGT) and the Treviño CROM, which had split from the Morones CROM, together with the independent electricians and miners unions. Because most labor organization was concentrated in a few urban centers, the smaller membership and divided representation of the Labor sector were compensated in some measure by disciplined action and unity of interest.

The third sector of the PRM, the so-called Popular sector, included a membership as functionally heterogeneous as those of the Labor and Farmers sectors were homogeneous. The real strength of the organization lay in the Federation of Government Employees' Unions, the FSTSE, representing both state and national bureaucrats. They were included here because President Cárdenas felt they should not have any directly shared political interest with nongovernmental organized labor. Certain nonindustrial unions, organizations of professional persons, youth groups, cooperative societies, and a number of miscellaneous organizations also acted through the Popular sector, which was divided into ten functional branches. In a sense it served as a catchall for any of the party's supporters who did not fit into another sector. As such, with the exception of the leadership of the other sectors, the Popular sector included virtually all of the former members of the old PNR.

It is hardly surprising that so diverse a membership had difficulty in organizing for action. Not until 1943 was it possible for a constituent convention to meet to set up the National Federation of Popular Organizations, the CNOP, which was to act as the formal mechanism uniting the member agencies. Even with the CNOP to act as a coordinating device, some of the components of the Popular sector have been restive. The FSTSE, for example, has sought a stronger role in the sector. Indeed, in 1946 and several times during the 1950's the government unions bid unsuccessfully for a sector of their own.

Considering its amorphous membership, the Popular sector was remarkably successful in obtaining patronage and in influencing policy. Undoubtedly this can be attributed to the nature of its membership for, as we know, in Mexico, the middle-class, professionally trained person represents a much higher degree of intensity of political action than does the less well-educated farmer or laborer. In the PRM as then constituted, and in the official party today for that matter, this group has political importance all out of proportion to its numbers.

Establishing a Military sector in the PRM touched off a tremendous furor. It was argued that the army had never acted officially in national politics, and that the precedent should be retained. In reply it was suggested that as the real power in Mexican politics, or at least the strongest single factor of power, the military's political activities should be brought out in the open where it could be held accountable for such activities. And it was true that at that time army officers held well over half of the more important positions in the government service, elective or appointive.

The military itself seems to have had little desire to be placed in the arena of politics. In December of 1940, after less than three years of existence, the Military sector was dissolved, with most of the officers holding elective offices passing to the Popular sector. This does not mean that the army divorced itself from politics. On the contrary, having returned to its old position behind the throne, the military's role in Mexican politics has remained strong and partisan. Acting through the Popular sector, although in recent years its activities have been somewhat less obvious than formerly, the military continues to wield a very important influence in policy-making.

23

"The Land Belongs to Him Who Works It"

Betty Kirk

Unlike Calles, whose agrarian ideal was the yeoman farmer and who was disappointed with the results of agrarian reform in Mexico, Cárdenas was fully committed to continued reform and to the ejido *system of communal land tenure. During his administration, approximately 40 million acres of land were distributed, and by 1940 nearly five million Mexicans, or one-fourth of the total population, lived on ejidos. In this reading, Betty Kirk, who was a newspaper correspondent in Mexico during the Cárdenas era, describes the effects of agrarian reform in the Laguna cotton district of northern Mexico, where collective ejidos were established, and the expropriation of two haciendas growing commercial crops in the state of Michoacán. Despite Miss Kirk's generally favorable report, it should be noted that, although the Cárdenas administration completed the destruction of the old hacienda system, rural prosperity was held back by the poverty of the Mexican soil and by the ignorance and technological deficiencies of the Mexican peasantry.*

The crusade which Zapata led and which was legalized by the constitution was apathetically applied for the next twenty-four years, until the presidency of Lázaro Cárdenas. During this period land was divided spasmodically, but no organized financing or direction of the divisions was made until the Cárdenas régime. And in six years Cárdenas broke up more estates and gave them to the peons, with financing from the newly created Ejidal and Agrarian banks, than were divided by all of his predecessors. The most dramatic of these divisions and the one which became the proving ground for the agrarian policy was the Laguna cotton district in the northern states of Coahuila and Durango.

During the last week in August, 1937, Minister of Finance Suárez

From Betty Kirk, *Covering the Mexican Front* (Norman: University of Oklahoma Press, 1942), pp. 109–118. Copyright 1942 by the University of Oklahoma Press. Reprinted by permission of the publisher. Italicized bracketed note in the text is by Helen Delpar.

invited a group of bankers and insurance men and Mexican and foreign newspaper correspondents to visit the Laguna district as his guests. We left Mexico City by train for the six-day trip to the vast cotton region, popularly known as "the Egypt of Mexico" because of its fine and abundant production. Arriving there, we found the heat sweltering and the air powdery with dust, but there was a spirit of intense activity. The land had been divided in October, 1936, by President Cárdenas personally, and this trip was made to inspect the results of a year of communal operation.

The entire Laguna region consists of 880,000 acres, of which only 250,000 are capable of cultivation because of the lack of water. In 1930, at the peak of private ownership, there were only 332 holdings in the region—131 haciendas, 93 ranches, 10 *ejidos,* 77 lots, and 21 parcels of land. The big estates were mainly owned by Spanish, British, German, and North American companies, and their fabulous profits were sent abroad to absentee landlords and stockholders.

The Cárdenas division broke them up, and in place of the 332 owners, 31,000 families numbering 150,000 people were given 220,000 acres of land. This served two principles of the agrarian policy by abolishing absentee landlordism and giving the peasants land, but it marked a shift not only in ownership but also in responsibility for development of the property.

.   .   .

Our headquarters for the trip were Torreón, from which we travelled by car and train to see the great experiment in operation. We found fine haciendas and good workers' houses left from the old régime, fields under cultivation and cotton being picked and shipped, and the first examples of the vast social program for education and emancipation which accompanied the economic phase. These included open-air theaters, sports fields, and schools. This program is administered by a council of social action in each *ejido* which supervises education, sports, hygiene, hospitals, theater, and lectures, all designed to make a modern, politically conscious Mexican out of the feudal peon. The social program is supported by 5 per cent of the total income of each *ejido.*

The region was divided into twenty-four zones, each directed by a zone chief directly responsible to the federal government. Each chief supervised from ten to twenty-eight *ejidos* in such matters as taxes, consumers' associations, financing, education, hygiene, and sports. Directly responsible to the zone chief was the labor chief of each *ejido,* elected by vote of his community. He instructed the farmers in cultivation, organization, construction, and social activities. His aide was a representative of the National Bank of Ejidal Credit, the federal financing organization.

Weekly charts were kept of the work of each individual, these serving as the basis for his pay when the crop was sold. *Ejido* charts of the progress of each community were kept and used as the basis for loans and financing. The unit of credit was the ejidal society to which the National Bank of Ejidal Credit lent money for maintenance, seeds, machinery, and livestock. This financial structure was the most important contribution of the Cárdenas régime to land division, for it enabled the farmer to operate with credit, as the *hacendado* had, until his crops were harvested. Former failures in land division were attributed to lack of financing.

The previous minimum wage in the district was 1.50 pesos a day, and the Ejidal Bank advanced this sum to each farmer for maintenance. When the harvest was sold the sum advanced was deducted from each farmer's share, plus an approximate 25 per cent to cover the cost of seeds, machinery, and livestock. The government had provided for that first year 330 tractors, 153 motors for electrical plants, 6,000 tons of cotton seed, 1,750 tons of wheat seed, and 23,500 mules. It also supplied a staff of agricultural and technical experts to supervise the farming. The remainder was divided according to the work each man had done, as recorded on his work chart.

The most radical change wrought in the status of the peasant was in this yearly lump profit, a sum in which he could never before have shared when on a salary basis, and which directly reflected the amount of work he himself had done. We were taken to what was, of course, the model *ejido* to see the Minister of Finance hand out to each peasant his profit for the year. The most industrious man received 1,450 pesos, the least industrious, 278 pesos. Before, such profits had always been shipped abroad to be spent in other markets, and the Mexican spokesmen pointed out that even though under communal operation production had slumped from the previous year, the money earned would be spent in Mexico to strengthen the Mexican economy and raise the general standard of living. The total amount given out by Señor Suárez that day was seventy-two thousand pesos to sixty-five men for the operation of the *ejidos* of Barcelona and Londres. Moreover, this profit represented only the proceeds from the cotton crop, and a fine wheat crop was yet to be harvested.

This was obviously a show place, for other *ejidos* in the region did not do so well that year. Some had plagues, others hailstorms; all suffered from insufficient water; some were definitely mismanaged and graft was rampant. Yet a leading banker who had lent money to the *hacendados* for years admitted that on an average only two out of five years in the Laguna were good years, depending on weather conditions, and that the profit made in the two years made up for the three years' losses. Moreover, all the financiers granted that no such

profound economic experiment could be judged after a year's operation, that its results could be appraised only after five or ten years.

It was fascinating to talk with these bankers who did not take the
die-hard attitude expected. All were willing to take the long view of
the ultimate national welfare, and they praised the experiment,
particularly the dam-building program which we saw in operation a
few days later. Luis Legorreta, manager of the conservative Banco
Nacional de México, said that the banks would continue to support
the government's program so long as no deficit occurred. Such a deficit
would lead to public unrest and the curtailment of the entire public
works program, and he advised a wide margin in calculations for
government expenditures.

A more enthusiastic appraisal was made by Alfonso Rivas, sub-
director of the Banco de Transportes. "My hat is off to Cárdenas,"
he exclaimed. "Although I am a conservative and don't see eye to
eye with his policy, when a man will refuse a bribe of 365,000 pesos
[$100,000] which was offered him not to divide this land, he com-
mands respect. His greatest weapon is his honesty. If the government
can find money to continue its program, it will be a success. The
government has to have money and I think it will be found in Mexico.
Cárdenas is attacking from all fronts because he has to. He can't build
dams until there are roads to transport materials, and he can't get
goods to markets and ports until there are railroads. Mexico is through
with revolution. We are inoculated against it by our own social serums.
We anticipate the demands being made by the people and satisfy those
demands as much as possible."

.   .   .

My invitation to see the actual division of the haciendas of Lombardía and Nueva Italia came both from President Cárdenas, via
Agustín Arroyo Ch., and from the *hacendado* himself, Don Ezio Cusi.
With such a welcome from the opponents in the drama I accepted with
alacrity. The invitations came at Lake Pátzcuaro, where I had gone for
a weekend on November 1, 1938. I left the lake and my weekend trip
stretched into two of the most absorbing weeks I have spent in Mexico.

Sr. Cusi, whose nephew Ezio I had known before, arranged for me
to go from Uruapán to the haciendas and be received there by his
managers. After a brief stay in Uruapán I was put on a truck going to
Lombardía and *tierra caliente*—"the hot lands." We drove for some
hours over miserable roads, passing en route the deserted hacienda of
Los Bancos, which had been divided four years before. It was a picture
of utter desolation, the formerly fertile sugar-cane fields only partially
cultivated by the *ejidatarios'* straggling plots. The Cusi truck driver
indignantly pointed it out as an example of the failure of land division and spoke glumly of the coming division of his employer's

estates. Los Bancos was in fact a glaring example of the futility of giving the land to the peons without financing and technical supervision to teach them to produce. But by that time I had learned that the very value of the Cárdenas program lay in its economic structure, supplied at the same time as the land.

We arrived at Lombardía at midday, and the Italian managers and Spanish overseer welcomed me graciously. The house itself is modest, not one of the luxury establishments customarily maintained by Mexican landowners. It was a strictly utilitarian building with a row of six bedrooms and a dining room opening onto a shady veranda, with kitchen and service rooms behind. I was given the best bedroom, which I yielded to President Cárdenas when he arrived a week later. Already installed in the hacienda were a number of young government agricultural engineers and Ejidal Bank experts, making preliminary surveys for the division. One had his wife and two babies with him, and it was interesting to hear the philosophy of a modern Mexican woman who loyally accompanies her husband on his many travels.

The week in the tropical setting of humming insects and rustling leaves went monotonously by as we waited for the President to arrive. It was my first visit to a hacienda, and it was satisfying to see at first hand the self-sufficiency of its feudal organization. The house and garden were set off in an enclosure made by high walls with an enormous entrance, like that of some ancient walled castle. Flanking these walls were the hacienda stores and paymaster's office, and there was always a detachment of soldiers quartered there to insure peace. Beyond straggled the village.

Included in this elaborate organization were factories for extracting lemon oil (a base for perfumes), an ice factory, a corn-grinding mill, a rice mill, a dairy, a bakery, a butcher shop, a general store, a hardware store, and workshops. Employment was given to caretakers, water controllers for the irrigation works, cowboys to handle the cattle, carpenters, iron workers, mechanics and truck drivers, burro drivers, loaders, pickers and packers for fruits and rice, planters, cutters, harvesters, and office workers. Lombardía was a little compact country all in itself, as was Nueva Italia, some miles away.

The hacienda was founded by Commendatore Dante Cusi, who had come from Italy to settle in Mexico's hot lands in 1898 during the Díaz régime. He settled in this valley between the foothills of the Sierra Madre mountains, but found it thirsting for water. As early as 1902 he began the vast irrigation works which now stretch for miles and which have converted virgin soil into the finest rice- and lime-producing region in Mexico.

At the time of the expropriation the two haciendas produced yearly

25,000,000 pounds of rice; 72,000,000 limes; 3,000,000 pounds of corn; 254,000 pounds of sesame; 20,000 pounds of *cascalote* (an oil used for tanning); 15,240 pounds of lemon extract; and 2,000 head of cattle. The irrigation system included forty miles of principal channels and two hundred miles of smaller ditches which irrigated half of the 150,000-acre estate. Moreover, this treasure house was capable of producing abundant sugar cane, cocoanuts, peanuts, and a vast number of perishable fruits and vegetables, whose production had not been pushed because of lack of transportation.

One morning, accompanied by an Indian *mozo* [*youth*], I rode on horseback across the fertile fields to see the Cusis harvesting their last crop. The air was humid, the sun dazzling, and it was like going into a fairyland to see the streams bedded with water lilies and the fragrant fields waving with the slender heads of rice. The *mozo,* too, loved the rice, and as he stood for me to take a picture he said softly, "They are beautiful, the rices . . ." Returning late from this trip, I found that a special Italian meal had been prepared, under the supervision of "Don Panchito" Ghibellini, the hearty old man who had planted the great lime orchards and called the trees his "children." That day of fiesta we had a luscious spaghetti and our dessert was whipped cream with honey, followed by fruits and cheese.

Late in the following afternoon, swiftly and silently the President arrived. After days of waiting he came, like an Indian fighting guerrilla warfare, with suddenness and surprise. He went first to Lombardía, where we had gone to meet him, and he entered its broad street between lines of girls dressed in China Poblana costumes, children, *ejidatarios,* and a band. He drove directly to the orchard near the schoolhouse, draped with bunting and flowers. There in the dense green light of late afternoon he sat and ate with the co-operative workers at bare wooden tables. The meal consisted of tortillas, barbecued meat, salad, and fresh cocoanut milk. That night he was serenaded by a *mariachi* band playing beneath his windows and by the throbbing *harpa grande,* the tom-tom of the tropics.

· · ·

The President was surrounded by politicos, like a bullfighter with his *cuadrilla.* These included Gildardo Magaña, governor of Michoacán and an old Zapatista, Gabino Vázquez, head of the Agrarian Department, Julián Rodríguez Adame, head of the National Bank of Ejidal Credit, General Francisco Múgica, Agustín Arroyo Ch., and Antonio Villalobos, head of the Labor Department. The next afternoon they went to the bull ring, which is the center for sports and ceremonies at every hacienda, and there the President received a great ovation. Governor Magaña made the official dotation, reading from a decree which repeated the words of Emiliano Zapata: "The land belongs to him who works it." The bull ring was decorated with palm fronds and jammed with men, women and children. The ceremony was repeated the next day at Nueva Italia and the Cusis were no longer the owners of their land.

Meanwhile, late at night I had seen men moving in and out of the office, talking with the Cusis. They were arranging payment for the equipment. One million pesos was paid a few months after the expropriation, and another million in the spring of 1940. This was for the lime trees, sixteen thousand head of cattle, farm machinery, buildings, rice mills, and the rice and lime crops then being harvested. No payment was made for the land. This same system had been used in liquidating the private properties in the Laguna.

⊷§ 24 §⊶

Expropriation of the Foreign-owned
Oil Industry

◆◄◉►◆

William Cameron Townsend

The most dramatic event of the Cárdenas administration was un-doubtedly the President's expropriation of the properties of foreign (British and American) oil companies on March 18, 1938. Although tension between the Mexican government and the companies had been almost continuous since the promulgation of the constitution of 1917, which vested direct ownership of subsoil deposits in the nation and permitted their exploitation by private firms only through concessions granted by the government, the motive for the expropriation was a labor dispute between the companies and the oil workers' union, which demanded higher wages, fringe benefits, and what would have been in effect a closed shop including white-collar employees. After the oil workers struck on May 28, 1937, the controversy was brought before the Federal Board of Conciliation and Arbitration, which, following the recommendations of a three-man investigating com-mittee, ordered that the workers be granted a substantial wage increase and other benefits. The companies then appealed to Mexico's Supreme Court, which ruled on March 1, 1938, that they would have to comply with the Board's decision. After last-minute efforts to reach a settlement proved unsuccessful and the companies indicated their unwillingness to abide by the Supreme Court's ruling, Cárdenas decided to nation-alize the oil properties, basing his action on an expropriation law passed in 1936. In this selection, William Cameron Townsend, a non-sectarian missionary from the United States and a close friend of Cárdenas since 1935, describes public reaction to the President's de-cision.

From William Cameron Townsend, *Lázaro Cárdenas, Mexican Democrat* (Ann Arbor, Mich.: George Wahr, 1952), pp. 256–259. Reprinted by permission of the publisher. This article appears as reprinted in James W. Wilkie and Albert L. Michaels (eds.), *Revolution in Mexico: Years of Upheaval, 1910–1940* (New York: Knopf, 1969), pp. 235–240. Italicized bracketed notes in the text are by Helen Delpar.

The companies expected the government to place their properties in a receivership which would have given them time to work. The government, hampered by the economic problems that the companies could have created had they been permitted to keep their fingers in the pie, would have found it impossible to have run the business successfully. The companies were in a better position to withstand a long drawn-out struggle than Mexico was. They thought, too, that by prolonging the conflict they would be able to profit from divided opinion among the Mexicans themselves and would be able to build up anti-Mexican opinion in the United States.

President Cárdenas, however, realized that every moment of delay made the companies more powerful in their position and placed the government more at their mercy. He determined to take from them their power to cripple the nation from within. Without serving notice to anyone, not even to solicitous [U.S.] Ambassador [Josephus] Daniels who might have been able to bring the companies to their senses had he been able to warn them how serious their situation had become, he went before the microphone on March 18, 1938, and announced his decree of expropriation against the seventeen oil companies. Speaking to the nation, he said:

> A total halt or even a limited production of petroleum would cause in a short time a crisis which would endanger not only our progress but also the peace of the nation. Banks and commerce would be paralyzed, public works of general interest would find their completion impossible, and the very existence of the government would be gravely imperiled because when the state loses its economic power it loses also its political power, producing chaos.
>
> It is evident that the problem which the oil companies have placed before the executive power of the nation by their refusal to obey the decree of the highest judicial tribunal is not the simple one of executing the judgment of a court, but rather it is an acute situation which drastically demands a solution. The social interests of the laboring classes of all the industries of the country demand it. It is to the public interest of Mexicans and even of those aliens who live in the Republic and who need peace first and afterward petroleum with which to continue their productive activities. It is the sovereignty of the nation which is thwarted through the maneuvers of foreign capitalists who, forgetting that they have formed themselves into Mexican companies, now attempt to elude the mandates and avoid the obligations placed upon them by the authorities of this country.
>
> The attitude of the oil companies is premeditated and their decision has been too deliberately thought out to permit the government to resort to any means less final, or adopt a stand less severe [than expropriation] . . . I call upon the whole nation to furnish such moral and physical support as may be needed to face the consequences that may result

from a decision which we would neither have wished nor sought had it depended on ourselves alone.

The people did respond with their full support. The President's bold stroke appealed to their patriotism and they became united as I have never seen them before or since. A great manifestation of confidence and support took place in the capital five days later, and it was my privilege to observe from a point of vantage that spontaneous mobilization of feeling on the part of the Mexican people.

The notes I made right on the spot will describe it:

I sit writing in a large room on the second floor of the National Palace which forms one side of the *Plaza de la Constitución* (*El Zócalo*). Here at crucial times throughout many centuries events of utmost importance in the history of Mexico have taken place. On a balcony nearby stands President Lázaro Cárdenas accompanied by members of his cabinet and scores of other officials watching the greatest popular demonstration which has taken place in this land during recent years.

The broad plaza, flanked on our right by the anciently solemn but stately cathedral, and on the left by the more modern Municipal Palace, is thronged with thousands of people, while thousands more march by beneath the President's balcony in a steady stream which will continue for hours and then flow on out into history as Mexico's second Declaration of Independence.

Just above where President Cárdenas stands waving a frequent recognition to the acclaims of the laborers and students as they march before him, there hangs the very bell which Hidalgo the priest rang one hundred and twenty-eight years ago in the far-off town of Dolores, announcing the intention of a handful of patriots to fight for the political independence of Mexico from Spain.

Last Friday, March 18, President Cárdenas figuratively rang the bell for economic independence by declaring that his government would not bow before the oil interests, principally British and Dutch, in their defiance of the Supreme Court which had found the demands of their employees for better wages and working conditions to be just. The impasse which resulted when the companies balked left the President no other alternative than to take over most of the oil industry.

Consternation has resulted in financial circles. The foreign colony here in Mexico City is decidedly partisan to the oil interests, fearing that what has been done will serve as a precedent for the confiscation of their own investments. Some declare their intention of selling out while they can and returning to their respective countries, though others say that they are making such large profits they will remain as long as they can buy more trinkets and can go more places with the same number of dollars.

President Cárdenas, in an effort to calm industry in its very reasonable fear of further confiscation, published a statement yesterday calling the attention of the public to the emergency conditions under which the expropriation law was resorted to in the case of the oil industry, and promising that it will not be applied to other enterprises. On the contrary, he promised that they will be given every encouragement possible.

The Bank of Mexico has had to redeem ten million *pesos'* worth of its bills with silver coin during the past few days, but the run seems to be over and plans have been formulated to mint fifty million more silver pesos so that there will be ample coin in circulation if the lack of confidence in bank bills should continue.

I stop writing long enough to step out onto a balcony and watch the Communist section march by. It consists of just a handful of demonstrators sandwiched in the multitude. They carry a large red banner which reads, "The Communist Party of Mexico," and a white and red one which says something about "On with the International Revolution." It is noteworthy today that the red and black emblems, which had almost supplanted the Mexican flag in parades here a few years ago, are less in evidence, while the national colors of green, white, and red are seen everywhere.

Labor unions, peasant leagues, and syndicates of schoolteachers and other federal employees have called a halt, temporarily at least, in their almost incessant petitioning for rights. The majority of the people have forgotten for the moment to complain against the rising cost of living, injustices, and this, that, and everything, in order to join in the nation-wide rally to the support of their daring leader.

Perhaps the Mexican Revolution has passed into a new phase as regards the psychological basis of its program. For a number of years past it has endeavored to teach the masses, long trained to subserviency, to rebel against all imposition and to demand their rights at every step. Very little was said about duty. The pendulum swung so far in that direction, especially during the first two years of the administration of General Cárdenas, who democratically insists that the only citizenry which can be properly and enduringly developed is one which is free and realizes that it is free, that at times chaos threatened not only laborers but also in the ranks of the schoolteachers and other government employees. Many observers wondered how a sense of duty would ever be instilled into them. The emergency of today, however, may perform the necessary miracle.

Two hundred thousand people are parading, carrying banners which express their approbation in terms such as these: "Down with imperialism," "The laborers desire the economic independence of Mexico," "General Cárdenas, you are the only one who has had the courage to defend our rights," and "President Cárdenas, we are with you in the enthusiasm of today and we will be with you in the struggle of tomorrow" (the economic struggle which will be necessary for Mexico to pay for the expropriated property).

The President, of course, must realize that he has bitten off a chunk which will require all his exceptional energy and that of his colleagues to chew to a point of semidigestion during the remaining three years of his administration. Everyone knows the government has been spending every *centavo* it could lay its hands on to promote development projects among the peasants where returns will be very slow to materialize. They know that for three months it has been hard put to meet its minimum obligations, due largely, it claims, to deliberate efforts on the part of the oil companies to embarrass it financially. How, then, can it hope to pay the large sum required to reimburse the companies even over the ten-year period which the expropriation law permits and at the same time meet the demands of the laborers?

Perhaps the rebirth of patriotism which is in evidence today will prove to be the solution of the situation. Not only the laborers, but the thinking citizenry in general realize that the honor of the nation is now at stake, and a do-or-die attitude seems to have been aroused. Both labor unions and government employees have declared in printed statements a willingness to tighten up their belts ten notches if necessary and sacrifice until Mexico has met the obligation with which she has saddled herself.

A united and duty-conscious Mexico *can* refund the oil companies. The industry which has been 90 percent foreign-controlled, something which we would never permit in the United States, will then be placed at the service of the nation. The living conditions of the laborers will be improved, and further exploitation will be directed by the consideration of national expediency rather than by the whims of foreign interests.

◆§ 25 ◆◆

Reaction of the Oil Companies

◆━━━◆━◆◆

E. David Cronon

After the oil companies realized that Cárdenas had no intention of rescinding the expropriation decree of March 18, 1938, and after the United States government acknowledged Mexico's right to expropriate the oil properties provided prompt and adequate compensation was made, the companies demanded a huge sum from Mexico, including payment for oil still underground. Settlements with both the American and the British firms were finally reached in the 1940s. In the meantime, as Professor E. David Cronon of the History Department of the University of Wisconsin shows here, the companies spared no effort to damage the reputation of the Cárdenas government and to block the export of Mexican oil.

With minor variations, watchful waiting was to be the companies' strategy for the next three-and-a-half years. The companies were convinced that they could accept nothing less than immediate compensation for their properties, including subsoil rights, without jeopardizing their position in other countries. They were certain, too, that the Mexicans could not successfully operate the oil industry alone. In any event, Mexico must be dealt with firmly so that no other country would be tempted to follow her lead. "If Mexico can get away with its present arbitrary act there is no safety for American property anywhere in Latin America or elsewhere," warned Thomas R. Armstrong, a Jersey Standard vice president early in July [1938], "and, sooner or later in some part of the world, drastic action will be called for." Laurence Duggan [chief of the State Department's Division of American Republics] believed the oil men were anticipating the early collapse of the Cárdenas regime, but [Josephus] Daniels [U.S. ambassador

From E. David Cronon, *Josephus Daniels in Mexico* (Madison: The University of Wisconsin Press; © 1960 by the Regents of the University of Wisconsin), pp. 207–211. Reprinted by permission of the publisher. This article appears as reprinted in James W. Wilkie and Albert Michaels (eds.), *Revolution in Mexico: Years of Upheaval, 1910–1940* (New York: Knopf, 1969), pp. 241–245.

to Mexico], who passed this report on to President Roosevelt, declared, "To me this looks like a vain hope."

Vain or not, the oil companies were doing everything possible to make President Cárdenas' position untenable. Immediately after the expropriation they launched a boycott of Mexican oil based upon their control of most of the world's tanker fleet and their obvious capacity to retaliate against independent tanker operators. By legal action they sought to tie up Mexican oil shipments abroad. They also persuaded a number of American manufacturers to refuse Mexico's prepaid cash orders for equipment needed to operate the oil industry. By 1940 this boycott was even being applied to American export firms suspected of supplying Mexico. When Westinghouse closed down its Mexican branch in 1939, [Ambassador] Daniels reported that the local company representative believed the move was the result of pressure by Rockefeller and power interests.

The companies' boycott of Mexican oil was helped by quiet support from the State Department. In 1939, for example, Secretary Hull blocked the purchase of Mexican fuel oil by American ships on a naval cruise, explaining in a policy directive: "This department as a policy matter of considerable importance would not consider it desirable for any branch of the United States government to purchase Mexican petroleum products at the present time." The State Department continued this ban on government purchases of Mexican oil until early 1942, some months after the general diplomatic settlement with Mexico. Moreover, it encouraged Latin American governments to take a similar stand against Mexican oil. Even when they were low bidders, American suppliers who offered Mexican oil were unable to get U.S. government contracts. When one such firm protested, it was told by the State Department's legal adviser that Mexico must not thus "reap the fruits of this wrongful act." The Sinclair interests discovered to their surprise and great unhappiness that acceptance of a settlement with Mexico in 1940 did not necessarily remove the taint from their oil. Jersey Standard quickly objected when Sinclair underbid it on a large Navy contract in the fall of 1940, and received State Department help in getting the Sinclair bid rejected. The Department also frowned on private operations in Mexican oil. An official advised the T.A.D. Jones Company of New Haven, when it sought approval of a profitable import deal, that it was "fishing in troubled waters." It seemed hardly a coincidence, too, that the representative year used by the department to set import quotas for foreign oil was 1939, when because of the boycott Mexican imports were at a minimum.

The oil interests also went to considerable pains to mobilize American public opinion. Jersey Standard's company magazine, *The Lamp,* began portraying Mexico as a strife-torn land of revolutionaries and brigands. Through their service stations, the companies warned American tourists against undertaking a trip into Mexico. Motorists were advised that there was danger of an uprising, their personal property might be in jeopardy, travel by car was unpleasant and hazardous, and even the Mexican railroads were unsafe. Wide publicity was given to the claim that Mexican gasoline was dangerously inferior. Its octane rating was alleged to be only 48, barely adequate to operate an automobile engine at minimum power.

Standard Oil of New Jersey made a special effort to publicize the companies' side of the dispute, sending a public relations expert to make the rounds of leading newspapers and magazines. At least one reporter, Seward R. Sheldon of the *Cleveland Press,* was offered an all-expense trip to Mexico if he would write a series of articles to "put the people right." Sheldon declined the invitation, but others went to Mexico to write highly partisan reports. For example, newspaper publisher Henry J. Allen, a former Republican governor of Kansas, toured Mexico briefly in the summer of 1938, and returned with a series of articles charging that Cárdenas was a dedicated Communist who was determined to establish a Soviet Mexico. One news service refused to handle the Allen articles as too obviously propaganda, but they were ultimately syndicated by the New York *Herald Tribune,* excerpted in the *Reader's Digest,* and sent out in pamphlet form by the Committee on Mexican Relations, an obscure group financed by Jersey Standard. After having thus qualified as an expert on Mexican affairs, Allen traveled about the United States demanding that the administration abandon the Good Neighbor Policy and force Mexico to return the oil properties.

Perhaps the most ambitious attempt to promote the cause of the oil interests came in July 1938, when the *Atlantic Monthly* published a special issue entitled "Trouble below the Border." Like the Allen articles, this was a thoroughly procompany analysis of the controversy, designed to persuade its readers that Mexico was sliding into dangerous chaos as a result of radical leadership. Daniels called it "rotten oil propaganda," a view that was reinforced after he learned from Duggan that the issue had been paid for by the companies. When the *Nation* exposed the source of the oil used to lubricate the *Atlantic*'s presses for this particular run, the magazine's embarrassed publisher could only retort lamely, "Well, we have our racket and you have yours." *Collier's* published a highly partisan article repeating company claims that Mexico's oil industry was rapidly breaking down under incompetent government direction, and charging that to Mexicans the term expropriate was "a polite, international word for 'steal.'" But when Mexico submitted an article in reply, *Collier's* refused to print it.

Writers who tried to be more objective in their reporting sometimes found it difficult to get their material into print, at least without significant editing. Anita Brenner, well qualified by years of residence in Mexico, did a balanced and informative article for *Fortune,* but after Daniels compared her original draft with the published version he predicted, "she will not recognize her own baby." Himself a journalist for more than half a century, Daniels winced at such threats to the integrity of his profession. . . . In view of the companies' careful efforts to mold public opinion, it was hardly surprising that a detailed survey of American publications in 1939—paid for by Standard Oil of New Jersey—showed that the press was overwhelmingly on the side of the oil interests in their dispute with Mexico.

❦ 26 ❧

The End of an Era

Albert L. Michaels

In 1940 Cárdenas was able to transmit power peacefully to former War Minister Manuel Ávila Camacho, despite the efforts of opposition candidate General Juan Andreu Almazán. President Franklin D. Roosevelt gave his blessing to the successful candidate by sending Vice President Henry A. Wallace to represent the United States at Ávila Camacho's inauguration on December 1, 1940. The administration of Ávila Camacho marked the beginning of a new era in Mexican history, often called the Thermidor of the Mexican Revolution, during which emphasis would be placed on industrialization rather than agrarian reform and on consolidating the gains of the Revolution rather than continued struggle. Professor Albert L. Michaels, the author of Article 21 as well as this selection, examines the reasons that led Cárdenas to choose the moderate, relatively unknown Ávila Camacho as his successor in preference to the more radical General Francisco Múgica, seemingly a more logical choice.

During the 1933 presidential campaign, Lázaro Cárdenas had defined the nation as "a territory whose natural wealth the people enjoy in common." In his six-year term Cárdenas conscientiously sought to make Mexico fit this definition. To a large degree he succeeded; his popular government divided much of the land, expropriated the oil holdings, and infused Mexican labor with a new sense of purpose. More important still, he encouraged both the urban and rural proletariat to form strong organizations, which theoretically could defend their rights no matter who the President might be. Furthermore, Cárdenas improved education, gave the Army a national identity, and established a truce with Mexico's Catholics. In 1940 Mexico was more closely integrated for the masses than it had ever been in all its previous history. Yet in 1940, for reasons that he has never explained, Cárdenas turned

From James W. Wilkie and Albert Michaels (eds.), *Revolution in Mexico: Years of Upheaval, 1910–1940* (New York: Knopf, 1969), pp. 273–278. Copyright © 1969 by James Wilkie and Albert Michaels. Reprinted by permission of Alfred A. Knopf, Inc. Italicized bracketed note in the text is by Helen Delpar.

over the government to Manuel Ávila Camacho, a soldier who stressed the importance of economic improvement over social improvement. There were several considerations that might have influenced this strange choice.

James W. Wilkie in his study of the Mexican federal budget and its effect on social change gives the following description of the results of Cárdenas' policies:

> Cárdenas himself seized the opportunity that the crisis in political revolution presented to undertake the social restructure of Mexico. He not only definitively reoriented the economy away from the agricultural hacienda system, he also proposed to change the educational system and swiftly to integrate the Mexican people into a nation, a program which had been delayed since Mexico's independence in 1821. We have seen that his programs had little practical effect on the life of the common man, who remained illiterate, shoeless, isolated, underfed, and without sewage disposal. A large number still could not speak Spanish by the time Cárdenas left office.

Cárdenas may have come to understand this by the end of his term; he certainly was no longer the unsophisticated popular nationalist who had entered office late in 1934. Like his predecessors, he may have come to the conclusion that Mexico had to develop wealth before it could achieve socialism. As Daniel Cosío Villegas once suggested to me: "Cárdenas had destroyed many things; perhaps he believed it was time to begin rebuilding."

The world situation no doubt also influenced Cárdenas' choice of Manuel Ávila Camacho. Cárdenas, a Marxist-oriented politician, always had hated and feared the world fascist movement. Mexico was one of the few nations to support actively the Spanish Republic against German and Italian aggression. The Cárdenas government officially protested fascist attacks on Austria, Albania, China, Poland, Belgium, and Norway. In 1938, in the midst of the oil crisis, Cárdenas secretly proposed to President Roosevelt that Mexico and the United States should support an economic boycott against aggressor nations, even though such a move would have ruined Mexico's German oil market. Later, in November 1940, Cárdenas stopped all oil exports to Japan. In the late 1930s, the Mexican government always made it clear that its sympathies lay with the Western Allies, and against Hitler and Mussolini.

In regard to presidential politics, Cárdenas must have felt that if a radical leftist like Francisco J. Múgica was to become president, the weak ties holding Mexico together might break, thus bringing on a civil war, such as Spain had experienced. If such a conflict developed, Mexico's middle classes and even the Army might be driven into the arms of cryptofascist groups like the *Sinarquistas*. On the other hand, a moderate soldier like Ávila Camacho would certainly have a better chance of uniting all Mexicans against the totalitarian threat than would have an intransigent radical like Múgica.

Unrest engendered by the world depression of 1929 greatly altered the fate of the official party's ideology. The economic crash of 1929 had destroyed faith in the laissez-faire capitalism, which had created prosperity in the United States. As a result even the newly rich like Calles and President Abelardo Rodríguez declared themselves in favor of strong state intervention in the economy. Seeking to keep political power and meet the economic crisis of the early 1930s, they decided that they could no longer justify gradual economic development within the capitalistic system. Lacking the mass appeal to meet the restlessness of the Mexican people, the *Callistas* [*followers of Calles*] turned to a more dynamic leader, Lázaro Cárdenas, who, to almost everyone's surprise, actually believed that the nation would only become united and peaceful if Mexico's wealth belonged to all of the people. Cárdenas strived to generate immediate social justice, and the Mexican proletariat responded to his program by giving him the mass support that he needed to supersede Calles.

The new concept of the nation rapidly spread to sectors previously hostile to the nationalism of the revolutionary government. The extreme left, heretofore internationalist, cooperated with the government. Justifying their position, the leftists, led by Vicente Lombardo Toledano, explained that nationalism was necessary in the struggle of an underdeveloped country against colonialism; however, they hoped that the necessity of having a nation would disappear in the coming world revolution. Even the Catholic right, which had previously opposed radical reform, took up popular nationalism. Authoritarian-minded Catholics flocked to the rabidly nationalistic Sinarquista movement, which promised to integrate the nation by halting class warfare. Both the extreme right and the extreme left had seen that they would have to espouse popular nationalism if they were to survive.

In 1939 political considerations again altered the face of the Mexican government's program. Faced with economic crisis and the rise of fascism, Cárdenas emphasized the unification of all Mexican classes over immediate justice for the proletarian class. In 1940 he presided over a campaign in which his hand-picked candidate abandoned the radical ideas that had inspired him in 1933. Cárdenas pursued this new policy, not because he had betrayed the Revolution, but because he was a pragmatic Mexican nationalist.

BIBLIOGRAPHY

Among the best books providing general coverage of the Mexican Revolution from 1910 to 1940 are Frank Tannenbaum, *Mexico: The Struggle for Peace and Bread* (New York: Knopf, 1950); Howard Cline, *The United States and Mexico,* rev. ed. (New York: Atheneum, 1963); and James W. Wilkie and Albert L. Michaels (eds.), *Revolution in Mexico: Years of Upheaval, 1910–1940* (New York: Knopf, 1969), a collection of readings. In *The Mexican Revolution: Federal Expenditure and Social Change Since 1910* (Berkeley: University of California Press, 1967), James W. Wilkie analyzes federal spending for social purposes and relates it to social change.

The contest between Cárdenas and Plutarco Elías Calles is recounted in John W. F. Dulles, *Yesterday in Mexico: A Chronicle of the Revolution, 1919–1936* (Austin: University of Texas Press, 1961), a detailed narrative stressing political events. Eyler Simpson, *The Ejido: Mexico's Way Out* (Chapel Hill: University of North Carolina Press, 1937) discusses agrarian reform in Mexico prior to the Cárdenas administration; the agrarian policies of the Cárdenas era and their consequences are described in Nathan L. Whetten, *Rural Mexico* (Chicago: University of Chicago Press, 1948). Three articles discuss conflicts between Church and state in Mexico during the Cárdenas years: Stanley E. Hilton, "The Church-State Dispute over Education in Mexico from Carranza to Cárdenas," *The Americas,* 21 (1964–1965), 163–183; Lyle C. Brown, "Mexican Church-State Relations, 1933–1940," *Journal of Church and State,* 6 (1964), 202–222; and E. David Cronon, "American Catholics and Mexican Anticlericalism, 1933–1936," *Mississippi Valley Historical Review,* 45 (1958), 201–230. On the rise of the CTM see Joe C. Ashby, *Organized Labor and the Mexican Revolution under Lázaro Cárdenas* (Chapel Hill: University of North Carolina Press, 1967).

Shirt-Sleeve Diplomat (Chapel Hill: University of North Carolina Press, 1947) is Josephus Daniels' account of his years as U.S. Ambassador to Mexico. Two contemporary descriptions of the Cárdenas years are *The Reconquest of Mexico* (New York: Oxford University Press, 1939), an extremely favorable interpretation by Nathaniel and Sylvia Weyl and *Reportage on Mexico* (New York: Dutton, 1941) by Virginia Prewett, an American reporter. For an analysis of the fate of the Revolution after 1940, see Stanley R. Ross (ed.), *Is the Mexican Revolution Dead?* (New York: Knopf, 1966).

[B] The Perón Era

❧ 27 ❧

Transformation of the Social and Political Structure

———◄◆►———

Gino Germani

Although Juan D. Perón (1895–   ) has lived in exile since his fall from power in September 1955, the phenomenon of Peronism remains a major factor in Argentine politics, and Argentina has not yet fully come to grips with the forces of proletarian discontent and economic nationalism which he unleashed. In seeking the roots of Peronism, historians usually focus on the consequences of several key developments in Argentine history after 1852: massive European immigration before 1914 and internal migration from rural areas to the cities after 1930; the concentration of landholding, which discouraged the formation of a rural middle class; the failures of the Radical Party between 1916 and 1930; and the moral and political bankruptcy of the conservative governments of the 1930s. In this selection, the Italian-born Argentine sociologist Gino Germani shows how these and other factors contributed to the emergence of Peronism in the 1940s.

From Joseph R. Barager (ed. and tr.), *Why Perón Came to Power* (New York: Knopf, 1968), pp. 110–126. Copyright © 1968 by Joseph R. Barager. Reprinted by permission of Alfred A. Knopf, Inc. Deletion in the text is by Joseph R. Barager. Italicized bracketed note in the text is by Helen Delpar.

The generation that assumed the task of developing Argentina into a modern national state was very aware of the contradictions between the simple rationalism of the independence-minded elite and the true nature of colonial society, which persisted during the first half of the nineteenth century as a result of the autocratic rule of the *caudillos*. Its members understood that no political reform would be possible until radical changes were effected in the social structure.

This generation was made up of "social realists" who used the philosophical and sociological thought of their time to understand the national reality, and they arrived at a distinct plan to effect substantial changes in the Argentine society. The essential measures for achieving this end were: education, foreign immigration, and economic development. These points summarize the plan of the so-called "Generation of 1837," of Sarmiento, Alberdi, Echeverría and others who formulated it and in part carried it out from the moment they secured power. But the ruling groups' action in fulfilling this program was no less contradictory than had been that of the revolutionary elite of May [*who directed the movement for independence*]: it should be remembered that in the end they constituted what came to be called "the oligarchy," a landholding bourgeoisie, despite its liberal motivation and sincere concern with transforming Argentina into a modern state. Undoubtedly, it was this position in the social structure that was the principal source of contradiction in its reformist efforts.

Let us see what happened with immigration. Its purpose was twofold: to "populate the desert" and to transform the population by giving it those features deemed necessary for developing a modern nation. In effect the ruling group tried to replace the "traditional" social pattern with one more appropriate for a modern industrial structure. At that time this transformation was regarded as a "racial" change and not the result of moving from one social structure to another. In the language of the times, it was a question of "bringing Europe to America," of Europeanizing the population of the interior, considered the major source of political instability and of backward economic practices.

With this in mind, the elite emphasized "colonizing" to make sure that the European immigrants would be rooted to the land. Although a surge of urban activities, industry, services, etc., also was desired, there can be no doubt that the immigration was definitely directed "toward the desert." What transpired only partially fulfilled these aims. Certainly the population was radically changed, and one of the features essential to understanding present-day Argentina is its large element of immigrant origin.

A radical change in the economic structure also took place with the emergence of Argentina as one of the world's leading producers of cereals and meats. But the social structure of the countryside was not changed as desired. No large and strong agrarian middle class, based on land ownership, emerged. Instead of "colonization" there resulted what some called a colossal land speculation that increased and reinforced the predominance of the great landholdings. By the early stages of massive immigration, the greater part of the most accessible and arable land was already in the hands of a few landholders. In 1914, after a half century of immigration, with foreigners representing no less than half the total active population, immigrants still made up only 10 per cent of the landowners. The traditional families had succeeded in maintaining and increasing substantially the latifundist pattern and in 1947 three fourths of the land was still concentrated in little more than 20,000 farming enterprises, less than 6 per cent of the total.

The legal pattern of land use was and continues to be land rental —or less favorable forms—and the place of a rural middle class was occupied in large measure by renters and small landowners, continuously exposed to all the favorable or unfavorable fluctuations of climate and the world market. Although some managed to prosper, the unfavorable economic conditions of the majority obliged them to be constantly moving in search of better working conditions and subjected them to all kinds of restrictions. In even worse conditions than these small landowners and renters were the landless peasants—salaried workers exposed to seasonal crop rotations, low levels of employment and low standards of living. One of the major and undesired results of this situation was the concentration of foreigners in the cities and the extraordinary urban growth.

TABLE 1
THE PROCESS OF URBANIZATION IN ARGENTINA 1869–1957

% Urban Population (Defined as those living in areas with 2,000 or more inhabitants)	Years
27%	1869
37	1895
53	1914
62	1947
65	1957

Undoubtedly, massive immigration and other innovations attempted by the elite directing the "national organization" from the second half of the past century onward meant a profound change in the country. But the social structure that thus emerged contained certain deviations from the ideal of achieving a stable base for a democracy. One of the most important impediments to democracy was the unfavorable rural structure and the resulting population distribution.

The elite wanted to populate the desert, and, in a certain sense, they did. But the population was largely concentrated in the cities; and instead of lessening the disequilibrium between the underdevelopment of the interior and the development of the Littoral, this further accentuated it. The consequences were made clear by the middle of the century.

The process of urbanization in Argentina developed in two great phases: the first, between 1869 and 1914, involved massive immigration from Europe; the second, corresponding to the period 1930/1935 to 1950/1955, was fed by internal migration on a massive scale.

The role of foreigners in the formation of the Argentine urban structure is clearly evident. Not only in cosmopolitan Buenos Aires, where 50 per cent of the population was made up of foreigners between 1869 and 1914, but also in the other cities where the proportion was also exceptionally high. Significantly, the larger the city, the greater the proportion of foreigners. Thus in cities of 100,000 and more inhabitants, more than one third—between 1895 and 1914—had been born outside the country. It should also be noted that in addition to this urban concentration there was another regional pattern. All the large cities were located in the Littoral zone, and foreigners generally settled there. As a result metropolitan Buenos Aires and the provinces of the Littoral always retained approximately 90 per cent of the immigrants.

This geographical concentration had a series of far-reaching effects on the social structure, involving the typical differentiation between "central" and "peripheral" areas with all its consequences for the political life of the country. Urban growth, combined with the expansion and transformation of the economy, inspired substantial changes in society: already, in the beginning of the present century, what we could call the traditional "boss" had been destroyed and replaced by figures more like the modern model. Also, as a result of other measures to spur economic development—attraction of capital, construction of railroads, legal reforms—the country became a great export center for cereals and meats. The new requirements of foreign trade, the impulse to internal activities given by great urban concentrations, and the accrued wealth of the country, stimulated the first industrial development.

Since the last quarter of a century modern industrial activity has emerged and expanded throughout the country, replacing the traditional handicraft methods; and although still centered on agricultural production, it had already reached a respectable volume by the first decade of the present century. At the same time the lower strata of the old society, largely rural, saw themselves replaced by an urban proletariat and a rapidly expanding middle class. Thus the "bipartite" traditional society (an upper class of large landholders versus a low stratum composed of the bulk of the population, with an intermediate stratum of little significance and usually identified with the upper class) was replaced in the central areas by the tripartite system (upper, middle, and lower classes). It could also be called multipartite, since the differentiation between levels, especially in the cities, becomes indistinguishable, and the structure assumes the image of a continuing series of overlapping positions in which the transition from one to another becomes difficult to perceive.

An Argentine middle class of a size and social and economic significance sufficient to be politically influential first appeared between 1869 and 1895. By the last decade of the nineteenth century it had become a group of great importance. It is necessary to remember that in the main it was an urban middle class, concentrated in the Littoral. Therefore, its weight is greater in the areas which play a central role in national life. Also, one must take into account the qualitative changes produced by the transition of the traditional boss to more modern types. The middle class, from its beginnings until the early part of the century, was composed mainly of men who had begun new activities: medium and small enterprises that comprised the commercial activity and nascent industry. Meanwhile the upper class— the traditional families—retained its broad control over the agricultural sector.

A smaller rural middle class was also formed from among the country people (campesinos) who achieved some prosperity and economic solidity. But this involved a minority group in comparison to the foreign immigrant masses and to the native rural population. Later, particularly after 1910, the middle class probably owed its growth largely to expansion of its "dependent" sectors—"white collar" workers, employees and public officials, professionals and technicians of the private and public bureaucracies. This change in the composition of the middle class also had political significance. In the lower, populous strata, the rural peons, the unskilled workers, the jobless, the old artisans, the domestic servants were increasingly becoming urban workers in industry, commerce, transportation, and services—that is, in activities carried out by modern enterprises and concentrated in the cities. This resulted in the movement of people from the "central" areas of the country to the cities, creating conditions favorable for the upsurge of proletarian movements which, in the pattern of the early stages of industrialization and urbanization, appear as social protest movements.

End of Limited Democracy and Political Participation
of the Middle Classes

The political significance of these changes is obvious: they brought about the entrance into national life of groups which had been separated from the old traditional strata. This implied the possibility (and necessity) that a functioning democracy—particularly in its most immediate manifestation, universal suffrage—would also include the recently formed classes. In other words, it involved political integration of the recently mobilized sectors of society.

Faced with this process, which would provide a base for the forming of a democratic state, the ruling elite did not seem disposed to share power, much less to cede it to the new groups being incorporated into the national life. The elite continued to aspire to a liberal democracy, in which participation was limited to the upper strata of society. Although in many other aspects the ruling elite's activities were progressive and open to greater participation of the popular strata in national life—for example, in education—there were certain limits which were very difficult or impossible to overcome in economic and political matters. In the first place, not only were the elite groups unable to renounce their monopoly of land, but they themselves profited from the economic transformation. Often the measures for development they chose were oriented more toward their own class interests than toward those of the nation. In the political field a prolonged struggle was necessary before the most progressive elements of that same "oligarchy" finally made universal suffrage possible and consented peacefully to participation in power by the new social groups. The first elections in which all the citizenry participated were held in 1916 and gave the government to men of the middle class, organized politically around the Radical Party formed three decades earlier.

This date, 1916, can be taken to mark the end of limited democracy in Argentina, and the beginning of representative democracy with full participation of the population, though it is difficult to fix rigid demarcations within such complex social processes. Moreover, this date was only the beginning of a long process which is still developing.

The transition from one type of democracy to another was characterized in Argentina by various features that helped make it particularly traumatic. In the first place, the country found itself in a somewhat paradoxical situation as a result of massive immigration. One essential but seldom remembered fact is that for thirty or forty years foreign-born people were much more numerous than natives. If one considers the effects of a double concentration—geographic and by age —the percentage of foreigners in categories most significant politically (male adults) and in the "central" zones (the capital and the provinces of the Littoral) one discovers the extraordinary fact that this figure reached some 50 to 70 per cent.

In terms of elections this meant that where participation in voting could have greatest importance, some 50 to 70 per cent of the inhabitants were not able to participate. In absolute figures, in 1895, of the 216,000 male inhabitants of the city of Buenos Aires, only 42,000 were native Argentines (and those naturalized amounted to less than 2 per cent). At this same date, in the provinces of the Littoral (Buenos Aires, Santa Fe, Mendoza, Córdoba, La Pampa, Entre Ríos), of over 600,000 adult males, 287,000 could exercise the right to vote as natives. If one considers the further drastic reduction in political participation derived from other social conditions, one can realize the full significance of the term "democracy with limited participation."

This problem of the lack of political participation by the majority of the population concerned the ruling groups of the era, but it is well known that in this respect the elite maintained its characteristic ambivalence. The stability of "limited" democracy was actually due in large part to this fact. It is very likely that the political effects of the appearance of the middle strata were considerably retarded by their predominantly foreign composition. The failure of the lower classes to form a party capable of representing them politically, was probably due to similar reasons. . . .

Landed property continued almost entirely in the hands of Argentines. Compare this with the situation in commercial and industrial development, where the managers of commerce and industry, and the industrial workers, were largely foreigners, and constituted a higher proportion of the middle class in the entire active population. Furthermore, in the lower, populous strata engaged in industrial activities (old handicrafts, domestic service) the native majority predominated. And of course among the rural population, especially in the interior provinces, natives also predominated. While the elite retained firm control over landed property, the middle class and the proletariat were formed in the cities on the basis of massive immigration.

As the children of immigrants became active and as the extraordinary proportion of foreigners began to lessen, these newly formed classes began to have a chance to exercise a *direct* influence on political activity. Here the word "direct" has particular importance. Obviously these majority masses, although marginal from the viewpoint of their electoral rights and of their political interest, exercised an indirect pull of great importance, although there are no studies or data that permit precise evaluation. In relation to the lower, populous class, the new classes nourished—as leader and as mass support—the great protest movements of the first decades of the century, and the middle strata provided the human element most propitious for the emergence of the movement that should have represented this sector politically in national life.

Thus in Argentina, the passage from elite government, with limited participation in democracy, to middle class government meant the incorporation of the foreign immigrant masses, or of their sons, into political life. But it is probable that the peculiar make-up of the population, and particularly the predominance of foreigners in the protest movements in the first decades of the century, meant a considerable delay in the formation of political organisms suitable for the urban proletariat. That element supported Radicalism, the expression of the middle classes, instead of forming a sufficiently strong party of their own (the Socialist Party had only local importance in the country's capital).

The Radical Party which governed the country for fourteen years until 1930 should have represented during that period all the new, emerging strata, but it did not fulfill that function. In fact, in no way did the Radical Party use power to bring about those changes in the social structure that might have assured a sounder base for the functioning of democratic institutions and tended to prepare the integration of all social strata as they emerged. It did nothing, or very little, to solve one of the basic problems of the country, the agrarian problem. Although until the end of this period conditions in the countryside were generally rather better than later on—and the stability of the rural population was much better, so that in those years there was less urban growth—the socio-economic structure of the countryside remained practically unchanged, since the means adopted were completely insufficient, when one considers the magnitude of the problem. With respect to the urban proletariat, the attitude of the Radical Party was no less ambivalent. Although numerous measures of social protection for the worker were adopted, the legislation was not only rather moderate, but it also often had no practical application. On the other hand, in spite of the climate of liberty enjoyed during the period, the workers' organizations did not see their functions facilitated. Legislation did not explicitly recognize the legal status of trade unions, although of course their functioning was permitted by the general dispositions of the Constitution. This lack of recognition, in an atmosphere where the higher strata openly opposed such organizations, made their work difficult and provided a very serious obstacle to the unions' role as a vehicle for progressive incorporation of the populous strata into the nation's political life. It is symptomatic that the Radical parliaments maintained the repressive legislation created by the oligarchy at the beginning of the century, opposing the first expansion of the workers' movements. In 1919 the Radical government did not hesitate to solve the social problems and commotion created by the postwar situation with a bloody repression.

The high percentage of foreigners during the era of emergence and development of labor movements probably served to impede the formation of a party that might have integrated them within the democratic structure of the country. On the one hand, in spite of their numerical and social importance in the population, they had to remain in a marginal position within the electorate. On the other hand, their foreign composition, combined with the internationalist ideology that so intensely characterized movements on the left during this era, probably contributed to placing such movements in an unfavorable light. This occurred precisely at the time when the incorporation of sons of immigrants was at its height, necessitating their firm identification with the new fatherland. One example is the undoubtedly nationalist character (in a democratic sense) of the UCR [Unión Cívica Radical] and its refined "isolation," particularly during World War I. . . .

Thus if the Radical Party, in spite of popular sympathy and support, was not capable of representing the proletariat politically, neither were the Socialist Party or the other organizations of the left. Moreover, as the Socialist Party "aged," it was gradually becoming more and more composed of middle class groups (owing to the intense ascendant mobility of the immigrants) and ended up representing only an alternate radicalism for the independent electorate.

Finally, the existence of "peripheral" areas, those large zones of the country in a state of underdevelopment, and the fact that the progressive incorporation of the inhabitants into national life was realized only in the central areas, in the Littoral and in zones of high urbanization—while the interior and the rural sections of the coast remained completely marginal—constituted another disturbing factor of fundamental importance for later development. In effect, it would have been essential for the political balance of the country (that is with regard to assuring the functioning of a representative democracy) that the strengthening of a democratic leftist party, endowed with the support and cohesion of the masses, be produced in the proper ideological climate; that is, within the tradition of leftist democratic thought such as occurred in the European countries that led the way in industrialization.

The Great Internal Migrations and Integration of the Popular Strata

Such was the situation in 1930, when as a repercussion of . . . the particular social structure of the country . . . and the world depression that rudely struck the Argentine economy, there was a change in the Argentine government. For the first time in many decades a constitutional government was overthrown by military intervention. This movement, which also reflected the new international political climate created by the emergence of Fascism in Europe, fundamentally signified the return of the "oligarchy" ousted from power by the Radical majority. But this "return" could not mean a return to the past and a kind of limited democracy in which political participation would be restricted to certain classes. It was to have meaning and consequences very different from the apparently analogous situation of a half century earlier. It was no longer a matter of the exclusion of the less developed sectors of the population as a result of the political "absence" or "passivity" of the less developed sectors of the population. Rather, the strata already fully "mobilized" would use compulsive means to ensure "exclusion." The principal means employed by those groups lacking the electoral support needed to secure power was systematic fraud, without the formal denial of the exercise of civil rights. Freedom of the press and of association were more or less respected, as were other rights sanctioned by the Constitution. But union activities encountered increasingly greater difficulties, and this, together with the frustration produced by the systematic manipulation of the popular will in elections, created a feeling of deep skepticism among the majority of people. This was a skepticism which continued to be influenced by the general crisis of democratic ideologies during the 1930's. Moreover, the parties of the opposition were not at the height of their effectiveness at this moment when the country was experiencing a new stage in its socio-economic development.

In effect, as a repercussion of new conditions created by the world crisis of 1929, two convergent processes were produced in Argentina: a new and decisive phase of industrialization was begun; and urbanization gained an unusual impetus with the massive migration to the cities from the country's interior. The intensity of these internal migrations was very great, and during the period of 1936–1947 the proportion of Argentines born in the provinces who moved to metropolitan Buenos Aires was equivalent to almost 40 per cent of the natural population increase of these same provinces. It was a mass exodus by which vast layers of people from the underdeveloped zones —masses until then completely on the fringes of the political life of the country—established themselves in the large cities and particularly in Buenos Aires.

It was a process in a way comparable to what had happened in the massive foreign immigration half a century before but with three great differences: (1) the rhythm was then much slower, since the growth of the urban population took place over at least three decades;

(2) the masses that exerted political pressure and led the movement for effective universal suffrage were not the immigrants themselves (who, because they were foreigners, did not participate except indirectly in political processes), but their sons; and (3) it was a matter of the recently formed middle class emerging, leaving a nascent proletariat in a subordinate situation. These great masses, transplanted rapidly to

TABLE 2

POPULATION OF THE BUENOS AIRES METROPOLITAN AREA*

INTERNAL AND EXTERNAL SOURCE OF ITS COMPOSITION (1869–1957)

Year	Total Population	% Born Abroad	% Born in the Interior	Average Annual Number of Migrants from the Interior
1869	250,000	47%	3%	
1895	783,000	50	8	8,000
1914	2,035,000	49	11	
1936	3,430,000	36	12	83,000
1947	4,720,000	26	29	
1957	6,370,000	22	36	96,000

* These figures for the metropolitan area, the city of Buenos Aires, plus the surrounding populated area of the province of Buenos Aires, are similar to those cited for the Federal Capital on p. 20 of the Introduction. The city of Buenos Aires and the Federal Capital are coterminous. [J. R. B.]

the cities and changed suddenly from rural peons, craftsmen, or laboring personnel into industrial workers, acquired a political significance without at the same time finding the institutional channels necessary for their integration into the normal functioning of the democracy. The repressive policy of the governments from the end of the past century until the beginning of the present, the ambivalence and relative failure of the governments of the middle class between 1916 and 1930, the severe limitations on the functioning of democracy after 1930, and the general disbelief and skepticism created by all this experience, coupled with the absence of political parties capable of expressing their sentiments and needs, left these masses "available" (*en disponibilidad*), making them a displaced element to be taken advantage of through whatever happenstance offered them some form of participation.

Meanwhile, other events also pressured Argentina; the expansion of Nazism in Europe and its first triumphs during the first three years of the war precipitated those events. A new military intervention in 1943, this time with open totalitarian designs, interrupted the conservative experiment with "democracy limited by means of fraud." But the social structure of Argentina, particularly at this stage of its evolution to an urban society and the type of masses "available" for use as a human base for a totalitarian movement, was very far from lending itself to a Fascist experiment of classic type, a simple reproduction of the Italian or German experiments. It was necessary to effect great changes in that scheme, and *Peronism,* which emerged starting with the military revolution, was the fitting expression of the particular conditions created in Argentina by an accumulation of old and new factors which we have tried to summarize.

There resulted, thus, another of the paradoxes in which the country's history abounds. A movement of the Fascist type set off a regime that was undoubtedly totalitarian in character, even though endowed with features very different from its European model: it was a type of authoritarianism based on the consent and support of the majority, which for the first time in sixteen years could express its wish in regular elections. This fact is of singular significance, since free elections were beginning to be transformed into the principal, if not the only, symbol of democracy, and had constituted one of the most insistent rallying cries of the parties of democratic opposition, particularly the Radicals, during the conservative regime.

❧ 28 ❧

Perón and Argentine Labor

◆◆◆◆◆

Robert J. Alexander

On June 4, 1943, when the government of Ramón Castillo was over-thrown by a military coup, Perón was a relatively obscure colonel in the Argentine army. Within the next two years he would become the most powerful figure in the government, holding simultaneously the positions of Vice President, Minister of War, and Secretary of Labor and Social Welfare. Although Perón could count on considerable military support for his ambitions, he was also aware of the desirability of building up a mass following, which he acquired through his policies as Secretary of Labor and Social Welfare. While in this position, Perón brought existing labor unions under his control, saw to it that large groups of workers were organized for the first time, and directed the enactment of social security legislation that covered most of the nation's work force. The process is described in this reading by Robert J. Alexander, Professor of Economics at Rutgers University and long-time observer of the Latin American labor movement.

During the 1930's and early 1940's, several significant changes occurred among the workers and in the trade union movement, particularly the CGT [Confederación General de Trabajo].[1] In 1930 immigration practically came to a halt. The urban working class, therefore, came to consist of second-generation Argentines and migrants from the countryside.

The second-generation workers were receptive to a native Argentine radicalism. The migrants from the countryside were politically illiterate. For them democracy had been a farce and so they were not impressed when someone who seemed to be helping them was accused

From Robert J. Alexander, *Labor Relations in Argentina, Brazil, and Chile* (New York: McGraw-Hill, 1962), pp. 167–181. Copyright © 1962 by McGraw-Hill, Inc. Reprinted by permission of McGraw-Hill Book Company. This article appears as reprinted in Joseph R. Barager (ed.), *Why Perón Came to Power* (New York: Knopf, 1968), pp. 181–198, *passim*. Deletions in the text are by Helen Delpar. Italicized bracketed notes in the text are by Helen Delpar.

[1] General Confederation of Labor. [H. D.]

of being a "Fascist." They, too, were good tinder for the fire which Perón was soon going to light.

At the same time, there was a growing tendency toward the bureaucratization of the labor movement. Trade union leadership had become a career in many of the larger unions. The labor organizations had begun to accumulate considerable property, not only headquarters buildings, but hospitals, summer camps, and other institutions built to provide social security and social service for their members.

Because unions had grown strong in such key industries as the railroads, it had become necessary for them to maintain at least an armed truce with the government. The romantic—and irresponsible—ideas of the old Anarchists, who used the unions as a weapon against the state, were not applicable to the new bread-and-butter unions which grew up in the decades before 1943.

Furthermore, there is considerable evidence that there was a growing gap between the leadership and membership of many of the unions. Attendance at union meetings fell off steadily during the 1930's, as did voting in union elections. Trade union membership became a duty rather than a privilege.

This gap was first exploited by the Communists whose influence grew in the late 1930's and early 1940's. The Communist-controlled Construction Workers' Union was the second largest organization in the CGT by 1943, and Communist influence was growing in a number of other organizations.

Finally, a large part of the working class remained outside the unions entirely. The packing-house workers, most of the metal workers, the workers on the "factory farms" of the sugar industry, and many other groups were unorganized. The trade union movement was heavily concentrated in Buenos Aires and its vicinity. Although there were some unions in the interior cities, nowhere was there the relative strength of the labor movement in the capital and its environs.

During the decades before the 1943 Revolution the important Argentine unions had established a pattern for labor-management relations that was adapted for his own purpose by Perón. Its two basic elements were collective bargaining and trade-union social insurance.

Collective contracts varied considerably in their geographical scope. In the railroad, textile, and shoemaking industries, there were nationwide collective agreements; in the printing trade, the hotel and restaurant industry, retail trade contracts were on a regional basis.

.   .   .

Negotiation of these contracts was conducted directly between the workers' and employers' organizations. The government played little or no part in the process and the Departamento Nacional del Trabajo was little more than a statistics-gathering agency. Settlement of disputes rising within the collective agreements was also handled directly through union-management grievance procedure. The unions were organized to present those problems which needed solution in the day-to-day relations of workers with employers.

The other emphasis of the union before the Perón period was the establishment of social security and social welfare projects. The most notable examples of these activities were the health and hospital programs of the two railroad workers' unions. These were administered by representatives of the unions, though they were financed by the employers with some help from the government. They provided complete medical care for most of the country's railroaders and their families.

. . .

At the time of the Revolution of 1943 there were four central labor organizations functioning. The old FORA [*the Federación Obrera Regional Argentina, an anarchosyndicalist labor organization established in 1905*] still had a few scattered unions affiliated with it in Buenos Aires and a few provincial cities. The Unión Sindical Argentina was somewhat larger and was still nominally Syndicalist in its orientation. Its most important affiliates were the Telephone Workers' Federation and the Maritime Workers' Union.

The CGT had split into two rival factions. This division arose from a struggle over the secretary generalship of the organization in its national congress in December 1942. One faction, based mainly on the two railroad unions, sought the re-election of outgoing Secretary General José Domenech. Most of the leaders of this group were Socialists.

The other faction sought the election of Francisco Pérez Leirós, also a Socialist and head of the Municipal Workers' Union. It was also led by Angel Borlenghi, Secretary General of the Commercial Employees' Confederation and a member of the Socialist Party. However, this group received its main backing from Communist-led unions such as those of the construction workers, metallurgical workers, and textile workers.

When the two factions disagreed over who had won a very close election, they split into two different organizations, each of which called itself the Confederación General del Trabajo. They were generally referred to as CGT 1 (that of Domenech), and CGT 2 (that of Pérez Leirós).

. . .

Government Direction of Labor Protest under Perón

The Revolution of 1943 brought about fundamental changes in labor-management relations in Argentina. Colonel Juan Domingo

Perón, who emerged as the leading figure in this revolution, sought to bring under his control the whole process of negotiation between workers and employers. Ultimately, he largely substituted the government's fiat for collective bargaining.

In order to achieve this complete government direction of the grievances of the Argentine workers and of the establishment of the "web of rule" in Argentine labor-management relations, Perón had to destroy first the independence of both the workers' organizations and those of the employers. By persuasion and force he brought the labor movement almost completely under his control. He was somewhat less successful in converting the employers and in quelling their opposition to him. Nonetheless, by the end of his regime, nearly all official organizations representing the employing class were under the domination of the Perón government.

Perón

Colonel Perón used the labor organization existing in 1943 as a level to boost him into power. At the same time he tied those organizations to his own destiny, and completely subordinated them. It is interesting to note the difference between Perón's attitude toward the labor movement and that of Vargas in Brazil. Vargas destroyed most existing labor organizations and established new state-controlled groups in their place. Perón, on the contrary, bent the existing trade unions to his will. Perhaps this was why he was never as successful as his Brazilian contemporary in completely destroying the independence of the labor movement.

Although Perón was successful in gaining control of the top leadership of the labor movement, he could never completely destroy the opposition in the rank and file, and there were numerous instances during his tenure in office when the lower-echelon leadership of the unions defied the President. The result of the Perón experience was the acceptance of the fact that the labor movement had become one of the great centers of power in the country's social, economic, and political structure.

The revolution that gave Perón his chance was motivated more by the army's fear of a pro-Allied government coming to power in the middle of World War II, than by any concern with social or economic affairs. The Army, which had been trained by German instructors, had for long been strongly pro-German, and in World War II was "neutral" in favor of the Axis. The prospect that the election scheduled for the end of 1943 might bring to power the pro-British landowner

Patrón Costas undoubtedly was at the root of the June 4, 1943, rebellion.

The military government which took office under the leadership of the new President, General Pedro Ramírez, dissolved Congress, which under the control of the Radical and Socialist parties had been the center of democratic and pro-Allied agitation for a number of years, and suspended freedom of the press.

Most important of all, as things turned out, the military regime suppressed CGT 2 on the grounds that it was "Communist-dominated," and ousted the leaders of some of the country's principal labor organizations, namely La Fraternidad, Unión Ferroviaria, and the Unión de Obreros Municipales, placing military officers in charge.

By September 1943 there were widespread demonstrations. The discontent was shared by an impressive number of retired generals and admirals who issued a statement calling for a restoration of constitutional government. Some of the younger members of the dominant military group saw that the regime was either going to become a violent dictatorship, in which case its tenure would probably be short, or it was going to have to seek support from civilian elements.

The first move was an attempt to win over the industrial middle class. This group had been discontented with the landowner-dominated governments and might have been expected to be friendly to a regime that had overthrown the last of these governments.

However, the industrialists had traditionally supported the Unión Cívica Radical, and they felt that ultimately this party would come to power when constitutional government was restored. They saw no point in mortgaging the future Radical government's position by making what they considered an unnecessary alliance.

The next move was to turn to the industrial working class. This group had also been unfriendly toward the landed oligarchy and had not received sympathetic treatment from any government since the first administration of President Hipólito Irigoyen (1916 through 1922).

Furthermore, a number of the military men already had contact with the labor movement. Colonel Juan Domingo Perón, the leader of this group, had been named Director of the Department of Labor soon after the June 4 revolution and had set about expanding its power and activities. Other officers closely associated with him had been placed in control of the unions taken over by the government. This group of military men conferred at length with leading trade union officials, in an effort to find out what it was the latter wanted and whether or not an alliance could be formed between military and trade union officialdom. These inquiries met with limited success.

The result of this change in direction of the June 4 revolutionary regime was the move in November 1943 to convert the old Department of Labor into a new Secretariat of Labor and Social Welfare, with cabinet status for its chief. The first Secretary of Labor was Colonel Perón.

Perón as Secretary of Labor

During the next two years, Perón rose rapidly, becoming Minister of War and Vice President, as well as Secretary of Labor early in 1944. He also set about to win over the workers. In doing so, he sought to convince them that only through his office could they get vindication for their grievances.

In his assault upon the labor movement, Perón used both the carrot and the stick. For those trade union leaders who resisted his blandishments he reserved prisons, concentration camps, and exile, and made it increasingly difficult for their unions to function. Meanwhile, many labor leaders who might have wished to resist Perón found that more and more of the rank and file were being won over by his promises and performance.

During the 1943–1945 period, Perón threw his efforts into helping the labor movement expand. There had been perhaps 300,000 to 350,000 organized workers in Argentina when he took office. Within a couple of years this number was increased several fold. Perón forced employers to recognize their workers' unions and to negotiate with them. He personally led campaigns among packing-house workers, sugar plantation peons, and various other labor groups in the interior of the republic. Where dual unions existed, he encouraged rival groups to forget their differences and to launch intensive organizing campaigns with the government's support.

On the other hand, Secretary of Labor Perón intruded his department into the field of collective bargaining negotiations. He first encouraged and then insisted that collective conflicts be brought to the secretariat for conciliation and decision. Many times, after collective negotiations conducted at the secretariat had been concluded, he presided over the formal signing of the new contracts. The workers soon came to the conclusion—which was frequently correct—that Colonel Perón had been more responsible for their increases and other benefits than had their own union leaders.

Finally, the Secretariat of Labor began an extensive job of enacting labor and social security legislation. In this field Argentina was considerably behind most of its neighbors in 1943.

This legislative work—by decree—extended into various fields. A more effective system of factory inspection was instigated. Social security legislation was enacted which brought under its scope the great majority of the country's wage- and salary-earning population. During the 1945 election campaign, Perón's successor as Secretary of Labor decreed that all employers must pay an extra month's pay to their workers at Christmas time. A number of legal, paid holidays were established.

His Control of the Labor Movement

The result was that by the middle of 1945 Perón had converted the trade union movement into a powerful personal political machine. He had conquered the Confederación General del Trabajo in the middle of 1944 when he had won its support for a government-sponsored Independence Day (May 25) celebration, the real purpose of which was to indicate political support for the regime then in power. Although certain unions remained hostile to Perón, their number was comparatively small by the end of 1945. The Unión Sindical Argentina was almost liquidated when most of its important unions joined the Perón-backed CGT.

The degree of support which Colonel Perón enjoyed among the workers was demonstrated in the events of October 1945. On the ninth of that month a military coup by hostile elements of the army resulted in his forced resignation and temporary imprisonment. However, the new military group was unable to rally the support of the civilian politicians and for over a week the country got along without any cabinet.

In the meantime, Perón's labor supporters began to mobilize. A major role in this action was played by Cipriano Reyes, the leader of the packing-house workers in the areas near Buenos Aires. These and other workers began to descend on the capital by train, truck, auto, and even by foot. Civilian opponents of Perón were forced to go into hiding, while the military group in charge of the government did not dare order their troops to halt the mobs.

As a result, on October 16, Colonel Perón was brought back from prison and the next day appeared on the balcony of the Casa Rosada, arm in arm with President Farrell, to address the cheering crowd of supporters. Although Perón did not return to any of his offices, he was from that time on in full control of the government.

A few days after Perón's restoration to power, a campaign to choose a constitutional President of the Republic was launched. Perón announced his candidacy, although he had no political party supporting him. To fill this gap, he organized three new political groups. The largest of these—which won a majority in both houses of Congress on February 24, 1946—was the Partido Laborista, organized by most of the principal trade union officials of the republic. A dissident group of Radical Party leaders who had thrown in their lot with Perón organized the "Renovated Radical Party," while a third group composed of miscellaneous elements announced their support for him on a so-called Independent ticket.

The opposition to Perón formed the Unión Democrática Nacional which consisted formally of the Radical, Socialist, Progressive Democratic, and Communist parties, and also had the backing of the Conservative Party. They nominated two old-line Radical politicians, José P. Tamborini and Enrique Mosca, for the posts of president and vice president, respectively.

The campaign was hectic. Both candidates were shot at several times. Although the opposition was allowed little use of the government-regimented radio, it controlled most of the country's newspapers. The opposition felt that they would win if the polling on election day were calm and honest. Although these were the conditions on election day, Perón won.

Organized Labor Under Perón

On June 4, 1946, Perón was inaugurated constitutional President of the nation. During the succeeding years, he and his wife set about destroying the independence of the trade union movement.

María Eva Duarte de Perón was the principal figure in bringing this about. She set up her headquarters in the Secretariat of Labor building and from there molded the trade union movement to her and her husband's will. Through repeated purges of the unions she removed those leaders who had thought that they were using Perón instead of the other way around. Ceaselessly active, Evita for six years kept constantly on the alert to oust any unionist of independent inclinations, while at the same time seeking to convince the workers that all blessings flowed from the Peróns.

The Ley de Asociaciones Profesionales

One of the most important measures used by the Perón regime to destroy the independence of the labor movement was the Ley de Asociaciones Profesionales. The significance of this measure was twofold. First of all, it officially put the power of the state behind recognized trade unions and implicitly obliged the employers to deal with them. In the second place, and equally important, the law for the first time made it essential for a union to acquire legal recognition before it could function effectively. Before 1945, unions wanting some kind of legal status registered as mere civil associations—on a par with a Rotary Club or charitable society. Many unions sought no kind of legal recognition whatever.

This law started off by defining a *"sindicato* or professional association" as a group "formed by manual or intellectual workers of the same profession or industry, or in similar or connected professions or industries, constituted for the defense of their professional interests." The decree then went on to say that these associations "can be freely established without necessity of previous authorization, always provided their objectives are not contrary to the morality, laws, and fundamental institutions of the nation."

Four types of workers' organizations are noted in the law. The first is the union having *personería gremial* [*that is, legal recognition as a labor union*]. The second type is a union with *personería jurídica,* or mere registration as a civil association, a category reserved largely for unions which have for one reason or another lost their *personería gremial.*

Third, there are "professional associations inscribed but without *personería gremial."* These organizations are registered in special files in the Ministry of Labor and "can act freely and can carry out . . . all those functions which are not expressly reserved to *sindicatos* with *personería gremial."* In some instances, where no *sindicatos* with *personería gremial* exist in the area of their jurisdiction, these groups can function as if they had such a status.

Finally, there are the workers' organizations which have no kind of government recognition whatsoever. These, as we have already noted, cannot function as normal trade unions. They cannot bargain with the employers, they cannot represent the workers in negotiations with the governmental authorities, and they cannot conduct any of the activities usually associated with a trade union.

.   .   .

The law provides certain minimum requirements for a union to gain *personería gremial.* These include having a minimum number of members and having statutes which provide adequate means for protection of the organization's property and collecting dues, and which set forth the officers, name, headquarters, objective, frequency of meetings and financial reports, as well as sanctions on members and means of modification of the statutes and dissolution of the organization.

Presumably the organization which represented the majority of the workers in a given trade or industry was to receive recognition and be granted *personería gremial.* In fact, the Peronista government used this decree on various occasions to destroy an existing union politically hostile to the regime in favor of a new group, which was Peronista.

.   .   .

The law sets forth conditions under which a union can lose its *personería gremial* and be succeeded by a rival group, although needless to say, these conditions were not observed in the case of anti-Peronista unions. According to the law it is possible for a rival union to be granted *personería gremial* "when the number of dues-paying members of the rival union during a continuous period of at least six months immediately previous to the request for recognition is superior to that of the recognized union; the latter then losing its recognition if it ceases to be sufficiently representative, although the authorities must also take into consideration the previously recognized union's contribution to the defense of its members' interests in deciding whether to strip it of recognition." Furthermore, in order for recognition to be transferred from one union to another such action must have the approval of the union losing *personería gremial,* "even if its membership is smaller" than that of its rival.

Many unions were squeezed out of existence by use of the Ley de Asociaciones Profesionales. Included were organizations of textile workers, shoe workers, hotel and restaurant workers, printers, clothing workers, shipbuilders, and maritime workers.

The Purge of the Unions

Evita went even further than this. She sought to destroy labor leaders who, even though they were supporters of Perón, had been union officials before the Perón regime. Between 1946 and 1951, there was a thorough purge of nearly all those leaders who helped put Perón in power during the 1943–1946 period.

.   .   .

An important part of Evita's work was assuring the workers that all their grievances would be channeled through and resolved by the Perón government. This was her "philanthropic" activity. One or two days a week Evita held court in the Secretariat of Labor building and received anyone with a problem. The President's wife became a combination marriage counselor, pediatrician, public defender, and Tammany Hall ward leader on those days. Ministers and other officials were in attendance, and would frequently be dispatched to set right some complaint. Few of those who visited Evita went away without the gift of a few hundred pesos.

The Eva Perón Foundation, which was a monopoly of all charity in the republic, carried out a similar function on a grander scale. In addition to building hospitals, children's homes, and similar institutions, it gave handouts to needy people and those stricken by some disaster. The foundation, though it received large "gifts" from unions, employers, and visiting foreign dignitaries, and large appropriations from Congress, never had to present any accounting of its funds. There is little doubt that much of the "charity" was given to the leading figures in the Perón regime most closely associated with Evita.

The result of all of this was that by the time of Perón's overthrow, most of the labor movement was a tool of the dictator. The top leadership consisted of unquestioning servants of the regime and their selection was made in the Ministry of Labor or in the Casa Rosada (presidential palace) not in the congresses of the unions which merely rubber-stamped the government's choices. There was no democracy in the middle and upper levels of the trade union movement—in the CGT, its provincial and city "delegations," or in the national and regional leadership of the industrial unions.

The only level on which a modicum of democracy was preserved was in the election of shop stewards and factory or workshop committees. Here the government allowed the workers in many unions to choose their representatives. However, in cases where these officials showed too much activity which the government interpreted as endangering its welfare, the CGT or the national leadership of an individual union would oust the offending unionists.

This degree of union democracy undoubtedly served two purposes as far as the Perón regime was concerned. In the first place, it kept it aware of discontent among its followers. In the second place, it served as an escape valve for the workers themselves, giving them some feeling of having a say in their organizations.

The Role of Eva Perón

————— ◄◄◆►► —————

National Investigations Commission

No account of Perón's career can overlook the contribution of María Eva Duarte (1919–1952), who was a minor radio and film actress when she met Perón in 1943. During the period from October 9 to October 17, 1945, when Perón was removed from his offices and imprisoned by military rivals, she proved her value by mobilizing labor support, which brought about his triumphant restoration to power on October 17. Shortly after this Evita was married to Perón. She became an important part of his government after he was elected to the presidency for the first time on February 24, 1946, especially through her contacts with women and with the descamisados, or "shirtless ones," who were the bulwark of the regime. In this selection, the National Investigations Commission established after Perón's ouster gives a critical assessment of her activities.

After several years of indoctrinating the masses and exerting himself in organizing his party, the dictator became aware that he had not succeeded in either effort. "A political force is not organized in five years," he said in his lectures on leadership, "because the task of persuasion, of education, of infiltration of the doctrine into the spirit of men cannot be achieved in so short a time. There is even less chance if the men coming to Peronism have come from different places, from different directions, with different tendencies and different orientations. We must ensure," he concluded, "that they go away forgetting old beliefs and doctrines and assimilating new ones. This is the work of generations." For that reason he put his trust in children and teenagers. . . .

As a beginning step he began to train women. Traditionally, the Argentine woman had remained aloof from politics, which, as with military matters and the priesthood, she considered the special province of men. In this regard world opinion had changed since the first Eng-

From Joseph R. Barager (ed. and tr.), *Why Perón Came to Power* (New York: Knopf, 1968), pp. 229–232. Copyright © 1968 by Joseph R. Barager. Reprinted by permission of Alfred A. Knopf, Inc.

lish "suffragists" claimed their right to participate in civic contests. These ideas had penetrated all countries, including our own, so that the concession of suffrage to Argentine women could not be postponed. The dictator took advantage of this. "If with the men's vote we have won by an enormous margin," he said on the eve of his second election, "with the women's vote we will win by a great deal more."

From the beginning of his public life he had at his side an unusual woman, different from nearly all other native Argentine women. She lacked formal training, but not political intuition; she was impetuous, domineering, and spectacular. Her early years had been difficult, until the disaster[1] brought her into close contact with the ambitious Colonel who linked himself with her. Thus began a collaboration unparalleled in history, though there are a few cases somewhat similar, among them Juan Manuel de Rosas and his wife Doña Encarnación Ezcurra.[2]

It is hard to determine precisely what each one contributed to their joint dictatorship. She accepted ideas, but she added passion and courage. The dictator simulated many things, whereas she scarcely ever did. She was a fiery little thing—indomitable, aggressive, spontaneous, at times barely feminine. Nature had endowed her with agreeable physical features, which she accentuated when good fortune permitted her to sport brilliant jewels and splendid gowns. In that way she compensated for her own unforgettable wretchedness and frustrations as an unnoticed actress without a future.[3] But this has little interest for what we are dealing with here. We must emphasize, rather, the adoration and, at the same time, the revulsion this woman aroused in our country during the six or seven years of the dictatorship. At one moment she seemed triumphant over all her enemies—when the CGT launched her name as a possible member of the presidential ticket—but that lasted only a few days. Then her "renunciation" was

---

[1] The earthquake that, in January 1944, devastated the city of San Juan, in western Argentina; Perón and Evita both participated in a national campaign for funds to aid the stricken area. [J. R. B.]

[2] Rosas was the dictator who exercised virtually absolute control over Buenos Aires and much of the rest of Argentina from 1835 to 1851. He had resigned as Governor of Buenos Aires Province in 1832, because the legislature would not grant him greater powers. While he was away campaigning against the Indians on the frontier, his wife, Doña Encarnación, manipulated provincial politics to Rosas' advantage, making it impossible for his successor to govern. As a result Rosas was recalled to take over with virtually unrestricted powers. [J.R.B.]

[3] Refers to Eva Duarte's career as a bit player in the Argentine cinema and her more prominent role in Argentine radio soap operas. [J. R. B.]

produced, imposed by factors that are not yet public knowledge.[4] As a result of her early death, the country was spared graver disturbances in the final period of the tyranny.

Eva Perón was the most extraordinary propaganda instrument the dictator had. Her jurisdiction over internal affairs, her decisiveness in difficult moments, her inexhaustible activity, and also her disdain for all conventional ways of doing things in social or political affairs served her well in subduing stubborn wills, maintaining lasting contact with the popular classes, organizing the feminine branch of the "movement," stirring up the multitudes, creating and fostering animosities, and above all exalting his [Perón's] name and his work everywhere and at all times. Her mission was not that of persuading but of promoting action, kindling passions, carrying out acts of vengeance. She was most likely sincere, because her scanty acting ability would not have permitted her to simulate so easily sentiments she did not have.

The dictator let "La Señora" go her own way. He knew that her sudden and unexpected attacks on their enemies reassured the common people more than his own discourses on indoctrination, that she reached the heart of the humble ones more than he did. He did not silence her words of delirious admiration for his person because they served him with the public. "Perón is a meteor burning with the desire to enlighten his century," she used to tell the most ingenuous ones, "he is not a politician, he is a leader, he is a genius, he is a teacher, he is a guide, no longer just of the Argentines, but of all men of good will. Our leader," she declared, "has come to fulfill in this difficult hour of world history the dreams and hopes of all peoples of all times and their inclinations for all the centuries. We do not wish to compare Perón with anyone. Perón has his own light. He is too great, and our leader can no longer be molested by the shadow of any sparrow." She lacked any sense of the absurd, so peculiar to the Argentines, and she was without modesty, although she repeatedly affected it.

---

[4] In 1951 an obedient CGT (General Confederation of Labor) conducted an all-out campaign to secure Evita the second place on a Perón-Perón ticket for the presidential election of 1951. In a dramatic scene Evita finally withdrew on the grounds that she was "too young" to be eligible. Most observers credit her withdrawal to military pressure on President Perón. If Evita had succeeded to the presidency, on the death or absence from the country of Perón, she would have been Commander in Chief of the Argentine Armed Forces. This was a possibility that even the most compliant Argentine officer did not find appealing. [J. R. B.]

≈§ 30 §≈

Justicialismo

George I. Blanksten

*While Perón was in power, foreign observers tended to consider him
an imitator of European fascists, but in recent years greater emphasis
has been placed on the Argentine roots of Peronism. Perón himself
advocated a social and political philosophy called* Justicialismo, *which
represented a "Third Position" located at the point of equilibrium between the four conflicting forces in society—idealism, materialism,
individualism, and collectivism. In this reading, taken from a book
published in 1953, George I. Blanksten, Professor of Political Science
at Northwestern University, discusses the origins of* Justicialismo, *which
he sees as an opportunistic attempt to divorce Peronism from fascism
after the Axis' defeat in World War II.*

The first recorded use of the word *Justicialismo* was made by Perón
in April of 1949. The occasion was memorable. A Congress of Philosophy, sponsored by the University of Cuyo, met at Mendoza. Some
two hundred philosophers representing nineteen countries attended
the affair. That in itself was not remarkable. What was remarkable
was that one of the philosophers was President Perón himself! He
presented a curious paper on a new philosophy which had been
brewed at the *Casa Rosada.* His speech revealed him to be more familiar with nineteenth-century German philosophy than many observers
had previously thought Perón to be. He talked facilely of the ideas of
two Germans in particular—Georg Wilhelm Friedrich Hegel, and
Karl Marx. Perón was critical of both. He said that Hegel's worship
of the concept of the state was intellectually sterile, and that Marxism
led to the "insectification of the individual." Perón would accept
neither equipping human beings with six legs nor "immoral individualism." If extreme collectivism was wrong, so was extreme individualism. What was needed was something between the two, a "Third

Position." The "Third Position" was *Justicialismo*. "What we have to search for," declared the philosopher Perón, "is the well-proportioned man."

.   .   .

As cultivated since 1949, justicialist thought has acquired a curious inheritance from the ideas of Hegel and Marx. As the two nineteenth-century Germans had developed dialectical approaches, so *Justicialismo* has its dialectic. As the Hegelian and Marxist systems were theories of conflict, so there is a justicialist conflict theory. Hegel and Marx, it will be remembered, held that society was given life and meaning by the fact that forces were in conflict within it. The more abstract Hegel called his opposed forces within society "thesis" and "antithesis"; Marx called them "classes." And the dialectics held that society moved or progressed only through continuing conflict between the opposed forces. Hegel and Marx believed that there were only two societal forces in conflict—Hegel gave both his forces abstract names; Marx called one of his classes "capital" and the other "labor."

While many points of difference existed between Hegelian and Marxist thought, the two were in agreement on the basic proposition that there were *only two* opposed forces involved in the struggle within the social organism, and that this conflict was resolved by the achievement of a species of "Third Position" between the struggling elements. Thus Hegel believed that the "Third Position" between his opposed "thesis" and "antithesis" was a "synthesis" (his perfect "synthesis" was called the "State"); whereas Marx held that "socialism" was the "Third Position" between the mutually hostile forces of "capital" and "labor." On the other hand, *Justicialismo* maintains that there are not two but rather *four* basically conflicting forces in society. These are "idealism," "materialism," "individualism," and "collectivism." Two propositions are central to the justicialist interpretation of the four forces. In the first place, each of them has a necessary and desirable role to play in society. Secondly, a constant conflict rages among the four.

According to *Justicialismo,* what is the proper societal role of each of the four elements?

First, *idealism* is legitimate in so far as it leads man to his destiny, "the complete possession of happiness, which is God." It is true that much idealism may be found in *Peronista* pronouncements. President Perón has said that "I have always believed that every human action, to be noble, must be based on an ideal"; and that his "doctrine is a doctrine of moral purity. . . . If it were an evil doctrine, I should be the first to oppose it, but being, as it is, nothing but good, we should aim at making it known everywhere and teaching it to every man and woman." The late Eva Perón, too, spoke at some length of the position of idealism in *Justicialismo.* "Humanity is living through tremendous days," she said. "A cold materialism ridicules gentleness; a solemn hostility attempts to separate men from the human simplicity that gives hearts warmth and feeling. Mixed ambitions have made man forget . . . the humble things which surround us, and man, who needs to love, has been converted into an indifferent being."

Second, *materialism* is necessary and proper in society to the extent that it provides man with the earthly necessities for the attainment of the goals of idealism. As one *Peronista* philosopher has put it, "man comes before the machine; the [Perón] revolution is not so much interested in the conservation and expansion of material wealth as such, but more in the preservation and perfection of the present and future human factor; in this sense the revolution is profoundly humanist and, as Perón himself has said in one of his speeches, involves a 'rise in the standard of living to a level compatible with the dignity of man and his general economic betterment, freeing man from economic slavery.' "

In the third place, *individualism* is legitimate in so far as it permits man to attain happiness through knowledge of himself as distinct from other people. In the justicialist view, "the individual is the first and most important element in society"; indeed, "that the individual should meekly accept his elimination as a sacrifice for the sake of the community, does not redound to the credit of the latter."

On the other hand, man, being a political animal, has need of society or the community, which is represented in *Justicialismo* by the fourth force, *collectivism.* This justicialist element aids man to achieve happiness in so far as he has need of the community or the collectivity. And the legitimate function of collectivism, in *Justicialismo,* is to preserve the community for the service of all men. "Man does not possess anything which belongs to the human community," a justicialist writer has said; and "when private interests are incompatible—or collide—with those of the community, then the authority of the state is applied to intervene directly."

Thus, each of the four forces is held to have a legitimate and proper role in human affairs. But, like the Hegelian and Marxist systems, *Justicialismo* is a theory of conflict. In justicialist dialectic, the four elements are continually in combat with each other, and mutual hostility is the theoretically natural and necessary relationship among them. Idealism is always at war with materialism, and individualism is never at peace with collectivism. From this theory of conflict emerges the justicialist notion of evil and of tyranny. Injustice, evil, and tyranny arise whenever any of the four elements is subdued and not permitted to exercise its proper and legitimate role in society. In justicialist theory, this unfortunate circumstance may occur in either of two types of situations: one of the four forces may triumph over the other three, destroying them; or any two of the four may ally against the other two and demolish them. In either circumstance, according to *Justicialismo*, the result is evil and fraught with injustice and tyranny.

Consider the forms of tyranny. Suppose idealism were to destroy materialism, individualism, and collectivism. This is probably easier for the Latin American than the "North American" to imagine, for the Roman Catholic Church occupies a peculiar place in the Hispanic-American states. Clerical dictatorships have indeed arisen in the Western Hemisphere. South Americans need look no farther afield for their illustrations than to Ecuador, where the fabulous Gabriel García Moreno presided over a theocratic regime from 1859 to 1875. In this dictatorship, man was a citizen only in so far as he was a practicing Roman Catholic; individualism, materialism, and collectivism were smothered; and the name of the country was changed to the "Republic of the Sacred Heart." In the end, however, even idealism disintegrated, the tyrant García Moreno fell at the hands of an assassin, and man became demoralized and "tired of God."

In the justicialist view, tyranny is no more tolerable if it results from a victory of materialism over the other elements. Materialism— property, the machine, the instruments of the "foreign imperialists"— can, according to *Justicialismo*, be as terrible a tyrant as any of the other forces. "One fine day, wise men, technicians, and teachers created the machine," said one justicialist writer, giving voice to a somewhat typically Latin-American antipathy for gadgets invented by foreigners. "The machine became a substitute for man. The machine was the instrument which permitted the organization of great commercial and industrial companies." These, in turn, deified property, another form of triumphant materialism at its worst. "*Justicialismo* affirms—in the 'Third Position'—that property cannot be an absolute right of anybody, and that it is necessary to abolish, not the right to private property, but the abuses of that right when improperly used."

So much for the tyrannical aspects of idealism and materialism. Individualism triumphant over the other forces can also bring despotism and injustice. In justicialist thought, anarchy is the rise of extreme individualism at the expense of the other three forces. *Peronistas* have little desire for individualism they regard as extreme. President Perón has said that "we must do away with the individualistic mentality." The reader need not be reminded at this point that individual liberty—a form of "extreme individualism," according to *Justicialismo*—has little place in the "new Argentina," and that the Constitution of 1949 stipulates, in approved justicialist fashion, that "the state does not recognize the liberty to undermine liberty." As interpreted by President Perón, this provision means that "individual freedom cannot signify an unlimited right, not only because this right must be in harmony with all other rights, but because at no time must it be turned into a weapon to be used against the essence of freedom itself. Only the protection of an irresponsible, uncontrolled liberalism has made possible the successful propaganda of despotic regimes which have ended by implanting in a democratic type of nation systems of rightist or leftist tyranny." Political individualism is bad enough to the *Peronista;* also intolerable is economic individualism. In justicialist terms, this involves "the resolve of the individualist to defend at all costs what he considers his inalienable right to make or sell whatever he likes, when and how he likes, and to engage in whatever business or industry he might think proper." According to Perón, "individualism of this kind leads to a society of inhuman egoists who think only of getting rich, although to do so it may be necessary to reduce millions of their less fortunate brothers to a state of starvation, poverty, and desperation."

Collectivism triumphant over the other forces is likewise tyrannical in *Justicialismo.* This is a point which the *Peronista* would probably have less difficulty in explaining to the "North American" than in elucidating on other aspects of the doctrine of Peronism. Spokesmen for the "new Argentina" say that they reject Hegel and Marx because both constructed systems providing for extremes of collectivism. "According to Hegel the individual is submitted to a historical destiny through the state, to which he belongs," Perón has pointed out. "The Marxists, for their part, would convert the individuals into beings all of the same pattern, with no landscapes or blue sky, part of a tyrannized community behind an iron curtain. What is very evident in both cases is the annihilation of man as such." And *Justicialismo* eschews traffic with this class of annihilation.

Thus, one type of tyranny results from domination and destruction of three of the forces by any one of them. *Justicialismo* holds, further, that there is a second form of tyranny. This occurs when any two of the forces form an alliance against the other two, and are able to destroy them. What masks does this class of tyranny wear?

Suppose that idealism and collectivism were to unite against materialism and individualism, achieving their destruction. This is the current justicialist definition of naziism and fascism, which Perón since 1945 has said are evil. His postwar condemnation of naziism and fascism—he calls them "collectivist idealism"—stems ostensibly from his sudden realization that they are similar to communism. In the view of the manufacturers of *Justicialismo,* naziism, fascism, and communism are alike in that all three are collectivist: "the only difference is that naziism and fascism have an idealistic concept of the state."

But, since 1945, that difference has not been enough to save them. Since the end of World War II, fascism and naziism have been bad. Perón has said so.

Again, consider an alliance of materialism and collectivism, resulting in the elimination of idealism and individualism. This is Perón's definition of communism. Justicialist writers have no love for it. In communism, they say, "man has arrived at the lowest point in his history. This will be his most bitter hour." *Peronistas* who know their doctrine say that they can imagine nothing worse than the destruction of idealism and individualism.

But what of a combination of materialism with individualism, to the exclusion of idealism and collectivism? This, according to Perón, is capitalism. And he does not like it. Capitalism, regarded within the justicialist framework as shorn of idealism and collectivism, is viewed by *Peronistas* as the "abuse of property." Perón calls capitalism "dehumanized capital." And "North Americans" may do well to note that Perón is a sworn enemy of capitalism as he understands it. Occasionally, when the United States is plunged into crisis, some "North Americans" complain that they had no forewarning of where the danger lay. They may do well to consider themselves forewarned by *Justicialismo. Peronistas* have asserted that "capitalism must be the enemy of this [that is, the Perón] revolution," and that *Justicialismo* "intends to abolish capitalism." Hear President Perón himself: "We think that if we are against capitalism we cannot preserve anything that is capitalist." He has said that "the political, social, and economic middleman must be eliminated," and that he "will not allow despotic capitalism to prevail in Argentina." Time was when Hitler and Mussolini told "North Americans" that their system was decadent. According to Perón, that system is decadent again. "Capitalism, glorious perhaps in the eighteenth century in its constructive stage, is arriving at its final stage," he has said. "New forms—as has been the custom of humanity throughout the ages—struggle and contend in the world to replace capitalism in its final stage."

Thus the high priests of *Justicialismo* have identified seven brands of tyranny. Four of them arise from the triumph of any one of the basic forces over the other three, whether the resultant evil be theocracy, all-inclusive materialism, anarchy, or complete collectivism. And three brands of tyranny spring from a victorious alliance of two of the elements to the exclusion of the other two, whether the product of the combination be fascism, communism, or capitalism.[1]

---

[1] Justicialist thinkers have said nothing about a combination of individualism with idealism. An alliance of materialism with idealism, or of collectivism with individualism, is held to be impossible in the nature of the system.

Can these tyrannies be avoided? *Peronistas* claim they have found a formula. Each of the seven tyrannies, it is argued, is a form of extremism, and what is needed is an arrangement which prevents extremism. This arrangement, says Perón, is *Justicialismo* or the "Third Position." Perhaps only a college professor would bother to point out that the "Third Position" is theoretically not "third," but rather eighth, in the sense that it is an alternative to the seven tyrannies. But—the dubious mathematics of *Justicialismo* aside for the moment—what is the "Third Position"?

It is an arrangement which guarantees each of the four basic forces the opportunity to exercise its proper role in society, neutralizes the conflict among the four, and prevents any one—or two—of them from dominating the others. In a sense, *Justicialismo* or the "Third Position" is the "new Argentina's" version of Aristotle's "Golden Mean," in so far as that concept sought the avoidance of extremes. The *Peronista* who knows his doctrine defines it thus: *Justicialismo* is "that doctrine whose objective is the happiness of man in human society achieved through the harmony of materialistic, idealistic, individualistic, and collectivistic forces, each valued in a Christian way." Or thus: "It would be a concordant and balanced combination of the forces that represent the modern state, designed to avoid strife and the annihilation of one of these forces; endeavoring to conciliate them, to unite them, and to put them in parallel motion to be able to form . . . a common destiny with benefit for the . . . forces and without injury to any one of them." *Justicialismo,* then, envisages a temperate social order compounded of "just the right amounts" of idealism, materialism, individualism, and collectivism.

How much of each is "just the right amount"? Or, to put the question another way, *where* is the "Third Position"? If *Justicialismo* were to be charted on a four-cornered diagram, with each of the corners representing one of the four basic forces, would the "Third Position" lie in the center of the diagram? According to Perón, the answer to that question is "no." He has said that "the 'Third Position' is not in any way a position of neutrality." How, then, can it be located? Each of the four forces must be assigned a value. In so far as justicialist writing has attempted to do this, the general tendency of *Peronistas* is to value idealism and individualism more highly than materialism and collectivism. It will be remembered that the four forces are assumed to be in continual conflict. The "Third Position," then, locates at the point of equilibrium among the four. Since idealism and individualism are assumed to be of greater value, that is, to have greater force, than the other two elements, the "Third Position" or point of equilibrium lies closer to idealism and individualism than to materialism and collectivism.

. . .

As employed by the "new Argentina," *Justicialismo* is called upon to justify *Peronista* policies operating on three levels. First, in the area of foreign policy, *Justicialismo* is the announced *rationale* of Argentina's "Third Position" between the United States and the Soviet Union. This matter will be explored more fully in a later chapter of this book. It might be noted at this point, however, that the "Third Position," being anti-Communist and also anti-capitalist, provides the ideological context within which Perón explains his anti-Soviet and also anti-"Yankee" foreign policy. Second, the "Third Position" is the official justification for the *Peronistas'* domestic economic policies. Peronism maintains a domestic "Third Position" between the rich and the poor. The regime says it is opposed to the "Oligarchy" and is the champion of the economically underprivileged but neither of these groups has lost or profited in spectacular economic terms in the "new Argentina." In effect, *Justicialismo* says in economic matters what Mr. Dooley once said of the "North American" President Theodore Roosevelt's anti-trust program: "On the one hand, bust the trusts; on the other hand, not so fast." Third, *Justicialismo* provides the ideational context for Perón's domestic political actions. Individual liberties are curtailed; federalism is reduced; political parties are restricted. But none of these, argues the "Third Position," is completely destroyed. All are saved from "extremism."

In the "new Argentina," justicialist doctrine comes completely equipped with a group of slogans which serve as battle cries or symbols behind which *Peronistas* rally. Consider some of the slogans of Peronism: "Dignification of Labor," "Elevation of social culture," "Humanization of Capital," "Faith in God," "Solidarity among Argentines." Many of these acquire their especial significance from the ideological framework of *Justicialismo*.

President Perón has declared himself to be very proud of the "Third Position," the "new Argentina's" contribution to the world of political philosophy. "When I think that we have been the first to announce this solution to men, and when I demonstrate that we have been the first to realize it, I can do no less than affirm my faith in the high destiny which God has seen fit to assign to our country," he told the congress in May of 1950. "My soul is filled with emotion when I think that the day cannot be far off when all of humanity, seeking some star in the night, will fix its eyes on the flag of the Argentines."

. . .

What is *Justicialismo?* It is more than a dubious political theory; it is a system of practical politics. *Justicialismo* is a juggler's act, a huge vaudeville performance. Perón is the clown, and Argentine special interest groups are the balls he juggles. The clown has seven balls.

They are called the "army," the "Church," the "Oligarchy," the "foreign imperialist," "labor," the "interior," and the *"porteños"* [*residents of Buenos Aires*]. *Justicialismo* is a juggler's act: the performer must keep all seven balls in motion, and he must remain equidistant from all of them. It is, in a sense, a tragic performance if the observer harbors sympathy for the clown. The juggler must preserve his "Third Position": he dare not catch one of the balls and call it his own, for the others will fall on his head and destroy him. This is not a performance that can be terminated successfully, for it is a species of marathon. The clown cannot catch all of the balls and accept ovations for a game well played. There is only one way the performance can end: at least one of the seven balls will fall on the juggler's head. Yes, *Justicialismo* is a vaudeville performance. It is not true that *Justicialismo* is "that doctrine before, during, and after which nothing happens." Rather, it is that performance before which the seven balls had a systemized relationship to each other, during which they are kept in dizzy motion, and after which at least one of them falls on the clown. The act can end in no other way.

Justicialismo says that there are seven tyrannies. This is true. For the juggler has seven balls, and at least one of them will kill him.

Perón gives and Perón takes away. Peronism is fluid and dynamic. The justicialist technique in politics means that the regime makes a studied and systematic practice of avoiding prolonged political honeymoons with specific interest groups. The juggler's seven balls are the interest groups, and Perón cannot perform unless all of them are kept in motion. There is much talk of the army, the Church, the "Oligarchy," the "foreign imperialist," labor, the "interior," and the *porteños*. Perón needs all of them. But none of them really belongs to him, for his is of necessity a "Third Position."

Consider the interest groups. The army will probably fall on Perón's head one day, but the "new Argentina" is the army's Argentina. The military is a major bulwark of the regime, but the army is in a constant state of potential rebellion. Some of its officers hated "Evita," and some hate the workers, the *descamisados*. In truth, the army and organized labor have little in common except the accident of the revolution. Perón dare not say his regime is the army's regime, for the other interest groups will rise against him; he dare not cling too long or too stubbornly to the others, for the army will destroy him. His is a "Third Position"; he can take no other.

Or perhaps it will be the Church that will destroy Perón. He needs the Church, but the government does not—cannot—belong to the clergy. Here, too, it is necessary to juggle. Again, consider the "Oligarchy." Perón needs the landowners and the capitalists, he cannot destroy them. Without the "Oligarchy" there is no "new Argentina," just as there was no old Argentina without the "Oligarchy." He dare not throw the "Oligarchy" away, yet he cannot call it his own. And what of the "foreign imperialist"? Let the Yankee explain it himself: "Where else can you get 12 per cent on your money?" Where is the "Third Position"? It is somewhere between more than 12 per cent ("extreme materialism") and no percentage at all ("extreme idealism"). "On the one hand, bust the trusts; on the other hand, not so fast." Mr. Dooley might well have been an Argentine.

And the workers, the *descamisados?* The juggler needs them, but they do not belong to him. And perhaps, as many Argentines predict, it may be labor that eventually destroys Perón. If it is indeed the seventh tyranny, communism ("materialistic collectivism") that terminates the performance, it will have been Perón who brought it. After all, no matter which one of the seven balls is dropped, it is the same juggler. And what of the *provincianos* and the *porteños?* They of the "interior" claim that Perón belongs to Buenos Aires; the *porteños* say, partly because Rosas represented the provinces of the "interior," that Perón reminds them of "Bloody Rosas."

Thus the seven balls. At least one will fall with lethal effect.

An intriguing question remains. Perón has said—and so it is the truth from headquarters—that *Justicialismo* envisages a temperate social order compounded of "just the right amounts" of idealism, materialism, individualism, and collectivism. How much of each is "just the right amount"? Beyond assigning greater values to idealism and to individualism than to the other two forces, *Perón does not say how much of each ingredient is the proper amount.* There is no objective standard for this; there is no quantitative formula, no mathematics, in *Justicialismo.* The "Third Position" is whatever Perón says it is; *Justicialismo* is whatever he does; and he is a juggler. Justicialist theory is, basically, a philosophy of opportunism.

❦ 31 ❧

Yesterday, Today, and Tomorrow

Mario Amadeo

The resignation of Perón on September 19, 1955 as a result of a military coup was followed by the establishment of a caretaker regime under General Eduardo Lonardi, who was himself deposed on November 13 because he was considered "soft" on Peronism. Under Lonardi's successor, General Pedro Aramburu, who was kidnapped by a Peronist group in 1970 and later found dead, more determined efforts were made to purge the government and the labor unions of every trace of Peronism. Some observers, however, saw Peronism as the result of a deep-rooted malaise in Argentine society which could not be healed overnight. One of these was Mario Amadeo, Minister of Foreign Affairs (and Religion) during the short-lived Lonardi government and Argentine Ambassador to the United Nations under President Arturo Frondizi. In an essay published in April 1956, Amadeo views Peronism as a flawed and ultimately unsuccessful response to Argentina's need for political and social transformation.

The reconstruction of the country, an essential objective of the revolution, involves a series of complex, visceral problems. Those problems, which assumed prominence at the very moment the regime was changed, are still awaiting an adequate solution.[1] Undoubtedly, they should be preoccupying the government that has the primary responsibility for facing up to them. But they also affect the nation's citizens, who share with the political authority responsibility for solving them.

The gravest and most urgent of those problems is the liquidation of the Peronist remains. Note well that we do not use the word "liquidation" in the sense of violent destruction; as when we say, for exam-

---

From Joseph R. Barager (ed. and tr.), *Why Perón Came to Power* (New York: Knopf, 1968), pp. 249–257. Copyright © 1968 by Joseph R. Barager. Reprinted by permission of Alfred A. Knopf, Inc. Deletions in the text are by Joseph R. Barager.

[1] Perón was overthrown in September 1955. Amadeo's essay was published in April 1956, during the provisional presidency of General Pedro Aramburu. [J. R. B.]

ple, the Russian Communists have "liquidated" the supporters of Beria or of Malenkov. Such a meaning would involve choosing a solution that, we hasten to say, is not the best one. No; when we refer to the liquidation of Peronism we mean the assimilation of that great sector of the Argentine population that gave its name to the fallen regime, to which, despite its mistakes and its failures, that group continues to be loyal. That mass sector is touchy and resentful. It looks askance at the movement that brought down its idol, and it takes refuge in an irrational and blind faith that soon they [the Peronists] will return to being what they were before [his fall]. Their motto and their war cry is: "Perón will return."

Well then; this position of uncompromising hostility must be overcome so that this mass sector may join spiritually in a task that is the patrimony and duty of all Argentines. Our country has been through an experience similar to that resulting from a war—a lost war. This is evident in the economic field, but so is it on the moral level. Unloosed rancors, unsatisfied aspirations, that indefinable state of uneasiness that accompanies defeat—these are the sentiments we can perceive in many of our compatriots and neighbors, the Argentines of 1956.

When a country finds itself in this situation, the first requisite for moving forward on the right road is to forge the compact unity of all the nation.

. . .

The success or failure of the attempt to unite the country depends, in good measure, on how one interprets the Peronist interval. There exists, in that regard, various versions, and it would be useful to review them systematically.

Thus the usual opinion among the socially conservative sectors is that Peronism was nothing but a nightmare, an evil period. Those sectors speak of "magnetic influence," of "collective suggestion," of "deformation of the conscience," and of other anomalies that reduce the problem to a question of pathological psychology. Those sectors consider that the Argentine populace have suffered a sickness, and that it is merely a question of submitting it to a vigorous cure. Once the period of treatment is over, everything will return to be what it was before; nothing will be left behind from the episode other than those vestiges a robust person would have from a case of the grippe or of the measles.

Others, in that same sector, are less simplistic, even though they perhaps are no less mistaken. These people agree that Peronism has been a more serious development than the first group claims and that it really has deeply stirred popular opinion. But they consider that Peronism has achieved that effect either through venality and corruption or by appealing exclusively to the lowest instincts of the common people. These people see nothing good or positive in the defeated movement. Peronism is the fruit of ignorance, as is superstition or quackery. This view has a binding effect only among the most primitive and uncivil sectors of the community. For them the question is settled with a little dose of re-education and a great dose of "beating." From the viewpoint of the anti-Peronists of the right, to "de-Peronize" is equivalent to "getting rid of rats."

For the anti-Peronists of our liberal left—the left composed of those intellectuals who today give direction to the revolution—the question is explained in terms of that sea where all rivers converge—Nazism. Perón and the Peronists were totalitarian Nazis who wished to impose on Argentina the system of Hitler and Mussolini. According to this viewpoint the ex-President was a doctrinaire thinker who, during his stay in Italy, had studied feverishly accelerated courses in the corporative system and had passionately resolved to apply that system in the *anima vili* of this innocent and democratic country. Consequently, these gentlemen cannot understand any other design but one in which all that is Peronist must be Nazi and all that is Nazi, Peronist. . . . For this sector, to "de-Peronize" is the same as to "de-Nazify."

Finally, there is another left—the anti-liberal and Marxist left; it finds fault only with the person of the Peronist chief and sees in that movement a form—crude and primitive but effective—of their fight against imperialism. As a result it was a little difficult for the men of this persuasion to explain how the petroleum contract with Standard Oil was a battle against imperialism, but contradictions do nc terrify a Marxist.[2] These individuals are disposed to go beyond Peró in their social reforms because they perceive that his shortcoming was not in having been too radical in his procedures but in not having been radical enough. This sector, in which the Trotskyite variety of Communists are the leaders of the outcry, implicitly proclaims the formula "Perón plus X" and intends to take charge of the proletariat left now unattached by the absence of the "leader."

.   .   .

For my part, I cannot accept the Peronist phenomenon as being exclusively a mark of inferiority, or a vestige of primitivism, or even less, the artificial adoption of an ideology foreign to our idiosyncrasy. I consider that Peronism is a very complex and very important phe-

---

[2] In his last year in office, Perón signed a contract with a subsidiary of Standard Oil of California to permit the exploitation of Argentine petroleum reserves under terms that were unacceptable to many Argentines. Even his own handpicked Peronist Party congressional leaders balked at supporting the contract. [J. R. B.]

nomenon and that one must differentiate between its positive and negative elements.

In the first place, I consider that Peronism has brought together, through failure, two transformations (some would say two revolutions) of diverse origin and destiny: an ideological and political transformation and a social renovation. Both were latent in the country, on June 4, 1943, and the sortie by the Army could have hastened the process but not provoked it. The country was living within discredited and outgrown socio-political structures, and was struggling to free itself of them. The June Revolution—purely military though it was in origin—brought about the propitious occasion that allowed the change to take place. Since everything was in crisis—ideas, institutions, parties, and men—everything tumbled down.

What, then, is the meaning and extent of these transformations, which Perón took over and put forward as the banners of the movement that carried him to power? In regard to the ideological and political transformation we will say little here. . . . It is enough, at this time, to note that the country no longer allows the existence of doctrines and institutional forms within which a disruption of the national order was fomented. It is possible that the political currents then reigning in the various European countries contributed by giving substance and style to that internal unrest; but it would be erroneous to attribute it exclusively to a process of contagion. To demonstrate that the institutional mechanism was no longer functioning normally, we only have to recall that in 1930, for the first time in seventy years, a revolutionary movement triumphed, and that the free vote established in 1912 had to be "corrected" by fraud. And finally, in order not to continue multiplying examples indefinitely, let us note that a great mass of the population, perhaps the majority, had definitely isolated itself from contact with the political parties. When a country's people isolates itself from civic life, it is either because it finds itself in the last stages of decadence, or because it is on the eve of a fundamental change. I believe that we were finding ourselves in the latter and not the former of those two situations.

The country was also longing for a great social renovation. In that respect it is necessary to admit that, at the time of the 1943 revolt, Argentina was one of the most backward countries of Latin America. And let it be clearly understood that we do not say this because we believe that the proletariat here was poorer or in more wretched circumstances than in other places or that it had less legislation for its aid and protection. On the contrary, the living conditions of the Argentine worker—rural or urban—were relatively humane and infinitely better than those of the majority of his Latin American counterparts. Compare, for example, the situation of a peon from one of our large farms with that of a Bolivian miner of that same epoch. If the housing of the Argentine worker was—and continues to be— defective, his level of nutrition was not a little superior to that of the middle class of any European country. As for social security laws, even if they were deficient and incomplete, they still formed a body of legislation that, in general, was respected.

The Argentine social problem was not so much one of a miserable and hungry proletariat as that of a nonexistent proletariat. It is very true that the tardy appearance of our working classes on the public scene was due, in part, to the lack of great industry and, in part, to the fact that until not many years ago those classes, in the urban sector, were composed of foreigners. But by 1943 the facts of the problem had already changed. World War II and the consequent economic isolation had given considerable impetus to industrial development so that several million urban workers were dependent on it. And as for the nationality problem, it had been resolved by the passage of time. The foreign grandparents and parents had been replaced by their native children and grandchildren, and their descendants became involved in the country's problems with the same interest and, from then on, with the same rights as the native, long-established traditional families. Some time the singular patriotism characteristic of the sons of the immigrants in this country must be analyzed.

The Marxist parties attempted to mobilize these forces before Perón, but they did not succeed, except in a very partial and fragmentary way. They did not succeed because, in the first place, they were employing ideological rather than emotional or temperamental concepts. In the second place, those ideological concepts, insofar as they were intelligible, met with the incoercible resistance of our workers against letting themselves be won over by extreme positions. It is a commonplace to say that Socialism can never pass over the Riochuelo,[3] and it will always be a mystery for the European from an industrial country that the only place where a conservative caudillo repeatedly triumphed without using fraud was in Avellanada, which had the largest agglomeration of workers in the republic.

Until 1945, therefore, the Argentine proletariat could not—even though desiring to do so—feel a sense of solidarity with the national destiny. No one had concerned himself with speaking its language, with understanding its innermost desires, or with contacting it directly. Lost in the past was the memory of Yrigoyen (who, strictly speaking, was not a proletariat caudillo). Governed by strangers, it

---

[3] The Riochuelo is the stream separating the city of Buenos Aires proper from the working-class districts of the neighboring province of Buenos Aires. [J. R. B.]

was inevitable that the Argentine working class would wholeheartedly follow a caudillo who seemed to express its sentiments clearly. Ideological transformation and social renovation, therefore, were being postulated by the historical conditions of the country at the end of the first third of the century. It would not have been impossible to consummate them in an orderly manner since the great wealth of the country and the peaceful disposition of its inhabitants were helping in the process.

The great and perhaps the only genius of Perón was in taking notice of the latent existence of these transformations and, putting himself at their head, utilizing the state powers the June Revolution had conferred on him and those that, soon afterward, he could snatch away from his comrades in arms. If he succeeded in doing it, it is undoubtedly because he possessed some of the gifts that denote a leader. He was speaking in clear, precise, and forceful language, designed for the multitude's simplistic attitude. And he knew how to say exactly what the mass of people wanted him to say. In this restricted sense, one could accept the interpretation that Peronism was a phenomenon of collective magnetization. But while this interpretation assumes that only Perón could create such a phenomenon, in our judgment he was merely the catalytic agent or unifying element of a movement that was obeying deeper motives than just his personal influence.

This is where that element of chance intervenes so that history is not a series of fatal deeds linked by the principle of causation but— like all that is human—possesses that ingredient of free choice that makes it impossible to guarantee its course. The free factor, in this case, was the personality of the man who put himself at the forefront of those transformations and impressed his stamp on them. His absolute lack of discrimination between good and evil, his total lack of the talents of a statesman, his monstrous and growing egocentricity, ought to provoke—as they did provoke—the tergiversation and the adulteration of a profound and legitimate desire for change. Thus it was that the ideological renovation was diluted in the puerile and stammering "Justicialist doctrine"; the political transformation into a constitutional reform that, although it does not have the diabolical outlines that now are assigned to it, turned out in the final analysis to be timid and lacking in technical skill. And the social renovation, even though the most effective and lasting work of the regime, dissipated itself in demagogic pyrotechnics. For that reason the Peronist adventure was, above all else, a great opportunity lost. And in the life of nations, as in the life of men, opportunity usually does not knock twice.

Perón, who as we have seen was much more the *medium* than the leader of the masses, exacerbated a problem that we share with all Hispanic America and that forms the crisis of this drama: *the divorce of the people from the governing classes*.[4]

BIBLIOGRAPHY

A bibliographical guide to the Perón era is provided by Fritz L. Hoffman in a two-part article, "Perón and After," *Hispanic American Historical Review*, 36 (1956), 510–528 and 39 (1959), 212–233. The years preceding Perón's rise are covered in Ysabel F. Rennie, *The Argentine Republic* (New York: Macmillan, 1945), while the origins of *Peronismo* are examined in Joseph R. Barager (ed.), *Why Perón Came to Power* (New York: Knopf, 1968). Also valuable as background reading are Robert A. Potash, *The Army and Politics in Argentina, 1928–1945* (Stanford, Cal.: Stanford University Press, 1969) and Félix Luna, *El 45: Crónica de un año decisivo* (Buenos Aires: Editorial Jorge Alvarez, 1969).

Robert J. Alexander, *The Perón Era* (New York: Columbia University Press, 1951) is an unfavorable assessment written while Perón was still in power; another contemporary work, María Flores, *The Woman with a Whip: Eva Perón* (Garden City, N.Y.: Doubleday, 1952) is also unfriendly toward its subject. Thomas F. McGann, "The Ambassador and the Dictator," *Centennial Review*, 6 (1962), 343–357 is a reappraisal of Spruille Braden's controversial ambassadorship in Argentina in 1945. On Perón and Argentina labor see Samuel L. Baily, *Labor, Nationalism and Politics in Argentina* (New Brunswick, N.J.: Rutgers University Press, 1967).

The causes of Perón's overthrow are discussed in Arthur P. Whitaker, *Argentine Upheaval* (New York: Praeger, 1956). The views of Argentine leftists toward *Peronismo* can be seen in such a work as Jorge Abelardo Ramos, *Revolución y contrarevolución en Argentina: Las masas en nuestra historia* (Buenos Aires: Amerindia, 1957). For *Peronismo* between 1955 and 1965 see Peter G. Ranis, *"Peronismo* Without Perón," *Journal of Inter-American Studies*, 8 (1966), 112–128.

---

[4] For another Argentine view of the problems of Peronism see Ernesto Sábato, *El otro rostro del Peronismo* (Buenos Aires, 1956), which was written in answer to Amadeo's essay. [J. R. B.]

[C] Aspects of the Cuban Revolution

✺ 32 ✺

The Roots of Cuban Nationalism

——◄●►——

C. A. M. Hennessy

*The transformation of Cuba into a communist state in the early 1960s
aroused strong reactions everywhere. In the United States, consternation over the "loss" of Cuba and alarm over the establishment of a
communist beachhead in the Western Hemisphere contributed to a
sharper awareness of the social and economic problems of Latin America. To Latin American leftists and aspiring revolutionaries throughout
the world, the new Cuba became a model to be emulated, especially
by other underdeveloped nations attempting to shake off the yoke of
"imperialist" exploitation. However, in a closely reasoned essay on the
roots of Cuban nationalism, C. A. M. Hennessy of the University of
Warwick stresses its uniquely Cuban character and concludes that although the Cuban Revolution "provides an inspiration to Latin American radicals, ... it is less clear that it provides a model." Professor
Hennessy is also the author of* The Federal Republic in Spain: Pi y
Margall and the Federal Republican Movement *(New York: Oxford
University Press, 1962).*

From C. A. M. Hennessy, "The Roots of Cuban Nationalism," *International
Affairs,* 39 (July 1963), 345–358. Reprinted by permission of the author. Some
footnotes deleted. Italicized bracketed notes in the text are by Helen Delpar.

When Castro gained power in Cuba in 1958 it seemed to the democratic Left in Europe, and to rebels without a cause, that here was a revolution on the new frontier. Cuba appeared to have produced a revolution with a difference. Neither capitalist nor Communist, it would break the ideological stalemate, and so provide a model for the uncommitted third of the world. Disillusion was all the more profound, therefore, when the Cuba crisis of 1962 appeared to provide confirmation that Castro's revolution was but 'a variant in the family of Communist revolutions'. It seemed that those who had argued that Castroism was the best insurance against Communism would have to eat their words, while those who had always held that Castroism was a cloak for Communism felt their case had been proved.

It is still too early for final judgments; the evidence is far too scanty and, above all, there is no simple explanation of Castro's complex personality. Until that can be explained, the revolution will make little sense—for in Cuban politics, as in those of Latin America generally, personalities are still the prime movers. But this much at least can be said: although Castro's motives may be obscure, and although his revolution has been overlaid by Cold War classifications, both he and it have their roots in Cuban history. For example, it is difficult to begin to understand Castro himself without considering the 19th-century nationalist José Martí (1853–1895), who has been a dominant intellectual influence on him. Unless, in short, the Castro Revolution is seen as a particular type of nationalist upheaval, closely conditioned by Cuban history, there is a danger that false analogies will be made with revolutionary situations elsewhere in Latin America.

It is too readily assumed that because Hispanic America shares a common language and the same colonial heritage there is a common unity and sense of purpose underlying the needs and aspirations of its many republics. Yet it may well be that the differences between them are more significant than their similarities. 'Hispanic America' and 'Latin America' are deceptively simple portmanteau terms behind which cluster the infinitely complex nationalist attitudes of a hundred and fifty years' separate existence.

There is a sharp contrast between those attitudes and the way in which Cubans think about their history and their national identity. On the mainland the independence movements at the beginning of the 19th century were nationalist only in a very limited sense, so that although they resulted in national states these were the most pathetic type of nation. They were without nationalist mythologies, and their limits were determined by the accidents of geography and the impermeable frontiers of Spanish administrative decisions. The creation of national mythologies thus became an obsession with many intellectuals: poised between a European culture towards which they had ambivalent feelings and, in a number of the new republics, an indigenous population which had remained largely uninfluenced by Western ideas, their task of finding a synthesis seemed insuperable. A further complication lay in the fact that in those countries where there was a minority of pure European stock (all except Chile, Argentina and Uruguay), the political nation as often as not excluded the indigenous peoples. An Indianist view implied a radicalism which ensured its rejection by the ruling groups. The great achievement of the Mexican Revolution was to make Indianism respectable, and to inspire other broadly based Indianist movements, such as Haya de la Torre's Indo-Americanism and the revolutionary nationalism of Bolivia.

The anti-Americanism which became an integral element in Latin American nationalisms had reactionary as well as radical overtones. Towards the end of the 19th century, fear of political dominance by the United States was sharpened by her expanding economic power, which threatened to disrupt a mainly static society and to sever the oligarchies' traditional links with Europe. The spirit of the *entrepreneur,* Protestantism and democracy were feared as much by the landowning oligarchy in the 19th century as trusts, concessions and corporations are by the radicals of to-day. But in those countries with large, unassimilated *mestizo* and Indian groups, anti-Americanism had an additional and dual character; it was both a symptom of a deep *malaise* arising from a sense of rootlessness and a positive affirmation of each country's uniqueness in terms of its Indian heritage. Mexican and Bolivian nationalists, and Peruvian *Apristas [supporters of the Peruvian political movement APRA; see Article 11]*, can to some extent base their nationalist mythologies on the records of flourishing pre-Spanish civilisations and on deeply rooted Indian cultures.

In this, at least, Cuba has been less fortunate. An island exposed to international rivalry in the Caribbean, her national identity has been continually threatened by foreign influences, in face of which her nationalists have had no pre-Spanish past or a flourishing indigenous culture on which to base a nationalist mythology. In spite of the work of the great Cuban anthropologist Fernando Ortiz, Afro-Cubanism as a movement cannot bear comparison with Afro-Brazilianism. The Spanish colonial legacy, and even North American racial attitudes, have been too strong for Cubans to have made, in racial terms, a virtue out of necessity.

A long gestation before independence was not enough in itself to give Cuban nationalism a sense of balance. The absence of a telluric basis for it tended to crystallise nationalist sentiment round the figure of Martí as it has also been a reason why the dynamic behind Cuban nationalism has often seemed to be little more than a febrile, hysterical anti-Americanism. It accounts, too, for the way in which, in Cuba, national myth-making has often lost touch with political reality. This was shown when the nationalists of the 1890s were prepared to devastate the island and so create the conditions for United States intervention rather than accept Spanish reforms. It has been shown, too, in Castro's own brand of nationalism when, on occasions, he has seemed prepared to invite the apotheosis of national martyrdom in the holocaust of a new war. There is also the fact that Cuban nationalism, whether in Martían or Castroist form, has always been couched in Latin American and universalist terms, not those of a narrow Cubanism. That is why the Castro revolution has seen itself as having the messianic mission of 'turning the Cordillera of the Andes into the Sierra Maestra of Latin America'.

Any analysis of Cuban nationalism must begin with a consideration of the island's social structure, not only because it has determined the form that nationalism has taken, but also because, in the case of Cuba, the axiom that nationalist movements are fomented, led and supported by the middle class needs some qualification. What middle class existed in the 19th century consisted of Spanish immigrants who, living in tight urban groups, failed to become assimilated, monopolised commerce, acted as bankers to debt-ridden *criollo* planters and were naturally a main support of the colonial régime. National independence was the objective of a small number of *criollo* lawyers, writers, liberal priests and students. Alienated intellectuals, rooted in no social class, make an early *début* in Cuban history but, unable to convert any but a small number of landowners to the idea of independence, and despised by the Spanish middle class, they were either forced into exile, like Varela (1787–1853) and Saco (1797–1879), or, like Luz y Caballero (1800–1862) and Mendive (1821–1886), they accepted the patient task of educational preparation. The few schools and the University of Havana, after its secularisation in 1842, almost entirely *criollo* staffed, became hothouses of nationalist sentiment.

Yet the decisive impetus to nationalism did not come from these elements but from radical landowners in Oriente who, for mainly economic reasons, revolted against Spanish rule in 1868 and thus began the Ten Years' War. That war was, in essence, the expression of a new nationalism which developed in response to the embittered frustrated nationalism of a declining imperial power which regarded Cuba as an integral part of Spain, and which refused to recognise her separate identity. Absence of easily exploitable wealth, and a small indigenous population, had discouraged any intensive Spanish colonisation of the island until after Spain had lost her mainland possessions. The economic boom and the sugar revolution of the early 19th century kept Cuba loyal, but this loyalty was rewarded only with relentless political and economic exploitation.

Nevertheless, the war ended in a stalemate because the Oriente landowners failed to win over the wealthier planters in the rest of the island, whose ideology, whether annexationism, reformism or autonomism, was always conditioned by fear of the democratic implications of the nationalists' creed.

The Oriente rebels were, in any case, themselves divided over the implications of the abolition of slavery, and it was only after the war had destroyed the economic basis of the slave-system, and with it slavery itself, that this main inhibiting factor in the nationalist revolution was removed. By that time, however, the initiative in the struggle for independence had passed to a small but vocal group of Cubans in Havana and in exile.

The particular significance of Martí in the history of Cuban nationalism lies in his appearance in the depressed 1880s, at the moment when the nationalist forces were leaderless and divided, and when the abolition of slavery made it feasible, for the first time, to create a mass nationalist movement which would draw its strength from groups other than discontented planters.

Sacrificing his health, marriage, happiness, and finally his life, to the cause of independence, Martí is both the greatest Cuban writer and the most famous of Cuban heroes. Born in Havana in 1853, the son of a Spanish sergeant and a Canary Island mother, his precocity attracted the attention of Rafael Mendive, the schoolmaster-poet, who became his spiritual godfather and from whom he inherited the intellectual tradition of nationalism handed down from Varela. Imprisoned at the age of 16 for sympathising with the rebels, forced labour in the chalk pits with common criminals left in him an undying hatred of colonial rule which was to keep him in exile for the rest of his life. Apart from a brief visit, and the few days before his death in action in 1895, he never returned to Cuba after he was exiled to Spain in 1871.

His four years of study in the turbulent Spain of the early 1870s convinced Martí that no justice could be expected from the *Cortes* or even from the distracted Republic of 1873. But his admiration for Spanish culture, and his ambivalent attitude towards his Spanish father, saved him from the type of Hispanophobia which has characterised many Latin American radicals. He believed that 'good' Spaniards could be persuaded to see the justice of Cuba's cause.

After spending some years in Mexico, Guatemala and Venezuela Martí settled in the United States, where he became one of the most perceptive foreign observers of the local scene. His experience in Mexico where his liberal friends, the heirs of Juárez, had been overthrown by Porfirio Díaz, and his experience in the Venezuela of Guzmán Blanco, from which he had been expelled for criticising the dictator, made him appreciative of democracy in the United States. Yet his stay in Guatemala, and contact with Indians there, made him recognise that American-style democracy would be inapplicable in a Latin American setting where, he felt, the indigenous peoples should play a cardinal, not a marginal, role in future developments. Indeed, in the United States he sensed very clearly the growing imperialist mood of the later 1880s, with its undertones of racial superiority. The first Pan-American Conference in 1889 was a warning light, and he began writing of the need for Latin America's second liberation, this time from United States economic domination.

Martí was a great Latin American figure and not just a parochial Cuban hero. Colonial censorship meant that during his lifetime he was better known outside the island through an unending flow of articles in the leading mainland papers. In his many-sided interests he is typical of the Latin American *pensador*. He was not only a committed intellectual but a brilliant political speaker, man of action and founder of the Cuban Revolutionary Party (PRC) in which he achieved the seemingly impossible task of uniting the notoriously divided exiles —bringing together illiterate negro tobacco workers of Tampa and Key West, sophisticated middle class exiles in New York and the wilful veteran generals of the Ten Years' War, Gómez and Maceo. It was his remarkable personality that won over these two hardened *caudillos* who were distrustful both of civilian control and of each other.

In Martí's populist creed the political nation was all-embracing; his notion of class harmony may have derived from a mystical sense of the brotherhood of all men, but it was also the result of an acute awareness that Cuba had no revolutionary class strong enough to bring a nationalist revolt to fruition. But, however useful in creating a sense of unity against the Spaniards, the populist myth collapsed in the bitter divisions of the early years of independence. The War of Liberation was not the short sharp struggle which Martí had imagined would forestall United States intervention, and in which a mass uprising would both overthrow Spanish power and temper a new nationalist spirit. Instead, it dragged on for three years and ended in the foreign intervention which he had so much feared.

Yet it is doubtful if even Martí could have conjured national unity out of the devastation of a three years' war of extermination, or if he would have been able to prevent those developments which were to determine Cuba's future as a monoculture economy. United States capital restored the sugar industry but at the price of perpetuating the *latifundia* and reducing the small cane planters to complete dependence on foreign-owned mills. Martí believed that political and economic independence were inseparable, and he had argued that Cuban democracy must be based on a small-holding peasantry in a diversified economy. Instead, a relentless process of centralisation extended the great sugar estates of the colonial period, thus inhibiting the growth of a rural middle class and creating a landless, agrarian proletariat.

The alienation of the rural proletariat from the land was paralleled by the alienation of the middle sectors[1] from a dynamic role in the state. The neo-colonial economy of the Republic left little room for the development of a Cuban middle class. There was no wholesale exodus of Spaniards, and those who remained kept their Spanish citizenship and pre-empted the best posts in the Church and commerce, while a deficient education system rendered many Cubans unfit for technical posts in expanding United States concerns. They could turn only to politics, government service, the professions and teaching. The social system of the republic perpetuated the Spanish legacy that public office should be made a source of private profit. Politics thus became the key to social advancement, and so little more than a squabble between factions for the ownership of government. Parties cut across group interests, and *personalismo* rather than principle determined party alignments. Implicit agreements that parties should alternate in power, and thus share out offices, broke down and *continuismo* became the main cause of 'revolution' as in 1905, 1917 and after 1928. But that type of 'revolution' meant merely a switch of government personnel, not a fundamental social or political change. Perhaps the most striking example of the spoils system was shown in 1948 when Prío Socorrás replaced Grau San Martín as President. Although both were members of the same party, 10,000 government posts nevertheless changed hands.

Government was, in fact, like the lottery which used to play such a prominent part in Cuban politics. Public life was permeated by a boom psychosis, with the middle sectors bidding against each other for government sinecures. In purely economic terms there might have been a middle class but in terms of self-identification and bourgeois culture values a middle class scarcely existed. Instead, there were what the Cubans themselves describe as the *'capas medias'* [*middle layers*].

---

[1] In any serious analysis of Latin American politics we need to be freed from a linguistic web of terms which are virtually meaningless in a Latin American context. Although "middle sectors" is open to objection, it avoids some of the implications of middle class. The Spanish merchants and bureaucrats of the colonial period might, with more justification, be described as a middle class.

There was no strong bourgeois tradition to offset the *rentier*[2] mentality which was one of the main legacies of the *criollo* plantocracy. Neither anti-clericalism nor anti-Americanism gave homogeneity to these groups, whose factionalism was the bane of Cuban politics. Living beyond their means to attain upper class status, patronising an enormous number of private schools, to the detriment of public education, and bombarded by the advertisements of a consumer society, they lived in a continual state of economic frustration and near-revolutionary ferment, plotting the overthrow of the political structure in order to hasten their accession to the upper reaches of the graft system.

The most coherent section, as might be expected, were the professional groups and the students. The common Latin American phenomenon of the under-employed intellectual can be related to the cultural legacy of the colonial régime, embalmed in a formalistic, literary and non-scientific university system. Critics, like Pozos Dulces (1809–1877), Martí and Varona (1849–1933), who argued that the educational system was totally unrelated to Cuba's needs, were voices crying in the wilderness. Law and medicine were the most oversubscribed professions, the one as a prelude to politics, the other because of its high status value. Although the rural areas desperately needed doctors, a disproportionate number remained in Havana where the opportunities for advancement lay.

The inability of society to absorb the products of the higher educational system exaggerated the dichotomy between 'generals and doctors'. *Caudillismo* based on the power of the army was not an evil of Cuban government until 1933. The disbanding of the army of liberation, under United States' pressure in 1900, prevented it from filling the political vacuum during the early years of independence, as had so often happened on the mainland, and its generals were forced to seek alternative ways of capitalising their prestige. Even after it was re-established in 1909, the army did not itself act as a political force. The generals, however, expecting to dominate politics by right, did so through manipulation of a patronage system in which lawyers were able to share in the pickings. Zayas, President between 1921 and 1925, represented the new symbiosis where the astute lawyer-politician managed a vast graft system in which generals were co-beneficiaries. Thus not even professional groups were united in their opposition to the *status quo,* and it was left to the rootless younger generation, faced with a bleak prospect as underemployed intellectuals, to provide the dynamic for a new nationalist conception of culture and politics.

---

[2] This term describes someone who lives off a fixed income, especially from bonds. [H. D.]

The ideas of the University Reform movement[3] had fallen on fertile ground in Havana University which, with its professors who did little or no work, was a microcosm of the graft in Cuban public life. From 1924, when students forced academic reforms on the government and began extension classes among the poor in the *Universidad Popular José Martí*, the University became both the focus of a regenerative movement and a centre of revolutionary politics. It was this lost generation of students, exiles in their own land, who re-discovered Martí with his nostalgic yearning for an idealised *patria* [*fatherland*] and his exile's vision of a socially united, racially harmonious and economically independent country. His stature grew as the expansion of United States cultural and economic influence brought a note of urgency to the intellectuals' search for national identity.

The concept of the 'frustrated revolution' of 1895 now helped to explain the contrast between Martí's dream of a rejuvenated nation and the reality of graft and corruption. In this interpretation, United States intervention, rather than the legacies of Spanish rule or indigenous weaknesses, was responsible for the distortions in public life, and for the diversion of Cuban history from the course which Martí had mapped out.

The Cuban belief that Spanish power had already been broken by the time the United States intervened in 1898, three years after the beginning of the War of Liberation, gave a keen edge to anti-Americanism, and the coincidence of national independence with a new phase of American imperialism made for an easy transference of nationalist antagonism from Spain to the United States. The attribution of all internal shortcomings to foreign intervention prevented a more fundamental analysis of the new republic's social *malaise*. There was also the fact that economic control from the United States, being more insidious than political control from Spain, precluded the possibility of heroic action.

After the post-war sugar boom broke in the early 1920s, American banks secured a dominant position in the sugar industry economy. By the late 1920s American interests controlled 70 per cent of sugar production and had become the financial prop of the unpopular régime of President Machado (1925–1933). The humiliating Platt

---

[3] This was inaugurated in 1918 in the University of Córdoba, Argentina. It aimed to break down the privileged colonial-style university, to secure student representation on governing bodies, to democratise entry and to give universities a specific function as challengers rather than defenders of the *status quo*. Its influence has been felt throughout Latin America, the earliest and best-known repercussions being in Peru where *Aprismo* grew out of the students' movement.

Amendment[4] and the repercussions of the 1929 crisis made anti-Americanism a main ingredient in the revolutionary movement which finally drove him from power in 1933. The revolutionary government of Grau San Martín, a university professor supported by university students, represented the radical nationalism of frustrated intellectuals, but it could rally little coherent support in the country at large. It was only to be expected that the United States would not recognise a régime which threatened nationalisation, but more significant was the hostility in Cuba itself of the two other revolutionary elements, organised labour, which was partly under Communist domination, and Batista's newly-promoted ex-sergeant officer corps.

Grau's reaction to the frustrated revolution of 1933 was to organise the nearest thing to a mass party in Cuban politics since Martí's P.R.C. Adopting the same name (although popularly known as the *Auténticos*) this party deliberately appealed more widely than to a specifically middle sector audience. But even so, Batista's power condemned him to 10 years of opposition. Ruling first through a succession of puppet presidents, and from 1940 to 1944 as president himself, Batista, supported by United States business interests, a pampered army and a tamed labour movement, could afford to ignore Grau whose potential nationalist support had been siphoned off by the Cubanisation law of 1933 (which compelled firms to employ 50 per cent. Cuban personnel), by the abrogation of the Platt Amendment in 1934 as part of Roosevelt's Good Neighbour policy, by the desperation of terrorist groups, like Guiteras' *Joven Cuba* which had been caught up in the mystique of violence, and by Batista's own brand of popular nationalism.

If Cuban reformers were frustrated during the 1934–1940 period, at least this could be explained in terms of Batista's corporate-style dictatorship. After 1944, when the *Auténticos* were in power, explanations were more difficult. Why did a revolutionary party fail to implement the neo-Socialist constitution of 1940 introduced by Batista, under left wing pressure as the Communists have claimed, in order to revive his waning popularity? Grau's failure to break the pattern of corruption, and even his extension of it into the labour movement in an effort to smash the Communist hold on the unions, discredited his party and led, in 1947, to the formation of a splinter party, the *Ortodoxos*. This now became the repository of revolutionary virtue and the refuge of yet another rootless younger generation. Although the Communists had attracted intellectuals of the calibre of Marinello, few

---

[4]An appendix to the 1901 Constitution, by which Cuban sovereignty was limited by the right reserved to the United States to intervene in the island should its interests be jeopardised.

were prepared to accept that particular type of discipline which, in the 1930s, demanded working agreements with Batista in preference to the democratic Left.[5]

The failure of the *Auténticos* reflected the personalities of its leaders, the whittling down of radical programmes through a need for working alliances in Congress, failure to stem graft and internal factionalism. It was a disaster for Cuba because it widened the sphere of corruption, further divided the middle sectors in the splintering of both *Auténticos* and *Ortodoxos* after 1952, and bred a cynicism about the abilities of Cubans to make democracy work. Except in the light of this failure of the democratic Left, Castro's revolution and his own political thinking make little sense.

Throughout the frustrating 1930s and 1940s the Martí cult gathered adherents, although an ambivalent attitude towards his writings reflected the divisions within the middle sectors where his popularity was greatest. The cult betrayed many of the characteristics of a sect mentality, providing a psychological compensation for a middle class lacking both power and faith in its own ability to change a society corrupted by United States influences. It provided a flight into a world of fantasy where, in the style of Rodó's *Ariel*, Cuban spirituality was contrasted with United States materialism and greed. But Martí's message became smothered in a torrent of words from those seeking a justification for present policies or a solace for past failures. Never was this more evident than in 1953, Martí's centenary and the first year of Batista's dictatorship, when over 500 articles on Martí were published. In contrast, there were those like Castro, to whom Martí was primarily a man of action, and for whom the cult provided not only the utopian vision behind the revolutionary movement but also a sense of continuity with the past and thus a means of identification with the heroic period of Cuba's history.

Castro's thinking has often been expressed in generalised Martían terms while Communism has implied a discipline which was neither in keeping with his need for self-dramatisation nor easy to reconcile with his earlier mode of thought. The relationship between Martí's Cuba-oriented humanism and Castro's Marxist-Leninism has not, so far, been

---

[5] With *personalismo* dominating politics, some intellectuals were attracted to Communism because of its demanding discipline and its impersonalism. The best example was perhaps Mella, the founder of the Students' Federation and first Secretary-General of the Cuban Communist party, assassinated under mysterious circumstances in Mexico in 1929. Continually quoted today, he is the Communists' hero, in contrast to Martí, the nationalist hero. A "Mella Institute" has recently been established at Havana University to popularise his life and work.

widely recognised; but, in interpreting the dialogue between nationalism and Communism, it would be unwise to underemphasise the emotional links which bind pupil to master which are recalled by the revolutionary slogan 'De José a Fidel'. Castro sees himself as a disciple who undertakes the second liberation of Latin America which the 'Apostle' had preached.[6]

'I carry in my heart the teachings of the Master', he said in his 'History will absolve me' speech of 1953, in which he also described Martí as the 'instigator of the 26th July'. The Communist condemnation of the Sierra Maestra rising as bourgeois romanticism was a just comment on the way in which Castro saw himself as a romantic hero figure in the Martí idiom. Even the landing from the *Granma* on an isolated part of the south coast of Oriente was a replica of Martí's landing in 1895. Castro cast himself in a role inspired by Martí's belief in the supreme importance of the individual leader. 'A man does not make a nation', Martí had written, 'but the nation at times may find its vibrant triumphant incarnation in a Man' and again 'Such leaders must be held sacred and the errors they commit forgiven them'. The role of the *líder máximo* [*maximum leader*] has been sanctified by Cuban tradition, and much of Castro's genius lies in the skill with which he plays on the *patrón* relationship, in which a sense of kinship is built up between the leader and his dependents.

If Martí's cult of the hero appealed to the histrionic side of Castro's personality, the vagueness and ambiguity of Martían ideology suited him for political reasons. Unlike his predecessor, Castro had built up no party in exile, his contacts in Cuba were tenuous and, although he might see himself as the chosen leader, he had been chosen by no one except a handful of immediate followers. It was therefore necessary for him to cast his programme in broad general terms, and he underplayed ideas of radical socialisation in order not to antagonise those potential supporters whose opposition to Batista was primarily political. An ideology of class harmony rather than class conflict was a tactical necessity. This does not mean that Castro was a concealed Marxist. In March 1962 he described his position in 1954 as that of a 'young man who was being guided towards Marxism and who was beginning to act as a Marxist'. But however much he may now think of himself as a Marxist, or rely on Marxists like Guevara, his is in fact a personalised version of Marxism in which echoes of his Martí affiliations are never far away.

Martí's social ideas were permeated by a mystical sense of unity, a secularised version of Christian love, which found one expression in

---

[6] Though, of course, Castro's personality has little in common with Martí, the self-effacing mystic.

his passionate feeling for the poor, and which embraced the ex-slaves whom he carefully drew into his revolutionary party. There should be complete racial equality in the new society. 'There is no racial problem', he wrote, 'because there are no races, only humanity'. He was, no less, a social romantic, stressing class harmony; the basic conflict was not between classes or races but between good and evil in which personal redemption could be found through self-sacrifice for the *patria*. Outside the *patria* true morality was impossible. Echoes of this Martían view are heard in Castro's often reiterated concept of the 'honest man', and his division of people into the selfish and the selfless, the exploiters and the exploited. The Revolution poses a stark moral choice—those who are against it are immoral and are so through self-interest. Freedom, in this view, seems to lie not so much in obedience to the Marxist laws of necessity as to the moral imperatives of Martí's secular religion. The moral fervour of the revolution was, and in many ways still is, Martían rather than Marxist in origin.

The idea of Cuba's messianic mission to liberate Latin America from the 'imperialist yoke' also has Martían rather than Marxist antecedents. Central to Martí's conception of nationalism was the idea that suffering exalts and purifies. Cuba's suffering during the Wars of Independence gave her a pre-emptive right to moral leadership in the struggle against foreign domination. His thought transcended a narrow Cubanism. 'In Cuba' he wrote, in words which are frequently repeated today, 'we are fighting not for the good of the island but to safeguard the independence of all Latin America by safeguarding our own'. He called Hispanic America back to the sense of common destiny which had been lost in the *caudillismo* and the chaotic early years of independence. He revived Bolívar's conception of a united Hispanic America as a counter to the United States' version of Pan-Americanism, which he saw, as many Latin Americans still do, as a sham designed to preserve artificial divisions which had been perpetuated by landowning oligarchies. When Cuba is described as *'una provincia de la madre patria de América Latina'* [*a province of the Latin American motherland*] the implication is that no Cuban action in Latin America can be termed interference because there are no real frontiers, only those which mark the boundaries of private fiefs created by landowning oligarchs who have betrayed the continent's destiny. Or, as Martí saw it, 'In America there are two countries and no more than two, with a very different soul because of their origin, background and customs, and only alike in their fundamental human identity'.

Castro's complete repudiation of the United States cannot be explained away as the result of pique or even of rational calculation. His anti-imperialism, imbibed from Martí, is directed against a suffocating spiritual patronage as well as against economic tutelage. The fact that

Cuban culture has lacked the resilience to resist Americanisation has only added force to the impulse to assert a new distinctiveness, and towards a breach with the United States.

The unsystematic nature of Martí's thought has made it easy for the Castro régime, by careful selection, to cite him as its precursor. His views on education, economics, the Church and the destiny of Latin America can be used to justify the revolution's changing programme—as in the 1961 campaign against illiteracy. But those of his maxims chosen as propaganda are often an uneasy mixture of platitude and profundity. However, his influence is implicit in Castro's conception of politics as a duty and as a national regenerating force, rather than as the satisfaction of particularist needs or the conciliation of opposed interests.

Castro has sought to re-create the lost paradise of Martí's populist myth. 'Of all the pages in the history of Cuba', he wrote from prison, 'perhaps those I must admire are not so much those about the exploits of the battlefields as those which deal with that gigantic task, heroic and silent, of uniting Cubans for the struggle'. His refusal to return to a 'permissive society' may be explained by a fear that it would only have led to factionalism, and to a weakening in the face of the United States. The concept of the nation in arms sustained the long struggle against Batista as it must also sustain that against the United States. Those who opposed Castro from 1959 onwards were, in his eyes, opposing the embodiment of the Martian ideal of a unified nation.

Communists are experts at adopting dead heroes of national liberation movements for their own, as may be seen from the cult in Cuba of the Nicaraguan patriot Sandino and of Martí's contemporary, the mulatto general Maceo.[7] Martí himself has been no exception: his works have long been known in Russia, and even Peking has celebrated a 'Martí day'. In Cuba he is still useful to the régime in spite of the official adoption of Marxist-Leninism. He can be used to emphasise the *Cubanidad* of the Revolution. In 1959, as in 1898, Cuba had no class strong enough economically to push through a nationalist revolution. On both occasions it was necessary for a foreign Power to underwrite the new régimes. Martí is the means by which Cubans can retain their national pride; equally his universalism, his Mazzinian emphasis on 'humanity' enables them to equate their own struggles with those of all countries which have suffered from imperialist exploitation. His advocacy of armed revolt, and his rejection, in the 1890s, of the view

---

[7] A mulatto army general who died in battle and who refused to accept the compromise peace of Zanjón which ended the Ten Years' War in 1878, is an obvious choice of hero in a period of no compromise, racial equality and army glorification.

that parliamentary activity through the Autonomist party would be the best preparation for independence, provides a reputable ancestry for the thesis, most forcefully expressed by Guevara, and shared by Peking, that the only way for revolution to succeed in Latin America is by armed insurrection on a Maoist-Cuban model. The *mambises* [*supporters of Cuban independence from Spain*] of the 1890s are the precursors of the *barbudos* [*bearded ones*] of the 1950s and the proto-types of the Latin American guerilla.

Persuasive though the Cuban thesis may be in the context of Latin American social structures, Cuba's revolution, like her history, is *sui generis*. It provides an inspiration to Latin American radicals, but it is less clear that it provides a model. If the roots of Cuban national-ism were different from those of the nationalisms of the mainland, so, too, is Cuba unaffected by many of the contemporary problems of the other republics. Compared with much of continental Latin America, the island has an equable climate with neither the difficulties of alti-tude nor semi-desert. It has no Indian problem; its negro population is extrovert and easier to assimilate than Indians with their distinctive cultures and often different languages. It is 60 per cent. urbanised, with its economy entirely dependent on Eastern-bloc aid. Even before 1961 it was fourth among the countries of Latin America in the num-ber of literates and third in the number of students receiving higher education. Uneven development, not underdevelopment, has been the cause of its social tensions.

Variations between the countries on the mainland are so great that no single revolutionary theory can apply to all. Yet it may well be that the determining factor in the Cuban revolution will be the same in future revolutions elsewhere in Latin America—the active student element within its disorganised and divided middle sectors. Success in Cuba has largely depended on the capacity of *déraciné* [8] middle sector students to provide revolutionary leadership, and to canalise incoherent mass peasant discontent. Interpretations of the Cuban Revolution often overlook what perhaps will come to be seen as its most striking feature—that it was a revolution between generations. Where the radical nationalist movements of the 1930s failed to draw youthful energies away from negative terrorism, Castro succeeded in concentrat-ing them in positive revolutionary action. The future of Castroism on the mainland may depend on failure or success in harnessing this po-tential revolutionary force.

The ease with which a nationalist movement has slipped into a

---

[8] Literally, un- or uprooted; alienated.

Communist-style régime is explained by the way in which Cuban nationalist ideology has been capable of adaptation to the needs of current Communist policy. But it would be unwise, for that reason, to assume that Castro's Communism bears a close resemblance to any other variety. Perhaps the current disagreements between Moscow and Peking may give Castro the wider room he needs for manoeuvre if he is to maintain himself in power.

Revolutions nowadays are too often interpreted solely in terms of how they affect the two rival blocs but, in this age of nuclear stalemate, ideological factors may assume greater importance and, to understand these in Latin America, the deeper roots of nationalist attitudes will have to be uncovered. Revolutions are sustained by utopian visions; without these they are but rebellions. The visions may be those of nationalist mythologies or socialist ideologies. It is the unusual interweaving of such threads which has given Castro's Revolution its unique texture.

On Cuban Political Economy

James O'Connor

There is virtually no aspect of the Cuban Revolution that has not stirred bitter controversy. The extent to which the Cuban peasantry supported or actively assisted Fidel Castro's 26th of July movement before the fall of Batista, the extent to which the Revolution was middle class in origins, leadership, and goals and was therefore "betrayed" by Castro's espousal of communism, the extent to which Castro himself had embraced Marxist-Leninist ideology before 1959—these are just a few of the topics that have provoked sharp debate among observers of the Revolution. All of these questions are touched upon in this selection by James O'Connor of the Economics Department of San Jose State College. He advances the thesis that the adoption of socialism between 1959 and 1961 was "a realistic and authentic response" to a stagnant economy characterized by monopoly capitalism, and that the social revolution was carried out with the acquiescence of the majority of the Cuban people. Professor O'Connor also wrote The Origins of Socialism in Cuba *(Ithaca, N.Y.: Cornell University Press, 1970).*

The thesis of this paper is that the social revolution in Cuba (1959–61) was inevitable in the sense that it was necessary for the island's further economic and social development. The nationalization and consolidation of industry, the collectivization of more than one third of Cuba's farm land, the complete reorganization of the labor unions and the banking and commercial systems, and thoroughgoing economic planning, rescued the island from permanent economic stagnation.[1] For this reason, Cuban socialism can be explained

---

From James O'Connor, "On Cuban Political Economy," *Political Science Quarterly,* 79 (June 1964), 233–247. Reprinted by permission of the publisher and the author. Some footnotes deleted.

[1] The shift of the great part of Cuba's trade from the United States to the socialist countries, and the reorientation of Cuba's foreign policy, do not directly concern us here. They are questions related to the transition from capitalist to socialist economy, but they seem to have had an independent

and understood in the context of the social structure of the old society
—not as the sour fruit of some "abnormality" or "conspiracy."

A corollary of this thesis is that any ruling group which failed
fundamentally to modify or replace Cuba's old economic institutions
could not count on a long and stable tenure. It also follows that the
political orientation of any political leader of "liberal" or conservative
persuasion who wished to retain power would have to shift more or less
rapidly to the Left to correspond with social reality.

The argument may be summarized as follows:

1. From a very early date the Cuban economy developed along capitalist lines. Pre-capitalist forms of economic organization—traditional, feudal, or mercantile—were in no way important features of
   the old society. During the twentieth century, the island's economy
   acquired the significant characteristics of monopoly capitalism, chief
   among which was the cartelization of markets. Monopoly controls
   blanketed Cuba's social economy and blocked the fulfillment of the
   island's true economic potential by wasting land, labor, and capital,
   and other economic resources.

2. Throughout the political revolution which triumphed in January
   1959, a small group of men acquired and retained the initiative.
   These men were non-Communists, and, while forming an alliance
   with the Cuban Communist party in late 1958 or early 1959, consistently kept the initiative during the social revolution of 1959–61.
   What is more, this social revolution was rapid, relatively peaceful,
   and defended by the vast majority of the Cuban people. These observations suggest that a social revolution of a specifically socialist
   character was not merely an ideological product, but a realistic and
   authentic response to social reality.

3. The political revolution was not marked by sharp class conflicts, and
   revolutionary programs drawn up before 1959 had appeal for nearly
   every Cuban social and economic class. Class conflicts developed
   out of the economic and political measures of the Revolutionary
   government which destroyed revolutionary unity by systematically
   discriminating against some classes and in favor of others and by
   polarizing political attitudes on the questions of elections, political
   parties, and relations with the United States. It is said that these

---

character as well. For this reason they are more simple, and at the same time,
more complex than the question of Cuban socialism itself. On one level of
analysis, it is obvious that the United States' refusal to trade with Cuba drove
the island to the Soviet Union. Looking deeper, one is compelled to inquire
into the nature of the relationship between the United States and Cuba for
clues to its deterioration. Clearly, the rapid socialization of the Cuban economy
contributed to the severance of ties between the two governments.

measures provide prima-facie evidence that Fidel Castro betrayed the original spirit and aims of the revolution (the betterment of the economic, social, and political condition of the Cuban people) when in fact they may have been the logical outcome of an attempt to realize these very aims.

I

From a very early date Cuba exhibited the main features of modern capitalist economy. Unlike most Latin American economies, Cuba lacked an important subsistence sector and nearly all segments of the population were integrated into the market economy. As early as 1899 over two thirds of the rural labor force were engaged in the cultivation of cash crops, while subsistence farming employed probably less than one quarter of the work force.

By mid-century the subsistence sector had been nearly totally submerged by specialized agricultural production for export and home consumption. Throughout the countryside the propertied rural middle class gave way to foreign capital, which exploited opportunities for large-scale production, and corporate and absentee ownership. Following the sugar crises of the nineteen-twenties a fine web of relationships began to bind together agriculture and high finance; the bankers also had a finger in commerce and, to a lesser degree, manufacturing.

The great part of the island's agricultural production was organized along monopolistic lines. Output restrictions, pegged prices, and other forms of monopolistic control blanketed sugar, tobacco, rice, potato, and coffee farming. In the key sugar sector, mill owners, growers, and wage workers all had powerful organizations. Outputs, wages, prices, and the distribution of sugar earnings were determined by the mill owners or growers cartels, or by a three-cornered bargaining relationship on the level of national politics.

In industry there were 150 employers' associations of one kind or another, many of them with wide powers over their members. Compulsory "producers' associations" dominated sugar and tobacco manufacture, and the great public utilities each had clear monopolies in their fields. As for the labor movement, it was, compared with the island's labor force, one of the largest in the world, and the central federation enjoyed unusual power over its affiliates. There was, besides, an extremely well developed "labor aristocracy" which had sealed off a number of important labor markets from outside competition, and which was mainly responsible for the extraordinarily low relationship between labor productivity and wages.

In short, the economic institutions which we are accustomed to associate with the high income capitalist nations overlaid the island's market system. It should be stressed that monopoly practices in Cuba's product and labor markets sprang up in the soil of a market economy. Restrictions in the rural economy were not of the type ordinarily associated with a system of traditional agriculture, and controls in the labor market were not those customary in mercantile or neo-mercantile systems. Cuba's economic institutions were capitalist institutions, historically specific to Cuba. These institutions had, by and large, a monopolistic character, as well. For this reason, they placed limits on the pace of Cuba's economic development by inhibiting the improvement of agricultural yields, wasting land, barring the wide introduction of a mixed, scientific agriculture, placing ceilings on labor and productivity, and, in general, on the ability of the economy to mobilize and utilize domestic and foreign capital efficiently.

In an economy which had been stagnating since World War II (ignoring temporary ups and downs in the sugar market), it should be unnecessary to emphasize the implications of these limits on economic growth for the nature and scope of the Cuban Revolution.

II

Against this background, the character of the political and social revolutions in Cuba is more comprehensible. In the *political* struggle against President Fulgencio Batista the decisive influence was apparently the dedication of a small band of young men. From the attack by Fidel Castro on the Moncada Barracks in July 1953, throughout the guerrilla war of 1957–58, until late 1959, when the Castro group firmly consolidated political power, not a single peasant revolt ignited the Cuban countryside. Passive resistance, surreptitious aid to Castro's forces, there were, to be sure; unlike a dozen other political revolutions, however, the peasant classes failed to grasp the initiative at any point in the struggle. Early in 1959 Comandante Ernesto (Che) Guevara, Castro's closest associate, appropriately described the Cuban peasants as the revolution's "invisible collaborators." The labor movement, in which over one half of Cuba's labor force was enrolled, figured even less prominently in the rebellion. It was in January 1959, after the regular army had received Castro's final blows, that the working classes shut down Havana's industry and commerce. Earlier, a general strike in April 1959 had been a total failure. The new Revolutionary government consistently retained the political initiative; the general strike in late January in the port city of Manzanillo protesting the leniency shown by the revolutionary tribunals toward war criminals was apparently the only major reversal of roles.

In the *social* revolution of 1959–61, the liquidation of Cuba's private property system was invariably initiated by the ruling group. The peasantry did not spontaneously seize and cultivate idle lands; with a handful of exceptions, they failed to claim even the small fields in which they labored until the new government formally turned these tracts over to them. To be sure, a decree published in February denied rights to land under the coming Agrarian Reform Law to any peasant who without authorization occupied properties belonging to someone else. More significant than the existence of the law is the fact that it did not have to be enforced. Nor did the urban workers and sugar mill laborers independently occupy the factories (this was a sharp departure from the abortive social revolution of 1933); rebel army or militia units at the direction of the central government took possession of Cuba's farm land and industry.

These two sets of events—the exclusive and individualistic flavor of the political revolution and the almost bloodless social revolution —are intimately connected. The social revolution was more or less orderly because the political revolution transferred power from one relatively small group of men to another, and because the masses of Cubans at the very least passively supported the social revolution.

In this context, it is significant that Cuba's is the only specifically socialist social revolution in history which was not authored by local Communist parties with or without the backing of the Red Army. Not until 1959, when the actual fighting had ceased, did Castro's 26th of July Movement win the open backing of the Cuban party (the Partido Socialista Popular, or PSP), although this is not true of some individual Communists who sided with Castro somewhat earlier, and, as might be expected, survived the 1962 spring and summer purges of old-line Communists almost to a man. The political careers of many of the old-line Communists were painfully brief. Subject to bitter public and private attacks by the 26th of July Movement's organ, *Revolución,* during most of 1959, the party members gained footholds in the new revolutionary organizations in 1960 *after* the major expropriations (with a few exceptions, most notably the trade unions in which they had always figured strongly and in two or three important offices in the National Agrarian Reform Institute [INRA]), helped shape the mass organizations and the new party, the ORI (Integrated Revolutionary Organizations), into their image of revolutionary associations in 1961 and early 1962, only to be deprived of many of their positions in the spring and summer of that year and replaced by non-Communist revolutionary personnel.[2]

---

[2] For the events in 1959 see the study by Maurice Zeitlin and Robert Scheer, *Cuba, Tragedy of the Hemisphere* (New York, 1963). The role of the party in

In connection with the question of the source of political initiative, it is important to point out that in the history of modern revolutions the Cuban experience was unique in another respect, and departed especially from the October Revolution. Irresistibly drawn to the peasantry in order to consolidate power, Lenin paved the way for the seizure of the estates. By this very measure, though, the central authority deprived itself of effective control of the land. Fifteen years passed before the rural economy was collectivized and integrated into the structure of the planned economy. The Cuban Revolution spared Fidel Castro an analogous problem, since the seeds of a planned rural economy were planted *simultaneously* with the transformation of land ownership. The fact that the Cuban farm worker and peasant never had the political initiative made possible the immediate collectivization of the cattle, rice, and sugar sectors of the rural economy. The fact that the better part of these sectors was already organized into large-scale producing units which had long utilized land, labor, and capital inefficiently made collectivization practical, feasible, and rational.

This development distinguishes the Cuban Revolution not only from the Russian Revolution, but sets it apart from the Chinese, the Mexican, and even the Bolivian experiences, as well. In Mexico the peasants at times had absolute initiative; until 1952 the Chinese leadership by force of circumstances emphasized individual ownership of the land; so did the Bolivian revolutionary group, and so it does today. The anti-feudal character of all these upheavals, though, was mirrored very faintly in Cuba, for reasons we have already discussed.

A summary of our argument to this point discloses that: non-Communist revolutionaries made a socialist revolution on an island where feudalism (or the neo-feudalism of pre-revolutionary Soviet Union, China, Mexico, and Bolivia) was largely absent, but where capitalistic, monopolistic controls were prominently featured. The PSP

1960 and 1961 is described in Theodore Draper's *Castro's Revolution: Myths and Realities* (New York, 1962). In this collection of articles is also "L'Affaire Escalante," which tries to interpret the purges at the top to North Americans. Monitoring of Cuban radio broadcasts and perusal of Cuban periodicals reveal that the purge had reached into the lowest levels of the ORI by mid-summer, 1962. This was confirmed by the author in August 1963, by another American, Maurice Zeitlin ("Castro and Cuba's Communists," *The Nation*, November 3, 1962), and by an anti-Castro writer in "Pero sigue la Purga," *Cuba Nueva*, May 15, 1962. That the PSP never had absolute initiative is unwittingly suggested by the leading exponent of the "revolution betrayed" thesis when he wrote that "if all had been going well in Cuba for the past year, the PSP's control might well have gone unchallenged. . . ." Draper, *Castro's Revolution*, 209.

never had the political initiative either before or during the key stages of the social revolution; the party, in fact, at first even opposed those sections of the May 1959 Agrarian Reform Law which encouraged collective production of agricultural commodities. The aim of the revolutionary leadership was to get the stagnating Cuban economy off dead center to improve the social and material conditions of the Cuban people. When they turned to socialist forms of economic organizations to realize this aim, they were supported by the majority of Cubans. From all of this evidence, one can clearly make a case that socialist economic planning in Cuba was less an ideological product than an expression of hard economic necessity.

III

Socialism—public ownership of the means of production—sometimes emerges from class conflict, and is invariably accompanied by more or less severe political warfare between classes. Cuba was no exception. The political revolution had a distinct classless character (at least no single class had the initiative during this phase of the struggle), but sharp class conflicts developed in the course of the social revolution. The emergence of these conflicts was accompanied by dramatic changes in the Revolutionary government's political line.

Beginning in mid-1959, after the Agrarian Reform Law put Cuba and the world on notice that a thoroughgoing social revolution was in the making, the Revolutionary government began to mark off sharply the "revolution" from the "counterrevolution." Departing from his previous position, Castro was the first to insist on the black and white nature of the struggle, an attitude that was quickly adopted by other government officials. Divisions and differences of opinion over revolutionary policy existed within the governing group—the struggle between the Castro group and the "old" communists is one instance—but the main lines of both domestic and foreign policy were (and are) seldom questioned, or in doubt. The extreme polarization of Cuban politics after mid-1959 is well exemplified in speech after speech delivered by Cuban government leaders. In this theme, the revolution and the Cuban nation are made one and the same, as indicated by Castro in early 1960: "To be a traitor to the Revolution is to be a traitor to the country. The destiny of our sovereignty is at stake. . . . We have decided that either we are or we are not a free country. And we are and want to be a free country."

From mid-1959 to the present, however, *genuine* cleavages in Cuban politics have been sharp and opposing opinions have been fiercely held, defining a political mood which corresponds in many ways to social and economic reality. From January 1959 on, a series of profound economic and social changes accompanied these inimical attitudes, and to a larger degree were responsible for them. There were no less than *fifteen hundred* decrees, laws, and resolutions during the first nine months of 1959. Unquestionably, nearly every new measure —especially those affecting the property system—drew some Cubans closer to the Revolutionary government and repelled others, leaving few indifferent. At the very least, each major law (the rent reduction and price control laws, agrarian reform, and the "intervention" of the utilities are some examples) compelled the ordinary Cuban to question his own political orientation; the most sweeping of these occasioned cabinet crises, resignations, flights abroad, and their cumulative effect led to the short war at Playa Giron in April 1961. The basis for the demand to choose sides—for or against the Revolutionary government—was therefore laid by the government's early economic and political measures. To make such a demand required some confidence that a sizable body of opinion would confirm the government's position. This suggests that the original revolutionary legislation might be likened to a whirlpool expelling odd debris, yet sucking in the hull of the ship. Be that as it may it is certainly likely that the slogan itself, together with the heady spirit in which it was launched, contributed to a political atmosphere in which a middle position became increasingly unrealistic and untenable. Castro's personality, after all, confers on the revolution a very special flavor. When he told an audience in the summer of 1960, at the time the United States acted to bar Cuban sugar from the mainland market, "In each cooperative we are going to build a town . . . with or without the quota. Each little town will have a school for the children of the members of the cooperative, with or without the quota . . . ," he conveyed a sense of boundless optimism apparent as early as the famous "History Will Absolve Me" speech in 1953 and by which his associates were invariably impressed. Reading through his speeches and declarations one is struck by the fact that the image of defeat, or even retreat, rarely, and then only reluctantly, appears. This nearly limitless confidence undoubtedly has affected Cuban politics and the island's economic development.

IV

That the new government chose to polarize opinion around the fundamental issue of its own support cannot be fully explained by Castro's optimism, however. It had the alternative—in place of isolating, indeed outlawing, any opposition, the logical climax of the government's actual policy—that of allowing his opposition to form into functioning interest groups. From there, employing the tactics of divide and conquer, he might have thwarted any potential majority coalition. These groups or parties would probably have ranged from the "left-opposition" of the small Cuban Trotskyite movement all the way to the moderate right of the large sugar and commercial interests (supposing that they had purged their numbers of pro-Batista elements). The leadership of the revolution, by playing one group against another, ceaselessly probing the weaknesses of each, might have retained power indefinitely.

Yet this policy seemed to have little relevance to the Cuban scene of 1959–60. Its usefulness is evident if in a crisis the ruling group cannot count on clear majority support; an example that springs to mind is British rule in India. Had the British rulers been foolish enough to imitate Castro's policy, they would have driven the opposition together, in the process probably creating a majority capable of threatening their own rule. Only a ruling group which anticipates majority support can for very long afford to alienate opposition elements so thoroughly that they are compelled to form strong working alliances. The Castro government appeared to be well along this path in the summer and fall of 1960 at the height of the first crisis with the United States.

Finally, the only dialogue between the "revolutionary party" and the "counterrevolutionary party" was literally at gun point. The social revolution had been consummated. Relations with the United States had totally deteriorated. And Castro, together with thousands of 26th of July Movement "liberals" and "reformers," had been radicalized and labelled "betrayers." Why did events follow this course?

V

Early in 1959, Castro was in every sense a popular hero whom many did not hesitate to compare with Martí. Among the island's nearly seven million people, few concealed their esteem, fewer still their respect. Even for the business community the future seemed promising. A leading business and financial organ reported that "American concerns with Cuban interests generally did not expect the change in Cuba's government to hamper their operations." In Cuba itself, the United States embassy took an optimistic view of the long-term investment possibilities. Some firms pre-paid taxes to help Castro consolidate his new government and others planned to accelerate investment programs temporarily postponed during the fighting. Business leaders in Cuba who "as recently as one month ago were gravely concerned about the revolution" apparently had undergone a radical shift in temper. Their doubts would soon return, however, for a rather elementary reason.

On the one hand, a wide range of pressing social, economic, and political problems, some of which had lingered on for years and others of which were fresh, containing unknown implications, confronted the triumphant rebels. In a hundred arenas, the new government struggled to make, implement, and enforce measures demanded by these problems. On the other hand, before assuming power, the Castro group had published or broadcast certain policy statements and decreed certain laws, enforced in those territories seized and occupied by the Rebel Army. Castro, the guerrilla leader, however, had embraced policies of a vague and ambiguous character; ideas were endorsed which Castro, the national politician, would later discard. The original (October 10, 1958) decree taking up the agrarian problem will do as an illustration. Article 2 promised all farm operators cultivating fewer than 27.2 hectares a plot of land of at least that size free of charge. This provision was directly incorporated into the major May 1959 Agrarian Reform Law. Where contiguous land was available this policy was carried out in practice. Article 6 of the October decree, which provided expropriated landowners with compensation, was also contained in the law of May 1959, although, with a handful of exceptions, it was not complied with. However, nowhere does the early law touch on the related problems of foreign properties or the *latifundium,* obviously political questions of a profound character. The vague reference to these problems in the introduction of the October decree could only raise more questions than it could answer. This is but one instance of the vagueness which seems to have characterized Castro's early outlook, and not a very conspicuous one at that. One authority has compiled a whole catalogue of other of the revolutionary's "broken promises."

A great many people were therefore understandably uncertain about the concrete steps the new government would take in the areas of economic development and domestic politics. The regime began to show its hand almost at once (by "intervening" the Cuban Electric Company, for instance), but the anti-Batista moderates whom Castro placed in the first cabinet made it a point to reassure the business community. President Urrutia himself proclaimed that Cuba needed and wanted foreign investments.

VI

With the benefit of hindsight it is tempting to conclude that Castro's group deliberately concealed their true designs from the Cuban population and opinion abroad as a tactical move to win all the support they could possibly get. It is not intended definitively to defend or refute this view here. It will be useful, though, to suggest that this hypothesis fails to exhaust the possibilities. Castro, for example, might very well have been confused or uncertain over the concrete problems—the agrarian problem, the question of economic development, and pressing political problems such as widespread government corruption, the fragile Cuban party system, and elections— which for years had been prominent features of the Cuban scene. The rebel leader, after all, surrounded himself with as varied a group of advisers as any national politician in memory: centrist careerist politicians, Keynesian economists, ex-and-would-be-bureaucrats, sincere liberals, professional revolutionaries, and amateur Marxist tacticians —there was very little advice Castro could not get if he wanted it. No less important, his own knowledge of Cuban economic and social life was apparently confined to three or four major areas. About the large class of small tenants and squatters in Oriente Province, the sugar industry, and the condition of the very poor throughout the island, he certainly knew a great deal. He had never been, however, in close touch with the problems of the tobacco farmers and other more or less well-to-do Cuban rural workers (apart from the sugar growers). And on the subjects of urban industry and trade and the city working class, he had much—as it turned out—to learn. In this connection, it is interesting to point out that in his first essay on the Cuban Revolution, Theodore Draper, who was later to develop the "revolution betrayed" thesis, wrote: "When Fidel Castro entered Havana . . . no one knew what he was going to do. It is doubtful whether he himself knew, except in the most general terms." As a matter of fact, this actively squares with Castro's own self-evaluation, expressed on numerous occasions, but never so frankly as in the famous "Marxist-Leninist" speech of December 1, 1961. Two months later he characterized the revolutionary leadership in these terms: "We were like a man with a vocation for music. But a man's vocation for music does not grant him a right to call himself a musician if he has not studied musical theory. When we started our revolutionary struggle, we already had some knowledge of Marxism-Leninism and we were in sympathy with it. But, by virtue of this, we could not call ourselves Marxists-Leninists. . . . We were apprentice revolutionaries."

There is also the possibility that both opinions, the one favorable to Castro, the other, because he is made out to be a deliberate liar, very unflattering, are partially true. In this event, the "conspirator" theory loses much of its bite; it is not hard to understand why a politician would hesitate to reveal plans which he knows may be unrealistic and never be put into action.

VII

Whatever the case, the fact is that his early support was extremely heterogeneous, and, for this reason, any policy would be bound to appear as a kind of betrayal to someone. No policy, though, would likely be considered a betrayal by everyone. To put it differently, few measures, and no really important ones, could possibly be universally popular; at the same time, every measure would heighten the loyalties of some of his followers. It was certain, therefore, that his universal popularity in January 1959 would be transitory. The struggle between the Association of Sugar Cane Planters and the Sugar Workers Federation over the issue of cane cutters' wages is a good example of the many class conflicts which would eventually spoil revolutionary harmony. On April 15, 1959, the new government decreed a fifteen per cent rise in the wage rates of the cane cutters. The cane planters (*colonos*) were ordered to pay the wage increases in full; they were to be reimbursed, however, by the mill owners, to the extent of one third of the extra wage costs. The *colonos* quickly voted among themselves to repeal the decree, arguing that the wage advance would make their farms "non-operational." Their protest was without effect. It goes without saying that the disputes which raged over the May Agrarian Reform Law and the Urban Reform Law a little later were argued strictly in class terms. And over the issues of elections and reconstruction of the Cuban political party system, and relations with the United States, it was the professional and middle classes which turned against the Revolutionary government. In the ranks of the poorer rural and urban workers and the marginal peasants there was little or no agitation for the reintroduction of the political forms and institutions dominating the Cuban scene prior to Batista's coup in 1952, nor was there great fear of the island's powerful northern neighbor.

While the economic and social measures divided the island along class lines to produce a kind of "reactive" class conflict, there was no mass agitation for the reorganization of the Cuban economy. The interventions and expropriations of 1959–60 clearly had the *support* of the majority of Cubans (even the relatively conservative sugar growers supported the seizure of the estates); but the poorer, underprivileged classes failed to *initiate* these actions. For this reason, an explanation of Cuban socialism which runs along the lines of pure "class struggle" doctrine is obviously forced and overly abstract.

This admission, however, does not rule out the possibility that Castroism and Cuban socialism were built on economic—not ideological—foundations. First, one cannot characterize the Cuban Revolution as primarily anti-feudal; quite the contrary, the Cuban economy exhibited all the main features of well developed (one is tempted to say, over developed) capitalism. What is more, Cuban capitalism was monopoly capitalism; *for this reason, the Cuban economy failed to grow as rapidly as existing technology, savings, and the supplies of labor and land permitted.* What inhibited the island's economic growth was not the absolute supplies of factors of production, but the way in which they were *organized.* Viewed in this context, it is highly suggestive that the "ideologists" apparently failed to have the political initiative at any time; we know that the Cuban Communist party did not make the revolution, and it remains to be proved that Fidel Castro was inevitably to term himself a "Marxist-Leninist." Finally, we know that it was possible more or less peacefully to forge socialism in Cuba, implying that most Cubans were ready (or at least willing) to accept a socialist economy, in marked contrast to the Russian experience.

Cuba, Castro, and the United States

——◄◆►——

Philip W. Bonsal

*Another controversial aspect of the early years of the Cuban Revolu-
tion was the initial reaction of the United States to the establishment
of the Castro government and the extent to which this reaction contributed to the alliance of Cuba with the Soviet Union. In this selection, Philip W. Bonsal (1903–   ), who was the American ambassador
to Cuba from 1959 to 1961, maintains that the United States did not
force Castro and Ernesto (Che) Guevara into the Soviet camp but was
"unwisely cooperative in removing obstacles to their chosen path."*

*Bonsal, who was ambassador to Bolivia at the time of his appoint-
ment, had been a telephone company executive in Cuba in the 1920s
and served in the American embassy in Havana in the 1930s. His father,
newspaper correspondent Stephen Bonsal (1865–1951), covered the
Cuban insurrection of 1895 and the Spanish-American War and wrote
two books on Cuba.*

Batista's military coup in 1952 and the apathy with which it was
received by the masses and all but a few leaders gave evidence of the
political bankruptcy which allowed Castro to flourish seven years
later. While the constitutional governments of Grau and Prío (1944
to 1952) had enlisted the participation of many representative and
devoted Cubans, the administrations themselves were generally regarded as corrupt, especially at the top, and dominated by vicious
political gangsterism at lower levels. The people had little faith in
their government or in the integrity of their political leaders.

In 1956, a number of distinguished Cubans made an effort to find
a constitutional way out for the dictatorship. Their effort, known as
the "Civic Dialogue," failed because of the intransigence of Batista
and those profiting from his rule. This was the point of no return in
the tragic course of Castro's rise to power.

Meanwhile, our representation in Havana was using its not incon-

Excerpted from Philip W. Bonsal, "Cuba, Castro, and the United States,"
Foreign Affairs, 45 (January 1967), 264–274. © Council on Foreign Relations,
Inc., New York.

siderable influence primarily in matters of concern to American business interests. These were numerous, important and generally constructive. They had contributed substantially to the economic and social development of the country. Taken as a whole, however, their impact was irritating, stifling and frustrating to the rising sense of Cuban nationalism.

Although Americans no longer controlled more than a third of the Cuban sugar production—the most modern and perhaps the most profitable third—our sugar interests played a major part in the varied and wide-ranging strategy to protect the United States quota. And many American companies owned or controlled vast Cuban cane plantations in spite of a clause in the Cuban constitution which established a policy of separate ownership of mills and plantations.

In addition, American interests dominated many key activities, including telephone and electric light and power companies, which operated in an atmosphere of general public hostility. A major railroad system serving the eastern half of the island was American-controlled. Crude oil was imported, refined and distributed by three large corporations, two American and one Anglo-Dutch. Exploration for oil in Cuba, still one of the great unfulfilled hopes (the Russians have not found any either), was largely carried out by American companies. The active exploitation of Cuba's important nickel resources was in the hands of Americans. Others were prominent in the fields of banking, retail merchandising and manufacturing of many different kinds. The cement plant which supplied the booming construction of Havana was American-owned and operated; so were, to a large extent, the hotels and gambling. Nor was our all-pervasive popular culture— except baseball—pleasing in all its aspects to those seeking the affirmation of indigenous values.

While the Batista government was giving these American interests in general benevolent treatment, and while it was attracting substantial amounts of badly needed private investment, it was itself becoming increasingly alienated from Cuban public opinion. A frenzy of self-enrichment was believed to have seized many of its high officials. Terrorism was met by a savage official counter-terrorism. Though much exaggerated later by the Castro propaganda machine, the number of murders by the Batista security establishment during those bitter years created thousands of deep hatreds—a potent element in the support for Castro. The corruption and the sadism of many Batista henchmen united most Cubans against the régime.

This widespread opposition did not look to the top leadership of Cuba's recent constitutional past. The so-called legitimate opposition which participated in the elections of November 1958 and lost to Batista's nominee was far from filling the need. Because of this vacuum, people's imaginations were captured by Fidel Castro who was conducting small-scale guerrilla operations in the remote fastnesses of eastern Cuba against Batista's armed forces more and more demoralized by the corruption in their midst and by the popular repudiation of the régime they served. The role of the guerrillas in bringing about the fall of the régime has been much exaggerated. However, by early 1958, most of the opposition elements were trying to work with Castro. The Communists were among the last to decide to support him.

After serving as Ambassador in Bolivia, I spent two weeks in Washington on my way to Cuba in February of 1959, examining material on the political beliefs and affiliations of Castro and his principal followers. On the basis of abundant though contradictory evidence, I concluded that Castro was not then a Communist, though some of his group, including his brother Raul, had Communist ties. It was clear that support for the new régime was widespread throughout Cuban society, and it seemed to me that many elements of that society, dominated by a relatively prosperous middle class with strong leanings toward the constitutional system then advocated by Castro himself, had far brighter prospects than the Communists eventually to control the government. The field of action of the new leaders would, I thought, be bounded by the nature of this community.

This diagnosis soon had to be modified. It failed to allow for the phenomenal personality and unprecedented charisma of Fidel Castro. It did not foresee the dearth of any acceptable leadership through which non-Communist elements might exert their influence. Indeed, many such elements abandoned the struggle and the country early in the game. Nor did the diagnosis take into account the use Castro was to make of sectors of the population hitherto vegetating outside the mainstream of Cuban development—the 15 to 20 percent of the people of working age unemployed or underemployed, the frustrated intellectuals who controlled the students, the subsistence farmers. From all these Castro drew his strength and they followed him as though he were indeed a redeemer. Castro was further helped at the outset by the attitudes of many people who, though not pro-Communist and certainly not anti-American, welcomed actions aimed at reducing American influence in the island as a reassertion of Cuban nationalism.

Castro turned out to be a cruel and extreme consequence of two factors: the shortcomings of Cuban society and of the Cuban-American relationship. Without him, the revolution made inevitable by Batista's excesses and by the politico-social failures of two generations would have been comparatively moderate. We soon learned that Castro was far more than an adventurer or a guerrilla leader, that he was perhaps the greatest demagogue ever to have appeared anywhere in Latin

America. He had a power to persuade with words quite independent of the intrinsic worth of the particular notions he might be advancing at the moment. As Theodore Draper makes plain in his works on Castroism, ideas are for Castro little more than servants of his lust for power. The same masses who in 1959 roared their approval of his democratic and then of his humanistic pronouncements shouted themselves hoarse approving his Marxism in 1961.

Through all Castro's gyrations, the only constant has been his determination to free Cuba from American influence (which he equates with domination) even at the eventual cost of submitting his country to the Soviet Union. It was not Castro's predilection for Communism but his pathological hatred of the American power structure as he believed it to be operative in Cuba, together with his discovery of the impotence of Cuba's supposedly influential classes, that led him eventually into the Communist camp. Only from that base, he thought, could he achieve his goal of eliminating American influence.

In early 1959, our government was aware of the almost unanimous support which Castro enjoyed in Cuba and of the hopeful attitude which he inspired in many of our own forward-looking people. Its attitude, therefore, was one of watchful waiting. In this period I saw Castro a number of times and had contacts with all the members of his cabinet, which then represented a variety of political and economic views. I made every effort in these contacts, and in talking with newspaper and magazine editors and many other influential citizens, to convey the good will of the people and the government of the United States. I stressed their satisfaction that the people of Cuba were recovering control of their destiny, and their conviction that relations between the two countries were mutually advantageous. However, I said, our government was willing to discuss any proposals for changes which the new régime might wish to advance. The actual and potential value of the American investment was stressed in an awareness of the régime's intention to investigate certain situations about which public opinion was exercised.

This effort, aimed at establishing a basis of coöperation and understanding with Castro and his followers, seemed to be making some progress with Cuban public opinion when it was interrupted by Castro's trip to the United States at the invitation of an association of American editors. The visit, which began in mid-April, proved a heady diet for Castro's voracious ego and may have given him a warped notion of the state of American public opinion. Our government strove to make a success of the visit, although it was not official. Castro was cordially received in Washington by the Secretary of State and by the Vice President. His party of over fifty included his top advisers in the economic field. We assumed these were disposed to discuss current economic relations and problems with us, but though we demonstrated our willingness to meet them halfway, we met a blank wall. There is reason to believe Castro forbade them to engage in any substantive conversations.

On Castro's return from his travels at the beginning of May, I met him at the airport and suggested an early renewal of our contacts. Although Castro agreed cordially, five weeks elapsed before the next interview and it was largely devoted to the agrarian reform law which had meanwhile been promulgated. I was surprised to note in a recent lecture by Senator Fulbright a reference to a statement purportedly made by Castro to an American newspaperman to the effect that "the American reaction to the agrarian reform of May 1959 made me realize that there was no chance of reaching an accommodation with the United States." The American reaction was friendly and understanding. Our legitimate preoccupation with the compensation of our citizens was reflected in discussions with Cuban officials over a period of months, during which the possibility of long-term bonds was contemplated. But the law was never really implemented. Most of the confiscations and other arbitrary actions of the Cuban authorities regarding the agricultural property of foreigners and Cubans had no sanction in the law.

Raul Roa was appointed foreign minister in June. He was far closer to Castro than was his distinguished predecessor, Roberto Agramonte, a man of principle. There followed an exchange of views in depth on all phases of Cuban-American relations, the climax of which was a five-hour interview with Castro at Roa's apartment the evening of September 5—after a number of implausible postponements. The atmosphere was relaxed and friendly. I reiterated the understanding sympathy of our government with the desires of the Cuban people for reform and renovation and went so far as to anticipate some of the elements of our more liberal policies toward Latin America of a year or two later. I described American economic interests in Cuba in terms of their potential for the progress of the Cuban economy and drew Castro's attention to the arbitrary treatment to which some of them had already been subjected. I endeavored to dispel a myth recounted to Castro with regard to one of these American enterprises. Referring to the rising tempo of vicious anti-American propaganda, I mentioned some of the outrageous statements being made by Ché Guevara in the course of his world travels. As many people before and since, I had the impression that Castro had given a polite and appreciative hearing to my views on subjects deserving mutual discussion and accommodation. Castro said something to the effect that I was perhaps giving too much importance to the propaganda excesses of young people working in an atmosphere of revolutionary enthusiasm not yet tempered by experience. The interview left me in a moderately hope-ful mood—soon to be destroyed by Castro's actions and words of the next few weeks.

During this period Castro must have come to realize how frail were the obstacles to his achieving complete power in Cuba. There were conspiracies against him, including one with Trujillo's support; he overcame them easily. He had some setbacks when expeditions which he organized and sent out from Cuba to destroy the governments of the Dominican Republic and of Nicaragua proved fiascoes involving (particularly in the Dominican case) considerable loss of life. But he must have been consoled in part for these failures when he noted how gingerly his interventions were treated by an inter-American com-munity supposedly devoted to the principle of nonintervention. Its attitude was symptomatic of the state of the continent's conscience at the time—an asset for Castro.

Also during these months, the issue of Communism came into sharper focus. Castro had often expressed opposition to Communism, but he gratefully exploited the red herring supplied by those in Cuba and in the United States to whom any proposal for a change in the status quo is *prima facie* made in Moscow. The remaining miasma of McCarthyism also served him well. Soon it became anathema for Cuban revolutionaries to express anti-Communist sentiments. Castro fired the head of his air force over this issue and, after a typical mob-manœuvre, eliminated, on the grounds of anti-Communism, the President whom he himself had picked. The final showdown on the issue came in Oc-tober with the arrest of Huber Matos, one of the rebel army's important leaders.

In the same week that Matos was arrested, an incident occurred which seemed finally to dash any hopes of establishing useful rela-tions. A plane piloted by the former head of the Castro air force evaded the vigilance of our authorities in Florida (regrettably not the only such case) and dropped anti-Castro leaflets over Havana where trigger-happy antiaircraft units opened fire on it. Their missiles came down in busy Havana streets killing two or three and wounding over forty people. Responsibility for the careless shooting devolved equally upon our authorities, in that the plane left Florida illegally, and the Cuban army. The government, after a fleeting moment of honesty in a soon-suppressed communiqué describing what had actually happened, lashed itself into a towering artificial passion over the alleged bombing of Havana with American connivance. A pamphlet put out by the foreign office described the incident as another Pearl Harbor. At the end of the week, Castro, addressing a mammoth gathering on this imaginary bombing, bellowed, shook his fist and foamed at the mouth to the roaring applause of the mob.

In late November, the cabinet was reorganized in a manner precluding any further possibility of rational dialogue between our two governments. Exchanges of statements continued on both sides, our aim being to demonstrate the degree to which we had shown patience, understanding and moderation in the face of hostility, prevarication and provocation, while Castro's purpose was to promote the beleaguered-citadel mentality which he had found so favorable to the extension of his authority.

In the circumstances, it became incumbent upon us to work out the policy we would now follow. A statement of our position, which I assisted in drafting, was issued from the White House toward the end of January 1960. It made the following points: (1) a reiteration of the United States's commitment to nonintervention in accordance with our treaty obligations; (2) the determination of the United States to do all in its power to prevent the use of its territory for the preparation of illegal acts against Cuba, although it was recognized that Cuban territory had been the point of departure for the launching of invasions against other countries; (3) the concern of the United States at the unfounded accusations directed against it by the Cuban authorities and its regret that its efforts to establish a basis of confidence and understanding had not been reciprocated; (4) a recognition of the sovereign right of the Cubans to engage in domestic reforms with due regard for their obligations under international law; (5) a determination on the part of the United States to defend the rights of its citizens in Cuba as provided under international law after they had exhausted their remedies under Cuban law.

This policy implied continued moderation and restraint on our part, denying Castro the chance to make political capital out of alleged American economic aggression. It could have slowed down the Soviet involvement in the Cuban economy, an involvement, in my judgment, more ardently desired at that time by Castro and Guevara than by Moscow. It would have given the Soviets the opportunity to counsel moderation instead of being forced either to act or to let Castro fall. And even if the policy had failed to prevent Castro's move into the Soviet orbit, it would have gained sympathy and support for our Cuban policy in inter-American and international public opinion by relieving us of responsibility for precipitating events or destroying existing ties. Further, it would have created more favorable conditions for local opposition to crystallize. And considering the state of disorganization and confusion then existing in the Cuban government, it was not Micawberish to hope that if events were not precipitated something might well turn up to alter the situation before Castro consolidated his security controls.

This policy lasted but a few weeks. Factors leading to its abandon-

ment included continued provocation from the Cubans, the visit of
Mikoyan to Havana in February (invading what had so long been an
almost exclusively American sphere of influence), and perhaps the
rising pressures of an election year in our own country. The proverbial
straw may have been Castro's outrageous allegation that we were responsible for the explosion and loss of life on a French munitions ship
in Havana harbor early in March. According to reports published in
later years, it was in that same month that our government decided
to train and equip Cuban nationals for armed action against the Castro
government, a decision wholly inconsistent with the policy we had
announced only two months earlier.

It is worth emphasizing that the January policy had been a considerable embarrassment to the Castro régime. On the other hand, our
new policy, which accelerated the break-up of the ties between the two
countries, was, I believe, welcomed by Castro and Guevara. We did
not force them into the arms of the Soviets but we were, in my judgment, unwisely coöperative in removing the obstacles in their chosen
path.

The first crisis provoked by our new policy involved a Cuban demand in May that the American and British oil refineries process about
a million tons of Soviet crude oil in the balance of the year, instead of
the Venezuelan oil they had been using. (This million tons was about
40 percent of total needs.) The companies had been most tolerant in
letting the government accumulate large foreign-exchange arrears covering crude oil already supplied; but they questioned the government's
right under Cuban law to order them to refine the Soviet oil. For its
part, the government wished to increase its purchases from the Soviet
Union and questioned the prices charged by the companies for the
crude oil they supplied. The companies would probably have reluctantly gone along with the government's request, seeking remedies
through the courts and eventually, if necessary, through channels provided under international law. However, early in June, I was informed by an oil company executive in Havana that he had a couple
of days earlier attended a meeting of representatives of the companies
in the office of the Secretary of the Treasury in Washington, at which
the Secretary had strongly urged the companies to refuse to refine the
Soviet crude oil. The companies accepted this recommendation.

The Cuban government, informed of the companies' negative decision, took over the refineries. The Soviets were now faced with the
necessity of doubling the original million tons of crude oil to be
shipped during the rest of the year to meet total Cuban requirements.
While this may have strained tanker availabilities, the Soviets accomplished the task in such a manner that the Cuban consumers were
hardly aware of any change in the source of supply. The revolution had

won a great and stimulating triumph, comparable to that of the Egyptians when they showed they could operate the Suez Canal without Western help. This was probably not the result contemplated by our government.

Early in July, while the outcome of the crude-oil crisis was still in doubt, President Eisenhower, using the discretion granted him by Congress, suspended the balance of the Cuban sugar quota for the year 1960 on the basis that under prevailing conditions Cuba was no longer a reliable supplier to the American market. The implication was clear that as long as conditions remained as they were Cuba would have no more market in the United States. The Soviets took the sugar we had refused. Cuban planters, cane-cutters, sugar-mill hands, dock workers—all those involved in the industry—went to work for the Russian instead of the American consumer. Castro and Guevara doubtless were highly pleased at our decision, the Russians perhaps less so. When my view on this decision was sought shortly before it was made public, I opposed it as nullifying the advantages we had derived from our previous policy. My belief was that if we were to modify the Cuban quota we should have done so only after negotiations with the Cuban government which would have made clear to all concerned the issues involved. I remain convinced that turning over to the Soviet Union the major responsibility for Cuba's sugar economy was a most regrettable step.

Within a month of the suspension of the quota, Castro had in retaliation nationalized the American sugar mills. Within three months he had taken over what was left of American investments and had made great progress in the elimination of private ownership of most productive assets in Cuba, including those of the Cubans themselves. The process was carried out in an atmosphere of heightened zeal and enthusiasm by those who felt that the fate of their movement depended on successfully meeting the challenge we had posed. Otherwise the revolution would have moved at a slower pace and might have met with strong resistance.

The rising revolutionary fervor was further stimulated by the realization during the summer that anti-Castro guerrillas were receiving arms-drops from a source generally assumed to be a United States agency. These guerrilla bands, brave as they were, posed no real threat to the régime. And the urban opposition to Castro was being deprived more and more of the positions of economic power which might have proved useful in furthering underground activity.

In this atmosphere, the break in diplomatic relations came as an anticlimax. It took place in early January 1961 as a result of Castro's demand that we reduce the establishment we were maintaining in Havana (very largely to facilitate the mass exit of Cubans from their homeland) to the level of the by then totally useless Cuban establishment in Washington.

In April 1961, 1,500 brave Cubans—selected, equipped, trained, financed, transported, misled and eventually (the survivors) ransomed by us—landed at the Bay of Pigs as the major element in an enterprise to free their 7,000,000 compatriots from Castro's military and security apparatus of something over 100,000 comparatively well prepared men and women. That fiasco, in conjunction with our replacement by Soviet Russia as Cuba's major economic partner, consolidated Castro's position. After the Bay of Pigs, the régime became so strong internally that even the missile crisis of October 1962, revealing as it did the true relative dimensions of the partners in the Castro-Khrushchev dialogue, failed to shake it.

Cuba, Historical Exception or Vanguard in the Anti-Colonial Struggle?

Che Guevara

Many of the points raised in the preceding selections are implicitly considered by Che Guevara (1928–1967), although his primary objective here is to explain his conception of the revolutionary future of Latin America. He contends that, despite certain exceptional circumstances, the Cuban experience can be duplicated throughout Latin America and that only a nucleus of guerrillas operating in the countryside can successfully initiate the revolution. This argument, of course, runs counter to Hennessy's conclusion that the Cuban Revolution is unlikely to serve as a model for other Latin American revolutions. Although Guevara's thesis has always been questioned by Marxists as well as non-Marxists, his death in Bolivia in 1967 during an unsuccessful guerrilla uprising, the apparent failure of other such movements elsewhere in Latin America, and Salvador Allende's 1970 electoral triumph at the head of a coalition of Socialists, Communists, and other leftists in Chile make it likely that Guevara's ideas will undergo even more severe scrutiny in the future.

Never in America has there been an event with such unusual characteristics, such profound roots and such far-reaching consequences for the destiny of the progressive movements in the hemisphere, as our revolutionary war. This has been the case to such an extent that some have characterized it as the cardinal event in our America, and the most important after the Russian Revolution, the victory over the military might of Hitler, and the triumph of the Chinese Revolution.

This movement, broadly heterodox in its form and manifestations, has nevertheless followed the general line of all of the great historical events of the century, which has been marked by the struggles against colonialism and the transition to socialism. Nevertheless, some factions

From Luis E. Aguilar (ed. and tr.), *Marxism in Latin America* (New York: Knopf, 1968), pp. 172–179. Copyright © 1968 by Alfred A. Knopf, Inc. Reprinted by permission of the publisher. Deletions in the text are by Luis E. Aguilar.

have sought to find in it a series of extraordinary roots and features that have been artificially inflated to the point of labeling them "determinant." There is reference to the exceptional nature of the Cuban Revolution, whereby it is supposedly established that the form and course of the Cuban Revolution are unique products of that revolution, and that the historic transition of the peoples in other countries of America will be different.

We accept the fact that there have been exceptional factors that have given our revolution peculiar features, and it is an established fact that each revolution depends on such special factors. But it is no less established that all revolutions will follow laws that cannot be violated by society. Let us therefore analyze the factors of this so-called special case.

The first, and perhaps the most important, the most original, is that telluric force called Fidel Castro—a name that in just a few years has attained historic significance and whose merits we consider worthy of comparison with those of the most outstanding figures in Latin American history. Fidel is a man of tremendous personal magnetism, destined to assume the role of leader in any movement in which he takes part. He has all the characteristics typical of a great leader: audacity, force, the desire to keep his ear attuned to the will of the people. But he has other important qualities: the capacity to absorb knowledge and experience, a grasp of the overall picture in a given situation, boundless faith in the future. . . . Fidel Castro did more than anyone else in Cuba to construct the now formidable apparatus of the revolution.

Nevertheless, no one can affirm that there were political and social conditions in Cuba that were totally different from those in any other country of the hemisphere, that it was precisely because of such difference that the revolution came about. Nor can it be charged that Fidel Castro made the revolution. Fidel directed the Cuban Revolution, interpreting the profound political unrest that was preparing the people for the great leap along the road to revolution. Certain conditions also existed that were not peculiar to Cuba but that could, with difficulty, be utilized again by other peoples, for the reason that imperialism—unlike some progressive groups—does learn from its mistakes.

The condition that we might describe as exceptional is that North American imperialism was confused and was thus never able to assess the true extent of the Cuban Revolution. By the time imperialism wanted to react, when it realized that the group of inexperienced young men who were parading the streets of Havana in triumph were clearly aware of their political responsibilities and had an iron resolve to carry them out, it was already too late.

We do not consider that there was anything exceptional in the fact that the bourgeoisie, or a large part of this sector, showed itself in favor of the revolutionary war, while at the same time it sought solutions that would make possible the replacement of the Batista government by elements that would be disposed to hold the revolution in check. Nor was there anything exceptional in the fact that some of the *latifundist* elements adopted a neutral attitude, or at least one of non-belligerency toward the insurrectionist forces. In this way, non-revolutionary forces in effect helped smooth the road to political power for the revolutionary forces.

By going one step further, we can point out another exceptional factor: in the majority of the localities in Cuba, the peasants had become proletarianized by the demands of the great capitalist, semi-mechanized farms and had attained greater class consciousness. But we must add that, throughout the original territory first dominated by the rebel army, there was a rural population of a different social and cultural origin than that which was to be found in the settlements around the large semi-mechanized farms in Cuba. In effect, the Sierra Maestra is a place where the peasants who go there to seek a new plot of land, which they wrest from the state or from some greedy landholder, find a refuge. The soldiers who constituted our first guerrilla army of peasants came from the latter group, a group that had already demonstrated in the most aggressive manner a love for the land and a desire to possess it, a group that displayed what might be termed the "spirit of the petty bourgeoisie." The peasant fights because he wants land, for himself, for his children, and wants to control it, to be able to sell it, and to improve his lot by working it.

Regardless of that spirit, the peasant quickly learns that he cannot satisfy his desire to possess the land without breaking up the *latifundia* system. Radical agrarian reform, which is the only way to give land to the peasant, runs counter to the interests of the imperialists, the large landholders, and the sugar and livestock magnates. The bourgeoisie is afraid to go against such interests; the proletariat is not afraid. Thus the progress of the revolution unites the workers and the peasants.

I do not believe that any other special factors can be cited. Let us now see what are the permanent bases for all social phenomena in America, or at least for those that bring about changes that can assume the magnitude of a revolution, such as that in Cuba.

First in chronological order, although not necessarily in order of importance, is the *latifundia* system. The large estate was the base of the economic power of the ruling class during the period following the revolution that was carried out in the last century in order to obtain independence from the colonial powers. But that class always lags behind the march of social progress, even though its more alert groups in certain places may change the form of their capital investment and at times make progress toward mechanized farming. In any case, the initial liberating revolution did not succeed in destroying the *latifundia* class, which continued to maintain a system of peonage on the land and invariably behaved in a reactionary manner.

The large landholder realized that he could not survive alone and entered into an alliance with the monopolies, the most vigorous and brutal oppressors of the American peoples. America was the battlefield in the internecine struggles of imperialism, and the wars between Costa Rica and Nicaragua, the separation of Panama, the struggle between Paraguay and Bolivia, etc., are merely facets of this titanic battle, a battle that was decided almost totally in favor of the American monopolies during the period following World War II.

What is underdevelopment? A dwarf with an enormous head is "underdeveloped," so long as his feeble legs do not support his body. That is what we are: countries with economies that have been distorted by the action of the imperialists, in subjugation to a single crop, a single product, a single market. This vicious circle produces what has become the common denominator of the people of America from the Rio Grande to the South Pole. That common denominator is the HUNGER OF THE PEOPLE, who are tired of being oppressed and exploited to the limit.

Thus, we see that there are these enormous and inescapable common denominators—the *latifundia* system, the underdevelopment, the hunger of the people—all which existed in that Cuba of before. . . . What did we do to free ourselves from them? We merely applied some formulas, which we have described on other occasions as our empirical remedy for the vast ills of our beloved Latin America.

The objective conditions for the struggle are provided by the people's hunger, their reaction to that hunger, etc. In America the subjective conditions are lacking; of these the most important is an awareness of the possibilities of achieving victory by following the road of violence against the imperialist powers and their allies within the country. These conditions are being created, however, by means of the armed conflict that begins to make the need for change more evident, by the defeat of the army by the people's army, and the subsequent annihilation of the former as an essential condition of any authentic revolution.

In pointing out the foregoing, we must repeat that the setting for this struggle must be the countryside, and that an army of peasants, working out of the countryside and seeking the noble objectives for which the rural population is fighting, will provide the great liberating army of the future, as it has already done in Cuba.

But there are also conditions that will make the struggle more difficult in other countries of America. Imperialism has learned its lesson and it will not let itself be taken by surprise in any corner of the hemisphere. The bourgeoisie of the various countries, despite their differences with imperialism, are in general incapable of maintaining a coherent position of opposition to imperialism: they fear the revolution more than they fear the despotic domination of the imperialists. The upper middle class is openly opposed to the revolution and does not hesitate to ally itself with imperialism and the feudal landowners in order to block the revolution's path.

Even when there exist great urban concentrations, it may be advisable to base the campaign outside the cities. The presence of a nucleus of guerrillas in the mountains maintains a continuing focus of rebellion. Something entirely different happens in the city; armed warfare against the repressive army can be carried to undreamed of ends, but only so long as there is a powerful force pitted against another force, not while there is only a small group. . . . There are no arms; they must be seized from the enemy. That is why the battle in the large cities must be initiated through a clandestine process designed to capture military groups or to continue to capture weapons, one by one, in a succession of surprise attacks. In the latter case, rapid progress can be made, and it cannot be denied that a popular rebellion, based on guerrilla tactics, would not be impossible within the city.

Dark days lie ahead for Latin America. Once the war against imperialism is launched, it is essential to be consistent, to strike hard where it hurts, without pause, never giving ground but moving constantly forward, constantly counterattacking, continually meeting any new aggression with ever stronger pressure from the masses of the people. This is the road to victory.

BIBLIOGRAPHY

Early writings on the Cuban Revolution are reviewed in John D. Harbron, "Cuba: Bibliography of Revolution," *International Journal,* 18 (1963), 215–223. A more recent and comprehensive work is Gilberto V. Fort, *The Cuban Revolution of Fidel Castro Viewed from Abroad. An Annotated Bibliography* (Lawrence: University of Kansas Libraries, 1969) which lists books and pamphlets published in English, Spanish, and Portuguese.

The background of the Revolution can be sought in numerous works, notably Wyatt MacGaffey and Clifford R. Barnett, *Twentieth-Century Cuba* (Garden City, N.Y.: Doubleday, 1965); Ramón Eduardo Ruiz, *Cuba: The Making of a Revolution* (New York: Norton, 1970); and Robert F. Smith (ed.), *Background to Revolution: The Development of Modern Cuba* (New York: Knopf, 1966), a collection of readings. Herbert Matthews, *Fidel*

Castro (New York: Simon and Schuster, 1969) is an adulatory biography by *The New York Times* journalist who introduced Castro to the American public in 1957. Lee Lockwood, *Castro's Cuba, Cuba's Fidel* (New York: Macmillan, 1967), is a photographer-journalist's account, in words and pictures, of several trips to Cuba in the mid-1960s including the text of a lengthy interview with Castro. A number of Castro's speeches are collected in Martin Kenner and James Petras (eds.), *Fidel Castro Speaks* (New York: Grove Press, 1969).

An excellent survey of changes in Cuban agriculture, education, and industry as a result of the Revolution is Dudley Seers, Andrés Bianchi, Richard Jolly, and Max Nolff, *Cuba: The Economic and Social Revolution* (Chapel Hill: University of North Carolina Press, 1964). Political changes are discussed in Richard R. Fagen, *The Transformation of Political Culture in Cuba* (Stanford, Cal.: Stanford University Press, 1969), while Maurice Zeitlin, *Revolutionary Politics and the Cuban Working Class* (Princeton, N.J.: Princeton University Press, 1967) and Carmelo Mesa-Largo, *The Labor Sector and Socialist Distribution in Cuba* (New York: Praeger, 1968) focus on labor. Castro's relations with the U.S.S.R. and with Cuban communists are examined in detail in Andrés Suárez, *Cuba: Castroism and Communism, 1959–1966* (Cambridge, Mass.: M.I.T. Press, 1967); also relevant is D. Bruce Jackson, *Castro, the Kremlin, and Communism in Latin America* (Baltimore: Johns Hopkins Press, 1969). Two books by erstwhile supporters of the Revolution are Teresa Casuso, *Cuba and Castro* (New York: Random House, 1962) and Rufo López-Fresquet, *My Fourteen Months with Castro* (Cleveland: World Publishing, 1966). For contrasting views of the Revolution by two American analysts, see Theodore Draper, *Castro's Revolution: Myths and Realities* (New York: Praeger, 1962) and *Castroism: Theory and Practice* (New York: Praeger, 1965) and William Appleman Williams, *The United States, Cuba, and Castro* (New York: Monthly Review, 1962). Other works of interest are Jaime Suchlicki, *University Students and Revolution in Cuba, 1920–1968* (Coral Gables: University of Miami Press, 1969); José Yglesias, *In the Fist of the Revolution: Life in a Cuban Country Town* (New York: Random House, 1969); Paul H. Sweezy and Leo Huberman, *Socialism in Cuba* (New York: Monthly Review, 1969); Viator [pseud.] "Cuba Revisited after Ten Years of Castro," *Foreign Affairs*, 48 (1969–1970), 312–321; and Boris Goldeberg, *The Cuban Revolution and Latin America* (New York: Praeger, 1965). Cuban history after 1762 is surveyed in Hugh Thomas' monumental *Cuba: The Pursuit of Freedom* (New York: Harper & Row, 1971). See also René Dumont, *Cuba: Socialism and Development* (New York: Grove Press, 1970).

Lester D. Langley, *The Cuban Policy of the United States* (New York: Wiley, 1968), is a brief survey of United States–Cuba relations since the early nineteenth century; Robert F. Smith, *The United States and Cuba: Business and Diplomacy, 1917–1960* (New York: Bookman Associates, 1960) emphasizes economic ties. Smith is also the editor of *What Happened in Cuba? A Documentary History* (New York: Twayne, 1963).

Ernesto Che Guevara has been the subject of several biographical studies including Daniel James, *Ché Guevara: A Biography* (New York: Stein and Day, 1968); Ricardo Rojo, *My Friend Ché* (New York: Dial Press, 1968);

Richard Harris, *Death of a Revolutionary: Che Guevara's Last Mission* (New York: Norton, 1970); and Luis J. González and Gustavo A. Sánchez Salazar, *The Great Rebel: Che Guevara in Bolivia* (New York: Grove Press, 1969). Of the many volumes of Guevara's writings that have appeared in English, the following may be singled out: Che Guevara, *Guerrilla Warfare* (New York: Vintage Books, 1968) and *Reminiscences of the Cuban Revolutionary War* (New York: Monthly Review, 1968); John Gerassi (ed.), *Venceremos! The Speeches and Writings of Che Guevara* (New York: Macmillan, 1968); Rolando E. Bonachea and Nelson P. Valdés (eds.), *Che: Selected Works of Ernesto Guevara* (Cambridge, Mass.: M.I.T. Press, 1969); and Daniel James (ed.), *The Complete Bolivian Diaries of Ché Guevara and Other Captured Documents* (New York: Stein and Day, 1968). Several of the selections in Luis E. Aguilar (ed.), *Marxism in Latin America* (New York: Knopf, 1968), deal with the impact of the Cuban Revolution and of Guevara's ideas on Latin American Marxists.

Glossary

adelantado [Sp.] A title held by many early conquerors of Spanish America. It conferred many powers and privileges upon them, including the right to govern any territory they conquered.

alcalde mayor [Sp.] An official responsible for the administration of a territory within the jurisdiction of an *audiencia*.

alcalde ordinario [Sp.] A member of a municipal council, who was also a magistrate, in colonial Spanish America.

audiencia [Sp.] A tribunal in colonial Spanish America that exercised administrative as well as judicial powers.

cabildo [Sp.] A municipal council in colonial Spanish America.

cacique [Sp.] A word of Arawak origin meaning Indian chieftain. It was used throughout Spanish America, but after the colonial period it was applied to any local boss regardless of race.

campesino [Sp.] Countryman, peasant.

capitão-mor [Port.] A district official in colonial Brazil with extensive military and administrative powers.

casta [Sp.] or caste A designation for persons of mixed racial ancestry in colonial Spanish America.

caudillo [Sp.] A leader, usually a dictator. Government by *caudillos* is known as *caudillismo*.

chapetón [Sp.] In colonial South America, a disparaging name for a Spaniard.

científicos [Sp.] A name applied to a group of influential Mexican intellectuals and government officials during the latter part of the dictatorship (1876–1911) of Porfirio Díaz. They were so called because of their emphasis on "scientific" methods of encouraging economic development.

colegio [Sp.] or colégio [Port.] A secondary or preparatory school.

compadrazgo [Sp.] or compadrio [Port.] Ritual kinship contracted between the parents and godparents of a child.

comuneros [Sp.] In colonial Spanish America, participants in a popular uprising against royal officials in Paraguay from 1721 to 1735 or in an insurrection to protest high taxes in New Granada from 1779 to 1781.

continuismo [Sp.] The continuation in office of a chief executive beyond his constitutionally prescribed term, usually by the expedient of amending the constitution to permit consecutive reelection.

corregimiento [Sp.] In colonial Spanish America, a territorial subdivision governed by an official called a *corregidor*.

Creole or *Criollo* [Sp.] In colonial Spanish America, a person born in America of Spanish parents.

descamisados [Sp.] Literally "shirtless ones." A name applied to the working-class followers of Juan D. Perón in Argentina.

ejido [Sp.] In Mexico, land belonging to a rural community. A member of a community who receives a plot of such land to cultivate during his lifetime is called an *ejidatario*.

encomienda [Sp.] The granted tribute of a group of Indians to a Spaniard in colonial Spanish America. The recipient of an *encomienda,* who was known as an *encomendero,* was obligated to safeguard the spiritual and physical welfare of his charges and to render certain services to the crown if the need arose.

fazenda [Port.]   A plantation.

Flota [Sp.]   See *Galeones y Flotas.*

fuero [Sp.]   A body of privileges granted to an organization or institution.

gachupín [Sp.]   In Mexico, a disparaging name for a Spaniard.

Galeones y Flotas [Sp.]   The collective name given to the two fleets of merchantmen and warships that sailed from Spain to the colonies each year. The fleet dispatched to Panama and northern South America was known as the *Galeones;* the Mexican fleet was called the *Flota.*

gamonal [Sp.]   In South America, a local political boss or strongman.

hacendado [Sp.]   Owner of an *hacienda,* a large landowner.

hidalgo [Sp.]   A member of the petty nobility of Spain.

jefe político [Sp.]   The chief administrative official of a district.

latifundium [Lat.; plural latifundia]   A large landed estate, especially one that is inefficiently or inadequately exploited. The prevalence of *latifundia* in a region is known as *latifundismo.*

mestizo [Sp.]   A person of mixed European and Indian ancestry.

mita [Sp.]   A word of Quechua origin used in colonial Peru for the periodic conscription of Indians to perform forced, paid labor.

oidor [Sp.]   A judge of an *audiencia.*

pardo [Sp.]   A free person of African ancestry.

patrón [Sp.]   A patron, master, or landlord.

peninsulares [Sp.]   Natives of the Iberian peninsula, that is, Spaniards.

pensador [Sp.]   Thinker, a term often applied to intellectuals in Spanish America.

pronunciamiento [Sp.]   An uprising or insurrection.

real patronato [Sp.]   The power of the Spanish crown to exercise patronage over the Catholic Church in America, particularly the right to make nominations to ecclesiastical office.

reduction   A mission village in colonial Latin America inhabited by Indian converts to Christianity and directed by members of the clergy.

regimento [Port.]   A set of instructions or rules.

repartimiento [Sp.]   Distribution or allotment. In colonial Spanish America, the word might refer to (a) the distribution of Indians to Spaniards, as in an *encomienda;* (b) the periodic conscription of Indians to perform forced, paid labor; (c) the forceable sale of merchandise to Indians by Spanish officials.

senzala [Port.]   A slave hut on a plantation.

sertão [Port.; plural sertões]   Backland or hinterland, especially the semi-arid interior of Northeast Brazil.

sesmaria [Port.]   A grant of land.

visita [Sp.]   An official investigation into the conduct of an officeholder or the administration of a province.

zambo [Sp.]   A person of mixed Indian and African ancestry.